Daniel Garrison Brinton

A Lenâpé-English Dictionary

From an anonymous ms. in the archives of the Moravian Church at Bethlehem, Pa.

Daniel Garrison Brinton

A Lenâpé-English Dictionary
From an anonymous ms. in the archives of the Moravian Church at Bethlehem, Pa.

ISBN/EAN: 9783337297763

Printed in Europe, USA, Canada, Australia, Japan

Cover: Foto ©Paul-Georg Meister /pixelio.de

More available books at **www.hansebooks.com**

PENNSYLVANIA STUDENTS' SERIES.

THE

PENNSYLVANIA

STUDENTS' SERIES.

VOL. I.

PHILADELPHIA:
THE HISTORICAL SOCIETY OF PENNSYLVANIA.
1889.

THE PENNSYLVANIA STUDENTS' SERIES.

Under the above title it is proposed to issue a series of volumes containing material of interest to the students of Pennsylvania history, but not suited to the volumes or magazine printed by the Trustees of the Publication Fund of The Historical Society of Pennsylvania.

The means necessary for the production of the first of the series has been generously contributed by a few members of the Historical Society, who desire that the entire proceeds arising from its sale shall be devoted to the production of works of a similar character. The money will be placed in the hands of the Treasurer of the Society, subject to the order of the undersigned, who will select the material to be printed and act as a committee of publication. Changes in the committee will be made, when necessary, by the Council of The Historical Society of Pennsylvania.

The edition of the volumes will be limited, they will be sold separately, and the price will be regulated by their cost; that of the first of the series, "A Lenâpé-English Dictionary," is $3 net. Copies can be purchased by addressing the Librarian of the Historical Society, 1300 Locust Street, Philadelphia. Checks should be drawn to the order of The Historical Society of Pennsylvania.

DANIEL G. BRINTON,
FREDERICK D. STONE.

A LENÂPÉ-ENGLISH DICTIONARY.

A LENÂPÉ-ENGLISH DICTIONARY.

From an anonymous MS. in the Archives of the Moravian Church at Bethlehem, Pa.

EDITED, WITH ADDITIONS,

BY

DANIEL G. BRINTON, A.M., M.D.,

PROFESSOR OF AMERICAN ARCHÆOLOGY AND LINGUISTICS IN THE UNIVERSITY OF PENNSYLVANIA,

AND

REV. ALBERT SEQAQKIND ANTHONY,

ASSISTANT MISSIONARY TO THE DELAWARES AND SIX NATIONS, CANADA.

PHILADELPHIA:
THE HISTORICAL SOCIETY OF PENNSYLVANIA.
1888.

PREFACE.

For about a century, beginning with 1740, Missionaries of the United Brethren, or Moravians, devoted themselves to the conversion and civilization of portions of the Lenâpé or Delaware Indians. These earnest Christian men studied the native tongue, reduced it to writing, and printed in it, for the use of their converts, a number of works of a religious and educational character. The history of their literary activity in this language has been recently traced elsewhere, in detail,* and need not be repeated here. While some of the results appeared in type, much of it remained in manuscript until the curiosity of scientific students led to its publication. Thus, in 1827, Peter S. Duponceau edited the Grammar of Zeisberger,† and sixty years later his English-German-Onondaga-Delaware Dictionary was printed by the private liberality of Professor E. N. Horsford.‡

These works of David Zeisberger—whose life found

---

* *The Lenâpé and their Legends;* by D. G. Brinton. pp. 74–109 (Philadelphia, 1885).

† *A Grammar of the Language of the Lenni Lenâpé,* in the *Transactions of the American Philosophical Society,* 1827.

‡ *Zeisberger's Indian Dictionary,* 4to, Cambridge, 1887.

an able and sympathetic narrator in the late Right Rev. Edmund de Schweinitz*—together with his printed "Delaware Spelling Book," were the chief sources from which the later missionaries drew their knowledge of the Lenâpé dialect; and unquestionably the present Lenâpé-English Dictionary was founded mainly upon the linguistic work of this proto-Lenâpist. So far as the history of the MS. is concerned, I can add nothing to what was stated in "The Lenâpé and their Legends," which is as follows:—

"It is probable that Mr. Dencke was the compiler of the Delaware Dictionary which is preserved in the Moravian Archives at Bethlehem. The MS. is an oblong octavo, in a small, but beautifully clear hand, and comprises about 3700 words. The handwriting is that of the late Rev. Mr. Kampman, who was missionary to the Delawares on the Canada Reservation from 1840 to 1842. On inquiring the circumstances connected with this MS., he stated to me that it was written at the period named, and was a copy of some older work, probably by Mr. Dencke; but of this he was not certain." †

---

* *Life and Times of David Zeisberger* (Philadelphia, 1871). This eminent Bishop of the Moravian Church died suddenly while the present work was passing through the press—a loss keenly felt throughout that respected Christian body and by a large circle of personal and literary friends beyond its limits.

† *The Lenâpé and their Legends*, pp. 84, 85.

The Rev. C. F. Dencke, here alluded to, was missionary to the Delawares at New Fairfield, Canada, for a number of years after the war of 1812. He was the author of a grammar of the tongue, now apparently lost,* and translated into it various portions of the New Testament. His death took place in 1839.

The MS. of Mr. Kampman was carefully copied and enlarged by the addition of words from the MSS. and printed works of Zeisberger, Heckewelder and Ettwein. These additions have, in the printed copies, been indicated by the capital letters, Z., E., and H. In this condition the MS. was submitted to the Rev. Albert Seqaqkind Anthony, a born Lenâpé, and perfectly familiar with the language of his nation as spoken by that colony of it resident on the Six Nations Reservation, in Ontario, Canada. In this colony, the usual dialect is the Minsi, and, as its members belong to a portion of the nation who were converted by missionaries of the English Church (to which Mr. Anthony belongs), the theological terms developed usually differ widely from those framed by the Moravians.

Mr. Anthony kept the MS. by him for some months, giving its contents careful attention, and subsequently the two editors met and passed in review every word in the Dictionary. The numerous notes and corrections in brackets, with an appended capital *A.*, are the emenda-

---

* A small portion of it is contained in some MSS. now in the possession of the Pennsylvania Historical Society.

tions suggested by Mr. Anthony from the present standpoint of the language and from the dialect of his ancestral sub-tribe. The latter differs somewhat from that employed by the compiler of the Dictionary. The grammatical forms employed indicate that this was the Unami (Wonami).

No attempt has been made to increase the lexicography by the insertion of words or forms obtained from the Delaware of to-day. All such, when mentioned, are by way of comparison only. It would have been easy to have extended the vocabulary. There are evidently some Lenâpé radicals and many themes which do not appear in this work. But the editors confined their efforts to presenting this work as exclusively concerned with the dialect as employed by the Moravian Missionaries; and hence, all additions to the vocabulary have been from their writings.

As is well known, the early Moravians were exclusively Germans; and in reducing the Lenâpé to a written idiom they made use of the German alphabet, without adding to it any phonetic signs. This alphabet was not ill adapted for the purpose. It could represent the gutturals and the vowel sounds of the Lenâpé with sufficient clearness. But there were a few sounds, and these frequent and important ones, which their Germanic ears did not differentiate.

The most prominent of these is the soft *th*, as in *with*. This is usually represented in the Dictionary by *s*. The true sibilant is, in reality, very rare; it scarcely exists. The soft *th* again appears wherever the Dictionary has an *x;* this is properly *k'th*.

The *h* is not a true aspirate, as in German, but rather a pause, as in the French *la Hollande*.

The terminal *k* is a strong, suddenly-checked expiration, which is, by some writers, not inaptly expressed by *q'* or *q!* Instead of the *k*, the Dictionary sometimes employs *que*, which appears to be identical in sound.

The labial *b* is very like a *p*, and probably alternates with it in the dialects.

The *g* is always hard, like the English *k;* the *j* has the value of the English *y ;* the compound *cy* is like the long *i* in *pine;* the syllables *gan* and *quan* are pronounced alike; and the diphthong *eu* has, at least in the Minsi of to-day, the value of *o* in *note*.

By observing these points and giving the remainder of the alphabet the German values, I had no difficulty in reading Dencke's translation of the Epistle of St. John to Mr. Anthony with such correctness that he understood it at once.

D. G. BRINTON.

A LENÂPÉ-ENGLISH DICTIONARY.

A, indeed, well.
Aan, to go; (*aal*, in Minsi. *A.*)
Abtschi, always;—*likhiqui*, at all times.
Abtschiechgochgihillen, to bleed to death.
Abtschihillak, the whooping cough; (*aabtschihillank. A.*)
Abtschihillen, to have the whooping cough.
Abtschinalan, to be afflicted to death.
Abtschinalittin, *Z.*, to die in battle; (they kill each other. *A.*)
Abtschinaluxin, to be afflicted, to be tormented to death.
Acheweli, *Z.*, necessary (dub., *A.*).
Achewen, bushy; a bush, thicket (dub., *A.*).

Achewiecheu, strong, spirituous.
Achewon, strong, spirituous; (archaic, *A.*)
Achgachemawachtin, to share with each other.
Achgahamauwan, to distribute to somebody.
Achgahikewagan, distribution, division.
Achgameu, broad, wide.
Achgegenummen, to choose.
Achge'gim, to teach, to instruct.
Achgegingen, to teach.
Achgegingewagan, teaching, information.
Achgeketum, *E.*, a teacher; (*A'achgckinket, A.*)
Achgelinquoam, to behold, to look; (arch., *A.*)
Achgelunen, to lie.
Achgeluneuch, *E.*, a liar.
Achgenindewagan, accusation, bad report.
Achgenindin, to blame one another.
Achgepchoau, to be deaf.
Achgepinqueu, to be blind; (to be blindfolded, *A.*)
Achgepinquot, blind.
Achgetaktschehellau, to jump over the fence; (*lit.*, to brace one's self for a jump, *A.*)
Achgettemagelo, merciful.
Achgettemakinaquot, poorly looking.
Achgigihawan, to mock or laugh at somebody; (arch., *A.*)
Achgigulan, to sleet.
Achgiguwen, to play, to be noisy, to be lively, to be jocular.

Achgiguwewagan, sport, pastime.
Achgiiki, mocking, jesting.
Achgikbi, elm, the elm tree.
Achginchen, to be quick of hearing.
Achgindamen, *Z.*, to count (also, to read, *A.*).
Achgiuchsowagan, drunkenness.
Achgiwalan, to deceive somebody; (arch., *A.*)
Achgiwalittewagan, deceit, fraud.
Achgiwalittin, to deceive, to cheat.
Achgonican, *or* Achquanican, *Z.*, a fish dam.
Achgook, snake.
Achgükbi, *Z.*, an elm tree.
Achgumen, dull, cloudy.
Achgumhok, cloud.
Achgumhokquot, cloudy; (*fig.*, to be still, *E.*)
Achgunnan, to clothe somebody; (*achgunha, A.*)
Achgussin, to burn the kettle; (dub., *A.*)
Achibis, to bind up or dress a wound; (dub., perhaps from *gachtun*, to bind, *A.*)
Achkindiken, to read; (*achkinsink*, to read, *A.*)
Achkiwelendam, to be disquieted, to be troubled in mind; (alludes to harsh occurrences, *A.*)
Achkiwitehewagan, irresolution.
Achochwen, to have bad travelling.
Achowalogen, to labor hard, to toil.
Achowat, hard, difficult, dangerous, painful, troublesome; (*achwat, A.*)
Achowelendam, to think difficult.

Achpa'mi, about, thereabouts.
Achpamsin, to walk, to walk about.
Achpanschi, beam, log for a house.
Achpateuny, *E.*, the east wind.
Achpekok, wound; (arch., *A.*)
Achpequot, wounded; *achpequat, Z.*, full of holes, from *pquihilleu*, it has a hole.
Achpin, to be there, to be at home.
Achpineen, abode, residence; *Z. epicnk*, where we are.
Achpiney, place to sleep on; *achpinink*, a bed, *Z.*
Achpi'que, flea.
Achpiquon, flute, fiddle (any musical instrument, *A.*).
Achpitawan, to be or abide in somebody.
Achpitpannik, ancestors, *Z.* (*lit.*, old residents, *A.*).
Achpitschiechen, to stop, to prevent.
Achpi'xu, full of fleas.
Achpoaliman, to mock somebody, to laugh at some one.
Achpoan, bread; *n'dapponhe*, I make bread; *achponhewak*, they make bread.
Achpoantit, piece of bread, small loaf.
Achpoem, roasted corn.
Achpoques, mouse; (*achpiques, A.*)
Achpussin, to roast, to broil.
Achquaneman, *H.*, a bushnet for fishing.
Achquanxowagan, lasciviousness, whoredom.
Achquetahen, to shoot at a mark.
Achquetschiechgugsin, to be tempted.
Achquetschiechtowagan, temptation.

Achquidhakamike, upon earth.
Achquin, to put on clothes; (*ehquink*, clothing, *A*.)
Achquindowagan, accusation, charge.
Achquipelawon, hoe.
Achquiwanis, blanket; (black or broad cloth, *A*.)
Achquoaici'lennees, *Z*., blackberries.
Achquoanan, to catch something with a net.
Achquoanemen, to fish with a bushnet.
Achquoani'kan, bushnet.
Achquoanquigeu, long timber.
Achschiechey, *Z*., a nest.
Achschikiminschi, fern.
Achsehhellen, to scatter, to disperse; (*seh'ellen*, *A*.)
Achsin, stone; pl., *chotachsin*, *Z*. (an archaic plural; now *achsinall*, *A*.).
Achsinemhoan, pewter spoon.
Achsinhittehikan, steel trap.
Achsinn'aminschi, sugar maple.
Achsinnigeu, stony.
Achtschingi, scarcely, hardly.
Achtschingiochwen, to venture to go.
Achtschinkhalan, to persuade somebody; to force somebody.
Achtschinkhewagan, disobedience; (*achtscheyinkgeusink*, *A*.)
Achtschipaptonen, to talk strangely, to speak roughly.
Achtschipilissin, to act strangely, to behave wonderfully.

Achtu, deer; (*achto'*. *A.*)
Achtuchwiecheken, deer's hair.
Achtuchwiminschi, red root.
Achtuhhu, plenty of deer.
Achwamallsin, to feel great pain; (to suffer in sickness. *A.*)
Achwangundowagan, lasting peace.
Achwangundowi, very peaceable.
Achwilek, hard, troublesome time; *achwileu*, (*A.*) it is a troublesome time.
Achwipisgeu, pitch dark.
Achwon, strong, spirituous; (forcible, violent. *A.*)
Achwowangeu, steep, high bank of a river.
Ahanhokqui, descended from, sprung from.
Ahas, a crow; (*ahasso*. *A.*)
Ahhino, a rich man; (dub., *A.*)
Ahiktek, a strowd.
Ahoalan, to love somebody; *ahoaltie'que*, *E.*, if you love.
Ahoalgussit, the beloved.
Ahoaltin, to love one another.
Ahoaltowagan, love.
Ahoaltowaganit, he that is love.
Ahoaltuwamallsin, to feel love.
Ahoaltuwi, loving.
Ahoatam, to esteem, to value.
Ahochwalquot, hard going, difficult travelling.
Ahotasu, *Z.*, dear, beloved (*ahoatasu*; does not apply to persons, but to things. *A.*).

Ahoweli, willful.
Ahowoapewi, strong; (power of endurance. *A.*)
Ajandamalquot, it is to be wished; it is desirable.
Ajandamoagan, desire.
Ajandamuwi, desired, wished for.
Ajanhelendam, to be indifferent, to be unconcerned.
Ajanhelendamoagan, indifference.
Ajanhissowagan, indifference, calmness of mind.
Ajapeu, buck.
Ajappawe, early in the morning.
Ajaskemi, for good and all.
Aje'ma, if, if only, if but; be so good, please.
Aji', take it.
Ajummen, to buy, to purchase.
Akquiwan, blanket; (black cloth. *A.* See *achquiwanis*.)
Alaaptonen, to break off in speaking.
Alachimoagan, rest; (the prefix *alach* is used to signify incapacity or inability. *A.*)
Alachimoatenamin, to rest happy.
Alachimuin, to rest.
Alagendowenke, after Sunday.
Alagischgu, day is spent.
Alahikan, a mark (to shoot at).
Alakqui, 'tis a pity!
Alakschachan, the wind ceases.
Alalechen, to cease breathing, to die; (dub., see *equilechlejeu*. *A.*)

Alalechet, the dying.
Alamachtagen, to stop fighting.
Alamikemossen, to stop working.
Alapenauwelendam, to leave off, to quit, to give up.
Alappa, to-morrow; (*ajappa. A.*)
Alappaje, early in the morning.
Alappiechsin, to speak fast.
Alasohen, to separate; (more exactly, to go asunder. *A.*)
Alawossin, to be unable to perform; to be incapable of doing.
Alemoagan, fear, apprehension; (arch., *A.*)
Alende, some.
Alett, rotten.
Alhakquot, stormy, rainy; land rain.
Alike, yet, still, nevertheless, however; for; already.
Allacquelendam, to be repentant.
Allamachtey, womb; (*lit.*, and generally, the inward parts. *A.*)
Allamawunke, *Z.*, under the hill.
Allamhakink, in the earth.
Allami, in there, therein, within.
Allamijey, in there, therein, within.
Allamuin, *Z.*, the war whoop (arch. See *Kowamo. A.*).
Allamunk, in there, therein, within.
Allamunque, in there, therein, within.
Allanque, star.
Allapehhellan, to rock somebody.

Allapi, *E.*, listen! here! (dub., *A.*)
Allapijeyjuwagan, activity, quickness.
Allauwin, to hunt.
Allemakewunk, on the north side of a hill.
Allemewachton, to carry abroad.
Allemi apuawachto, — *tangawachto*, — *tatchawachto*, — —*tepawachto*, falls in price;—*tatchittin*, to decrease.
Allemih'hillen, to pass by, to fly; (*ellameh'hilan. A.*)
Allemiminschik, sarsaparilla.
Allemitschellachton, to roll along.
Allewussowagan, majesty; (*lit.*, greater power; a comparative form. *A.*)
Allogalan, to send somebody.
Allogalgussin, to be sent.
Allogagan, servant.
Allogaganin, to keep a servant.
Alloge'wagan, work.
Allohak, strong, powerful; more powerful; (a comparative form. *A.*)
Allohakasin, to teach, to instruct; (*lit.*, to have power over another. *A.*)
Allohumasin, to show.
Alloku, lean; poor; (probably for *alloqueu*,—it is too bad, it is inferior. *A.*)
Allokuwagan, leanness.
Alloquepi, hat; cap.
Allouchsit, strong, mighty.
Allouchsoagan, strength.

Allowat, strong, mighty.
Allowelemuwi, valuable.
Allowelendam, to esteem highly; to prize above everything.
Allowelendamoagan, great esteem, high estimation.
Allowigamen, to overcome, to subdue.
Allowihillen, to leave over.
Allowilek, that which is above everything, most weighty.
Allowiwi, more, yet more, much more; rather;—*mehek*, greater.
Allum, dog; (more exactly, any domesticated animal. *A.*) (Compare *moekaneu* and *linchum*.)
Allumaptonen, to say on.
Allumes, little dog, pup; (young of any domestic animal. *A.*)
Allumhammochwen, to set off by water.
Allummahen, to throw.
Allummeuchtummen, to go away weeping.
Allummochachton, to carry away.
Allummochwalan, to bring somebody away.
Allum'sin, to go away.
Allumtoonhen, to say on.
Alluns, arrow, bullet; (especially and originally, arrow. *A.*)
Allunshikan, bullet mould.
Allunsinutey, shot bag.
Alod, for, yet.
Am, well, indeed.

DICTIONARY. 19

Amakquitehemen, to cut off; (*amank'itshen*, to knock off. *A*.)

Amamchachwelendamen, to suffer.

Aman, fishing line, rope; *n'dapi aman*, *H.*, I come from fishing with a hook and line; (*aman*, properly, cord, string. *A*.)

Amanatak, fishing line.

Amandamen, to feel.

Amandamoagan, feeling.

Amandamuwi, sensitive.

Amangachgenimgussowagan, the being elated by praise.

Amangachpoques, rat.

Amangamek, large fish.

Amanganachquiminschi, Spanish oak.

Amanghattachcat, coarse linen.

Amangi, big, great, large.

Amangiechsin, to speak loud, to cry out.

Amatschiechsin, to speak brokenly.

Amatschipuis, turkey buzzard.

Amatschisowapasigan, the herb "colt's foot."

Ambeson, *Z.*, an Indian cradle.

Amechachwilawechtowagan, chastisement.

A'mel, *Z.*, a hammer.

Amemens, child.

Amemensuwi, childlike, childish.

Amementit, babe.

Amemi, pigeon; (*memi*. *A*.)

Amendchewagan, disobedience, stubbornness.
Amentschinsin, to praise, to give honor.
Ametschimi, often ;—*ne leep,* there was more done.
Amiga, long, a long time.
Amimi, *Z.,* a dove. See *Amemi.*
Amintschindewagan, praise.
Amintschiuchsin, to disobey.
Amintschiuchsowagan, disobedience.
Amochol, canoe, boat.
Amocholes, little canoe.
Amocholhe, poplar; (the buttonwood or sycamore ; *lit.,* the boat wood, as canoes were made from it. *A.*)
Amoe, bee ; wasp; (a generic term for the kind. *A.*)
Amoewiwikwam, bee hive.
Amoquigachschechin, to bruise the finger nail.
Amoschimoe, spike buck ; yearling.
Amueen, *Z.,* to angle.
Amuigenan, to raise somebody up.
Amuin, to arise.
Amuiwagan, resurrection.
Anakan, pl., *all,* mat made of rushes.
Anatschihuwewagan, care, cautiousness.
Anatschiton, to take care.
Andhanni, bullfrog.
Anechwunaltey, bark canoe.
Anehku, bark; (*anechuin. A.*)
Anena, by little and little ; by degrees ;—*ikalissi,* the more, more and more.

Anenawi, by little and little, by degrees;—*mcheli*, the more, more and more.
Anetassoagan, *Z.*, helplessness.
Aney, road, walking road, path.
Angellen, to die; (*lit.*, going to decay, may be applied to animate objects during life. *A.*)
Angellowagan, death.
Angellowi, mortal, deadly.
Anhoktonhen, to interpret.
Anicus, *Z.*, a mouse, a ground squirrel; pl., *anixak*.
Aninsihhillen, the young of a bird or fowl.
Anischik, thank'e; thanks.
Anixi gischuch, (the month in which the ground squirrels begin to run) January.
Ankhittasowagan, loss.
Ankhitton, to lose.
Anoschi, shoe-string.
Anschiwi, more by degrees.
Ansenummen, to take together.
Ansiptikin, to bind up into sheaves.
Apachgilentschachsin, to warm the hands.
Apachtoquepi, crown.
Apachtschiechton, to display, to set something up; to attach one's self to, to fix upon.
Apagihen, to come from planting.
Apaligen, to tread upon; (*achpaligen*. *A.*)
Apallauwin, to come from hunting.
Apalogen, to come from work.

Apami, in vain.
Apanachen, to come from cutting wood.
Apatschin, to come back, to return.
Apel, apple.
Apemikemossin, to stop working.
Apendamen, to enjoy, to make use of.
Apendelluxin, to be made partaker.
Apendelluxowagan, the being made partaker.
Apensoagan, *Z.*, enjoyment, fruition.
Apensuwi, useful, enjoyable.
Apipachgihhillen, to bud, to shoot forth.
Apit, by the way.
Apitchanehhellen, contrary mind.
Apitschi, after a little while, by and bye.
Apittehikan, anvil; (*lit.*, where one thing is struck upon another. *A.*)
Aptatschin, to freeze to death.
Aptelendam, to grieve to death.
Aptonagan, word; chapter; (strictly, a word. *A.*)
Aptonaltin, to speak with each other.
Aptonen, to speak.
Aptuppeu, drowned.
Apuangellen, to die easily; to die quickly.
Apuat, easy, easily.
Apuawachto, cheap.
Apuelendam, to think easy.
Apuichton, to make easy, to make light.
Aputschiechton, to turn the wrong side out.

Ascaletschi, unripe.
Aschanquussin, to be cast away; to be rejected.
Aschite, then.
Aschowin, to swim; *aschowill, n'daschwül,* I swim.
Aschowitchan, raft.
Aschtehhellen, to go or cross over one another.
Aschtetehasik, *Z.*, the cross †; (*aschtetchican, A.* The former refers to the stick, the latter to the symbol.)
Aschukiso, poor, worth nothing, beggar.
Asgask, green; *askeu, Z.* (this means "raw;" *askasqueu,* it is green, for a leaf, etc. *A.*)
Asgaskachgook, green snake.
Asgelendam, to wait with impatience.
Aski, must, necessitated, obliged.
Askiquall, grass, herbs.
Askiwi, raw, green.
Aspenummen, to lift up.
Aspenuxin, to be lifted up.
Aspin, to ascend; (*ispin. A.*)
Aspinachken, to lift up the hand.
Aspochwen, to go up, to ascend.
Aspoquen, to raise the eye.
Assisku, mud, clay.
Assiskuju, muddy, dirty, marshy.
Assisquahoos, earthen pot; *assiskequahos, E.*
Assisquohasu, daubed with clay.
Assisquohen, to mix clay.
Atenkpatton, to quench fire.

Atschimolehan, to relate to somebody.
Atschimolsin, to consult, to hold counsel.
Atschimolsoagan, counsel, advice.
Atta, no, not ;—*am*, not at all ;—*auwen*, nobody ;—*hasch*, no, never ;—*ihaschi*, never, nevermore ; at no time ;—*ülewi*, not at all true ;—*kocku*, nothing ;—*tani*, by no means.
Attach, moreover, beyond, above.
Attago, no, by no means.
Auchsin, to be hard to deal with.
Auchsu, (of beasts) wild, untractable ; (of men) avaricious, difficult to deal with.
Auchsuwagan, Z., fury, anger.
Awechemos, creature, cattle.
Awe'hellea, Z., a bird (this is the generic term now in use. It means self-suspended, referring to the flight of birds. *A*.)
Awehhelleu, bird, fowl ; (applied to large fowls, etc. *A*.)
Auweken, to make use of.
Auwen, who, somebody, which ;—*ha?* who then ? *ma*, who is there ?
Auweni ? who is it ?
Auwih ! oh ! (exclamation of pain.)
Auwijewi, yet, however.
Awelemukunees, young buck.
Awelendam, to be certain, to be sure.
Awendam, to suffer pain.

Awendamoagan, suffering.
Awendamowanglowagan, painful death.
Awendamuwi, painful.
Awessis, beast.
Awonn, fog, mist.
Awossachtenne, over or beyond the hill.
Awossagame, heaven; (*lit.*, the place beyond or out of sight. *A.*)
Awossake, behind the house.
Awossakihakan, that side of the plantation.
Awosschakque, over the log or tree.
Awosseki, over the leaf; (dub., *A.*)
Awossenachk, over the fence, behind the fence.
Awossenuppeque, over the lake.
Awossi, over, over there, beyond, on the other side, behind.
Awossijey, over, over there, beyond, on the other side, behind.
Awossin, to warm one's self.
Awullakenim, to laud, to praise.
Awullakeniman, to praise somebody.
Awullakenimoagan, praise.
Awullsittamen, to obey.
Awullsittamsewagan, obedience.
Awullsittamuwi, obedient.
Awullsu, good, fine, pretty; (animate, pl. *auwulsuak;* inanimate, *auwultu,* pl. *auwultol,*) (from *wulissu*). *A.*

C

B.

Bambil, (pl. *ak*) book, letter; (applied to any writing or writing material. *A.*)
Bambilenutey, pocket book.
Beson, medicine, physic; (out of use. *A.* See *chappik;* it is for *mbeson*, q. v.)
Bihilewen, to be hoarse.
Biminaten, to spin ; (see under P.)
Bingtschwanak, *E.*, the pupil of the eye.
Bischi, yes, indeed, to be sure ; (*biesch*, H. ibid.)
Bischik, yes, indeed, to be sure.
Bischuwi, wilderness ; (arch., *A.*)
Blaknik, flying squirrel.
Blenhotik, black snakeroot.
Blœu, *Z.*, a turkey cock. (*Ploeu*, turkey of either sex. *A.*)
Bochwejesik, *Z.*, joint of the foot.
Bochwinan, to skin an animal.
Bohhuhachqua, basket wood.
Bohhuhan, to peal off the rind of a tree.
Bokandpechin, to bruise the hand.
Bonihen, to lay on (wood on a fire).

C.

Ceppitsch, *Z.*, a conspiracy.
Chaasch, eight.
Chaasch tcha pachki, eight hundred.

Chaaschtchenachke, eighty.
Chaihoak, *Z.*, clothes-lice.
Challanunschi, sumach.
Chammap, *Z.*, fed (he or it was fed. *A.*).
Chans, elder brother.
Chanson, bedstead.
Chasquem, Indian corn.
Chauchschisis, old woman.
Chauwalanne, fork-tailed eagle.
Chawachto, dear, high priced.
Cheiho, *Z.*, the body (means that which is whole, entire. *A.*).
Cheinutey, saddle bag.
Cheli, much.
Chelit, a great deal.
Ches, pl. *ak*, skin; leather; *machtschilokees*, *Z.*, a leather string. (*Choi*, a pelt. *A.*)
Chesimus, younger brother or sister.
Chessachgutakan, leather breeches.
Cheweleleney, manifold.
Cheyjantup, *Z.*, a scalp.
Chinqualippa, great buck.
Chiquasu, patched, mended.
Chitquen, deep water, high water.
Choanschikan, Virginian (virginity ?).
Chokquinen, to cough.
Chokquineu, *A.*, he has a disease with coughing.
Chokquinewagan, cough.

Chottschinschu, big trough, large bowl; *chotachsun,* Z., a large stone.
Chowasquall, old dry grass.
Chumm, daughter-in-law; (*lit.,* my daughter-in-law. *A.*)
Chuppecat, deep, high water.
Chwelensowagan, pride.
Chwelhammook, great many deer tracks.
Chweli, much, many; *chweltol,* as many; *chwelopannik,* there were many.
Chwelokunak, many nights.
Clagacheu, *H.,* it is aground, or, rests on something.
Clahican, *Z.,* a steel trap.
Clamachpin, *Z.,* to sit still; *clamachphil! H.,* sit still!
Clamhattenmoagan, *Z.,* steadiness.
Clammieche, *Z.,* to lie still.
Clampeechen, *Z.,* still or standing water.
Colassu, *Z.,* sweat by a bath.
Combach (quall), *Z.,* leaf, leaves of a tree; *cumbachquiwi,* it is full of leaves; compare *wunissak* (arch., *A.*).
Commoot, or, **Commootgeen,** *Z.,* stolen.
Cub'bachcan, thick; *cubbachcan packchack,* a thick board; *cubbachcan schackeef,* a thick skin.
Cuwe, *Z.,* pine tree; *cuweuchac,* pine wood (properly *p'koweu,* it is sticky, alluding to the resin. *A.*).

D.

Dachiquamen, to patch, to mend.
Dachiquoagan, a patch.
Dajasgelendam, to desire ardently, to wait for with much concern.
Dalakihillen, to tear, rend in two.
Dalaktschetechen, to fall and burst open.
Dallumens, tame creature; (any domestic animal, see *allums*. *A*.)
Damachgigamen, to tread under foot.
Damaskhikan, a scythe.
Damaskhiken, to mow.
Damaskus, muskrat; (dub. mod. *chuaskquis*. *A*.)
Dawamhican, *Z*., the jaw bone.
Delachgapachgunk, in the cleft of a rock.
Dellemangan, the thick part of the arm; (thy, *etc*. *A*.)
Dellsoagan, manner, custom, habit; (thy habit. *A*.)
Demasxalo, a file.
Despehhellan, to have the smallpox.
Despehhellewagan, smallpox (dub., *A*.).
Dulheu, *Z*., the bosom, breast (with possessives).

E.

E—e, *H*., Yes (lazily).
Echgoquijeque, ye serpents.
Eemhoanis, spoon.

Eenhawachtin, to pay one another, to satisfy each other.
Eenhawachtowagan, payment, reward.
Eenhen, to pay.
Eenhiken, to pay; (*enhe'ken. A.*)
Eesgans, *Z.*, a needle (arch., *A.*).
Eet, perhaps, may be.
Egohan, *H.*, yes, indeed!
Eh! Eh! exclamation of approbation.
Ehachgahiket, distributer, divider.
Ehachpink, place; *ehachpit, Z.*, his place.
Ehachpit, his place, his habitation.
Ehachpussitunk, gridiron.
Ehachquink, clothing.
Ehachquit, etc., his cloth, etc.
Ehachtubuwing, *Z.*, a cup.
Ehalluchsit, the mighty and powerful.
Ehamhittehukuk, battery of a gun lock.
Ehangelikgik, the dead; (arch., *A.*)
Ehasgitamank, watermelon.
Ehelamek, ribbon.
Ehelandawink, ladder.
Ehelekhigetonk, ink.
Ehelikhique, at which time.
Ehelilamank, well, spring, fountain; (a running or flowing spring. *A.*)
Ehelinguatek, stove pipe.
Ehendachpuink, a table.

Ehenendhaken, to speak a parable.
Ehes, muscle; clam.
Eheschandek, window.
Eheschapamuk, *Z.*, a bottle; (anything of glass. *A.*)
Ehoalan—(pl. Ehoalachgik), beloved, dear.
Ehoalgussit, the beloved.
Ehoalid, my lover.
Ejaja, etc., where, wherever or whither I go, etc.
Ekajah! aye! aye! exclamation of surprise.
Ekamejek, broadness.
Ekamhasik, broad.
Ekee! ay! exclamation of surprise.
Ekesa! *H.*, for shame!
Ekhokiike, at the end of the world.
Ekih! O my! exclamation of pain.
Ekisah! exclamation of indignant surprise.
Ekoqualis, raspberry.
Eksasamallsin, to feel less pain, to feel better.
Eksaselendam, to diminish, to disesteem.
Eksaselendamoagan, restraint, abridgment.
Eksasi, less.
Elachpaje, this morning.
Elachtoniket, he that searcheth, seeker.
Elalogen, what to do.
Elamallsin, how to feel, to feel as.
Elangellen, to be leprous; (*lit.*, to perish miserably. *A.*)
Elangomat, friend, relation; (*lit.*, a member of one's family. *A.*)

Elangomellan, my friend.
Elauwit, hunter; (*chalowit. A.*)
Elawachtik, so dear.
Elek, as it is, as it happens.
Elekhammajenk, our debts.
Elekhasik, as is written.
Elelemukquenk, what we are destined for.
Elemamek, everywhere; (*lit.*, as it lies; the sense "everywhere" not now known. *A.*)
Elemamekhaki, all over the country; (*lit.*, "the way the land lies." *A.*)
Elĕmi, to-day once, sometime to-day;—*gendowewagan*, this week;—*kechokunak*, in a few days;—*nipink*, this summer;—*siquin*, this spring;—*lowank*, this winter.
Elemiechen, along the road.
Elemiechink, by the way.
Elemokunak, one of these days.
Elemukulek, in the bend of the river.
Elemussit, he that is going away.
Elenapewian, thou Indian!
Elewunsit, as he is called, so he is named; (*eliwinsit. A.*)
Elgigui, as, like as, in like manner, like that; so, so as, so very; as much so, as well as; (after compar.) than; —*ametschimi*, as often as, so often;—*mcheli*, as much as.
Elgigunk, as big, as wide as.

Elgigunkhaki, as big and wide as the world is; all the world round.
Elgilen, as tall as, as big as.
Elgixin, to be worthy.
Elhokquechink, at his head.
Eli, because; (in questions) then; (in compos.) as, so, what.
Eligischquik, to-day; (sometime during to-day. *A.*)
Elikhikqui, at this time.
Elikus, ant, pismire; (*eli'ques. A.*)
Elilenin, as is usual with one, as is customary.
Elinaquo, as this, as that, as the other.
Elinaquot, so, so as, also, likewise.
Elinaxit, as he appears; his appearance, figure, look.
Elinquechink, before, in presence of.
Elitehat, as he thinks.
Elitton'henk, sermon; (concerning a sermon. *A.*)
Eliwi, both.
Elke ! *H.,* wonderful!
Elogalintschik, messengers.
Elogamgussit, messenger.
Elsija, etc., as I am, as I do, etc.
Elsit, as he is minded, as he does.
Eluet, as he saith, his saying.
Eluwak, most powerful.
Eluwantowit, God above all.
Eluwi, most.
Eluwiahoalgussit, the beloved above all things; best beloved.

Eluwikschiechsit, the most holy, holiest.
Eluwilissit, the most gracious one.
Eluwitakauwussit, the best, the supremely good.
Eluwitschitanessit, the strongest.
Eluwiwulik, the very best, the supremely good.
Eluwussit, the Almighty, the most powerful, the most majestic.
Enapandikan, the hind sight of a gun.
Enda, where, whither.
Endchappin, as many as are here.
Endchekhamman, as much as one owes.
Endchen, as often as.
Endchi, as much as, as many as.
Enendhaken, to speak a parable.
Enendhakewagan, parable.
Epia, etc., where I am, etc.
Epigachink, foundation.
Epit, he who is there; inhabitant.
Equiwi, under; beneath.
Equohellen, to depart this life, to die.
Es, yet.
Eschauwessit, side.
Eschiwi, through.
Eschochwalan, to help somebody through, to carry some one through.
Eschochwen, to go through, to drive through.
Eschoochwejupetschundchenk, it penetrates my heart.
Espan, *z.*, a raccoon.

Espenni, lift it up.
Esquande, door; entrance (threshold or place of entrance; not a door. *A.*).
Esquo, not yet.
Esquota, not yet.
Esseni, stony, flinty; (from *achsin.*)
Etachgilowank, last winter.
Etachginipink, last summer.
Etek, where it is.
Etschigapawin, to step between, to stand between.
Etschihillat, mediator.
Eweken, to make use of; (*ewehen'. A.*)
Ewenikia, etc., who I am, etc.
Ewochgehikan, stirring ladle.

G.

Gachene, if, whether.
Gachgamun, roasted corn; (alludes to the noise made in eating by crunching the grains. *A.*)
Gachgamuniminschi, hoop-ash.
Gachgenummen, to break off.
Gachhachgik, wild bay.
Gachkappawi, soon, early.
Gachpallan, to pull somebody out of the water; (*gochpenna. A.*)

Gachpattejeu, southeast; (there are now no expressions for such divisions of the compass. *A.*)
Gachpattejewink, toward the southeast.
Gachpees, twin.
Gachpilgussowagan, binding, tying.
Gachsasu, dried.
Gachsummen, to dry.
Gachtalquot, it is to be wished, it is desirable.
Gachtelawossin, to be dry for thirst; (*gachtoseu. A.*)
Gachten, dry.
Gachti, almost nearly; close by; *wsami*, almost too much.
Gachtin, year.
Gachtingetsch, next year; (*gachtinge'. A.*)
Gachtonalen, to persecute, to seek to kill; (*gachto* signifies wish or desire. Like *gatotamen. A.*)
Gachtonquoam, to be sleepy; (radical is—*quoam*, referring to sleep. *A.*)
Gachto'tam, to desire, to lust.
Gadhammawachtowagan, last will, testament.
Gagachgelunen, *Z.*, to tell lies.
Gagachti, almost, very near.
Gagiuhokewagan, deceit.
Gagiwanantpehellan, to be dizzy; to be giddy in the head.
Gagun, stocking; (legging. *A.*)
Gahan, shallow; low water (not in use. *A.*).
Gahowes, mother; (*g'ichk*, my mother. *A.*)

Gakelunenhen, to make to a liar.
Gakloltowagan, quarrel, dispute.
Gakpitschehellat, Z., a madman, a fool (a fool. *A.*).
Gamenowinenk, on the other side of the great sea.
Gamunk, over there, on the other side of the river, over the water; (*gamink. A.*)
Gandhatton, to hide, to conceal; *n'danthallen hackey*, Z., I hide myself in the earth.
Gandhikan, setting pole; (a pole with which to push a boat. *A.*)
Gangamattok, bad action, bad behavior; (out of use. *A.*)
Ganschala'muin, to cry out.
Ganschapuchk, big rock; (a boulder. *A.*)
Ganschapuchken, rocky, full of rocks.
Ganschelalogen, to do great wonders.
Ganschelalogewagan, wonderful work.
Ganschelendam, to wonder, to be surprised.
Ganschewen, to roar, to make a great noise; (*guanschewell. A.*)
Ganschhittaquot, it makes a terrible noise.
Ganschilallogen, to perform a miracle.
Ganschinaquot, it is surprising.
Gashikan, dishclout; (a skin or cloth for rubbing. *A.*)
Gasihhillen, to decay, to fade.
Gaskhamen, Z., to notch.
Gatatam, to want, to desire; *gatotamen*, Z., to long for.
Gaton, to hide, to conceal.

Gatschiechtowagan, mystery, secret.
Gattamen, to desire, to long for.
Gattati, come! be willing! well!
Gatti, near, almost.
Gattonachsin, to persecute, to seek to kill.
Gattopuin, to hunger, to be hungry.
Gattosomuin, to thirst, to be thirsty.
Gattungwam, *Z.*, sleepy, drowsy (arch., *A.*).
Gauwin, to sleep.
Gauwoheen, to lie down to sleep.
Gawi, *Z.*, the hedgehog; pl., *gawiak*.
Gawunsch, *Z.*, briars (*gawinsch*. *A.*).
Gawunschuwitschik, gooseberries.
Gebtschaat, foolish fellow, clown.
Gechgauwiwink, *Z.*, a bed.
Gechgelandamink, bridle-bit.
Gechkschutteek, *Z.*, an oven (a stone. *A.*).
Gechpilgussowoagan, *Z.*, a knot.
Geeschtek, hot.
Gegachxis, lizard (not in use. See *tucchque*. *A.*).
Gegauwink, bed.
Gegekhoat, thy chosen, thy elect.
Gegekhuntschik, the elect, the chosen.
Gegepchoat, the deaf; a deaf person.
Gegepinquot, blind; a blind person.
Gegeyjumhen, to rule, to reign.
Gegeyjumhet, ruler, governor, head chief.
Gegeyjumhewagan, rule, government.

DICTIONARY. 39

Gegochbisik, *Z.*, a belt, a girdle; (*gochbisink. A.*)
Gekschiechtigehend, washing tub.
Gektemagelemuwi, merciful.
Gektemagelowagan, mercy.
Gelackelendam, *Z.*, levity.
Gelantpepisit, tied about the head.
Gelelendamen, to be of opinion.
Gelen'nin, to take hold; (or, to hold in the hand. *A.*)
Geliechhammen, to sow, to stitch.
Gellenummen, to take along.
Gelohittamen, to disbelieve.
Genachgihan, to take care of somebody; (*genachgcha. A.*)
Genachgihat, overseer; preserver.
Genachgiton, to take care of.
Genam, to thank.
Genamoagan, thank.
Genamuwi, thankful, grateful.
Gendachgussin, to climb up; (*gelachgusi. A.*)
Gendatehundin, to drive in a nail.
Gendelemuxin, to be condemned.
Gendelemuxowagan, condemnation, damnation.
Gendelendam, to condemn.
Gendelinget, he that condemneth.
Gendowen, Sunday; (*lit.*, a day of worship. *A.*)
Gendowewagan, week.
Gendowewuniwi gischquik, Sunday.
Gendsitaja, ball of the foot; (hollow of the foot. *A.*)

Gendsitat, ball of the foot; (as above. *A.*)
Gentgeen, *Z.*, to dance (*gintkaan. A.*).
Gentsch, a little while ago;—*linitti*, just now, not long ago.
Geptschat, *H.*, a fool; pl., *schik.*
Geschiechek, pure, holy; (*lit.*, washed; not used now in a moral sense. *A.*)
Geschiechsit, pure, holy; (as above. *A.*)
Geschiechton, to wash.
Geschtek, ripe, done, cooked.
Geskundhak, pumpkin; (out of use. *A.*)
Getaam, *Z.*, the hazel nut.
Getanittowit, Great Creator, God; (rather, the great spirit. *A.*)
Getisgamen, to drive out; (*ge'tsche'gamen. A.*)
Getschachgenummen, to loosen, to untie.
Getschihillalan, to betray somebody; (out of use. *A.*)
Getschihillalittin, to betray each other.
Getschihillalowet, traitor.
Gettemageleman, to help somebody, to relieve some one, to compassionate some person.
Gettemagelemuxowagan, the being shown mercy, favor, tenderness.
Gettemagelensin, to be humble.
Gettemagelensit, one that is humble.
Gettemagelensitawan, to humble one's self before somebody.
Gettemagelensuwi, humble.

Gettemagelentin, to be kind to each other, to be merciful toward one another.
Gettemagelin, to be merciful.
Gettemagelowagan, mercy.
Gettemagelowaganit, he who is merciful.
Gettemageluwi, merciful.
Gettemaki, poor, miserable.
Gettemakitschitanengussin, to be a miserable slave.
Gettemaxin, to be poor, to be miserable.
Getteminak, fortunate, happy; (not in use. *A.*)
Getteminakuwagan, felicity, happiness, gladness.
Gewit, sleeper.
Gichgehhelleu, a fowl with young ones.
Gichtamen, *Z.*, to be lazy; (*gichtämeneu*, he is lazy. *A.*)
Giechgi, near by, close by, toward.
Giechgigawachtowagan, nearness.
Gigauwinasu, *Z.*, borrowed (not in use. *A.*).
Gigischquik, this day past.
Gigitowalan, to speak with somebody, to talk to some one.
Gigitschimuis, summer duck.
Gihim, to encourage, to admonish.
Gihiman, to admonish somebody, to exhort some one.
Gilkissin, to laugh; (*achgilkissin. A.*)
Ginanikamen, to have good, sharp teeth.
Gintsch, a little while ago, if; (after negat.) unless, except;—*linitti*, a little while ago, directly, presently.
Gintschglennin, to push.

D

Gintschimuin, to sound, to crow.
Gintschtschingussit, messenger.
Gintschtschinman, to send somebody; (to appoint somebody. *A.*)
Gischachgeniman, to judge somebody.
Gischachgenindewagan, impeachment, accusation.
Gischachgenutasu, concluded, settled, determined.
Gischachgenutemen, to conclude.
Gischachpoanhe, the bread is done baking.
Gischachsoagan, enlightening, shining.
Gischachsummen, to enlighten.
Gischachtek, clear, light.
Gischachteu, it is clear, light.
Gischalo'gen, to finish a work.
Gischambeso, bound, tied.
Gischamocholheu, the canoe is finished.
Gischapan, daylight, daybreak.
Gischatschimolsin, to have resolved, to have decreed.
Gischeleman, to create with the mind.
Gischelemuxit, creature.
Gischelendam, to hatch or meditate something good or bad; to lie.
Gischelendamen, to make, to cause.
Gischenachk, the fence is finished.
Gischenaxin, to be ready, to be prepared.
Gischgu, day.
Gischguniwi, by day, in the daytime.
Gischhakihen, to be done planting.

Gischhatteu, ready.
Gischhittelawan, to hit somebody.
Gischiechen, to be ready, to be done, to be finished.
Gischigachink, grounded.
Gischigin, to be born; (to ripen, to mature. *A.*)
Gischigu, born.
Gischihan, to create with the hands, to make something.
Gischikenammen, to increase, to produce fruit.
Gischikewagan, *Z.*, procreation, reproduction.
Gischikheu, to finish a house, to make a house ready, to put a house in order.
Gischileu, it has proved true.
Gischipenauwelendam, to have considered, to have made up one's mind, to be ready.
Gischitehen, to be determined.
Gischiton, to make ready, to prepare, to finish.
Gischkschagokan, saw.
Gischkschagotamen, to saw.
Gischkschasgokan, scythe, sickle.
Gischkschummen, to cut with a knife.
Gischquik, day.
Gischquike, by day.
Gischuch, sun, month.
Gischuchwipall, sunbeams, rays of the sun.
Gischuteu, warm, lukewarm.
Gischuwalheu, ready packed, ready laden.
Gischuweu, warm.
Gischuwewickwam, warm house.

Gischuwikwamikat, warm house.
Giskhammen, to chop.
Giskhaquen, to cut with an axe, to chop.
Gispuin, to be satisfied, to have eaten enough.
Gissa! exclamation of indignation.
Gissai! exclamation of indignation.
Glakelendam, to be merry, to make sport; (to be excited. *A.*)
Glatten, frozen.
Glelendam, to be of opinion.
Glikatepi, hobble; (girth of a saddle. *A.*)
Glikatepiso, hobbled.
Glikenikan, sumach.
Glistam, to hearken, to listen.
Glittonepi, bridle; (*lit.*, tied in the mouth. *A.*)
Gloltowalan, to maltreat somebody; to use some one ill; (out of use. *A.*)
Gluphokquen, to look back; (from root *glupk*, back (adverb). *A.*)
Gluppiechton, to turn about.
Gluppihilleu, turned about.
Gluxu, *Z.*, he laughs; *glüksowak*, they laugh.
Gochgachgaschowin, to swim over.
Gochgahhellen, to overset.
Gochpelolakan, canoe rope, boat line.
Gochpiwi, from the water.
Gochquoapetechin, the pulse; (*k'hokpetechin*, the rebounding, the pulsation. *A.*)

Gock, wampum, money; (*keekq'. A.*)
Gohan! yes, exclamation of approval!
Gojachti, for the most part, mostly, nearly; (arch., *A.*)
Gōkhos, owl; (generic for any owl. *A.*)
Gokhotit, little owl.
Gomuus, *Z.*, the neck (arch., now use *ochquecanggan. A.*).
Gopens, about, thereabouts.
Gophammen, *H.*, to shut close.
Goppachtenemen, to take out of the water.
Goquehemen, to reject, repel, push back, repulse; refuse, avert.
Goschgosch, hog.
Goschgoschigawan, hog sty.
Goschgotit, little pig.
Guhn, snow.
Guka, *Z.*, mamma, mother.
Gulaqueen, good evening; (*anixit gulaqueen,* I am glad that you have lived till evening. *A.*)
Gull, shilling; (*kquill. A.*)
Gulukochsün, *Z.*, a turkey cock (refers to the upright position taken by the fowl, but not now in use. *A.*).
Gulukquihillan, to be lame; (out of joint. *A.*)
Gulukquot, lame; (with a joint, or jointed. *A.*)
Gunagen, to stay out long.
Gunalachgat, deep.
Gunammochk, otter.
Gunaquot, long, tall, high; (especially, high. *A.*)
Gunaweke, yet, awhile.

Gunaxin, to be long, to be tall, to be high.
Gunaxit, long, tall, high.
Gundakan, throat.
Gundaschees, watersnake.
Gundassisku, deep mire, deep mud.
Gundassiskuju, deeply marshy.
Gunelendam, to think it a long time; to think a thing long.
Guneu, long.
Gunigischuk, daily.
Gunih, a long while.
Guninschu, trough.
Gunitpoquik, mighty; (not in use. *A.*)
Guntam, to swallow.
Guntschitangen, to exhort, to admonish.
Guntschitangewagan, admonition, exhortation.
Gutginquechin, to look back.
Gutgisgamen, to drive back.
Gutgu, knee.
Guthattachgat, single thread, untwisted.
Guttandamen, to taste.
Guttapachki, one hundred.
Guttasch, six.
Guttasch tcha pachki, six hundred.
Guttasch tche nachke, sixty.
Güttenummen, to take off, to pull off.
Guttgennemen, to return something, to give back.
Ganschiechsin, to cry aloud.

H.

Ha, ha! exclamation of laughter.
Hackiálachgat, *Z.*, a cellar.
Hagiach, *Z.*, beans, earth-beans.
Haken, coal; (not in use. *A.*)
Hakey, body, self; (*w'hakey*, his body; always with possessive pron. *A.*)
Hakeyiwi, bodily, corporeal.
Haki, earth, ground.
Hakiachxit, bean.
Hakihakan, field, plantation.
Hakihen, to plant, to farm.
Hakihet, planter, farmer; (*ek'hakihet*. *A.*)
Hakink, under;—*untschi*, from below.
Hallachpis, *Z.*, wild hemp.
Hallemiwi, eternal, eternally.
Hallepangel, barrel, cask (not a native word. *A.*)
Haniqus, ground squirrel; (any kind of squirrel. *A.*)
Hapichque, *Z.*, a rib (*opichque*, a rib; *opochquan*, all the ribs. *A.*).
Happa, yet a little while; a little longer.
Happachpoon, chair; saddle; bench; seat.
Happenikan, pincers.
Happi, with it, in the bargain.
Happis, a band for carrying burdens.
Haschawije, square; (*lit.*, many corners; *schaweje*, one corner, a square corner. *A.*)

Haschi, ever, at any time.
Hattape, bow.
Hattawaniminschi, dogwood; (not now used. See *taquachhakaniminshi.* *A.*)
Hattees, sinew.
Hattelü, having.
Hatten, he has, it is there.
Hatton, to put, to place, to fix; (to put in a place. *A.*)
He, he! exclamation of laughter.
Helleniechsin, to speak the Indian language; (from *lenno,* man. *A.*)
Hempsigawan, *Z.*, a tent.
Hickachquon, shin; (*w'ichkachquon,* his shin bone. *A.*)
Higihhillen, the water falls, abates.
Hikan, ebb tide; (at the ending of the flow. *A.*)
Hikpesemen, to boil water in till dry.
Hilleu, commonly.
Hitguttit, little tree.
Hittandelitewagan, instruction.
Hittuk, tree; (the prefix *M'* is necessary. See *Mehittuk.* *A.*)
Ho, exclamation of vociferation.
Hobbenis, turnip; (*lit.,* a small tuber, potato, etc. *A.*)
Hob'bin, *A.*, a potato.
Höh, exclamation of surprise.
Hoh, exclamation of joy.
Hohoh, exclamation of joy.

Hokes, bark of a tree; (some particular bark not now known. The usual word is *anschuin*. *A*.)
Hokeyall, himself.
Hokquoan, pothook; a chain.
Hokunk, above, above the earth;—*li*, upward;—*untschi*, from above.
Hoos, kettle, pot.
Hopexu, kidney; *hope'xuac*, pl., *Z*. (not in use. See *totcloos*. *A*.)
Hopikan, rib; (*opichquai*. *A*. See *hapichque*.)
Hopiquon, foreshoulder.
Hopoakan, a pipe for smoking; (arch., *A*.)
Hopochquan, side.
Huh! exclamation of vociferation.
Hukqui, chin; (*w'ikqui*, his chin. *A*.)
Hukquomilan, hail; (*mukquomelan*. *A*.)
Hummak, *Z*., head lice.
Huppeechk, rain worm.
Husca, very;—*mcheli*, very much; (*husca, wisca*, properly means new; *kange*, is very, as *kange wulit*, very good. *A*.)
Huscateek, very much, very much so.

I.

Ichauweleman, to let somebody have the preference.
Ichauwelendam, to prefer; (*tachauwelendam*, to desire to give one an advantage. *A*.)

Ichauwi, rather.
Ihiabtschi, still, to this time.
Ihih! exclamation of grief.
Ijabtschi, yet, still, nevertheless, however.
Ika, there, yonder;—*talli*, there, over there;—*untschi*, from there, thence; (*nellak*, is used locatively with these terminations, not *ika*. *A*.)
Ikali, thither; (*nellakli'*. *A*.)
Ikalissi, further, still further; still more.
Ikalitti, a little further.
Ikih! exclamation of grief.
Ilau, *H.*, a war chief; (properly, a man of valor, one experienced in war, not necessarily a chief. *A*.)
Ili, however, nevertheless, still, yet, though;—*matta*, not even, *allowi matta*, let alone;—*wsami*, quite too.
Ink (suffix), in, in the, on, out of.
Iwi! exclamation of grief.

J.

Jagatamoewi Gischuch, July; (from *amoe*—honey bee month. *A*.)
Jaga'wan, hut, house; (not in use. *A*.)
Jahellaap, net of yarn; (not now known. *A*.)
Janewi, always, at all times.
Japeechen, along shore, along the bank, on the river side.

Japewi, on the bank, at the edge; a high bank.
Jawi, on one side.
Jechauwelendam, to love better, to prefer; (see *Ichauwelendam.*)
Ju, exclamation of joy.
Ju, well!
Ju, here, hither;—*endalauchsit*, man;—*shaki*, so far as here;—*talli*, just here;—*undach*, this side;—*undachqui*, here, hither, this way;—*wuntschi*, from hence, for that reason, therefore.
Juch, well!
Juchnall, hither.
Juchnook, well!
Juchta, now (used in petitioning or interrogating).
Juhuh! exclamation used in calling.
Juk, these.
Juke, now, presently;—*gischquik*, to-day;—*likhiqui*, at this time, about the present time;—*petschi*, till now, hither;—*untschi*, henceforth.
Jukella! ah! oh that! would that!
Juketeek! oh that!
Jukik, these.
Julak, there.
Jullik, these.
Jun, here; through here; there; this one;—*talli*, here.
Juque, now.

K.

Kaak, wild goose; (*kaag'*. *A.*)
Kajah! wonderful! exclamation of wonder.
Kakey, thyself.
Katschi, don't, let it alone! (doubtful. *A.*)
Katschiwoak, besides, further, again.
Keecha? how much?
Keechen, a few times.
Keechi? how much? (how many? *A.*)
Keechitti, a little.
Keechoguni? how long?
Kehella! yes! exclamation of approval!
Kekschittek, a stove.
Kepe, thou also, thou too.
Kepene, we also; (*ki lonawitsch*, the form *ke* in these words is not in use. *A.*)
Kepewo, ye also, you too.
Kepoak, they also.
Ki, thou.
Kichgematgeu, *Z.*, a thief.
Kichkinet, *Z.*, a guide (from *kichkican*, a mark or sign; *kichkinet*, one who understands the marks. *A.*).
Kigin'amen, to know, to be acquainted with.
Kiginolewagan, sign, token.
Kigischgotum, green grasshopper.
Kih! exclamation of pain.

Kihhican, *Z.*, a boundary (a line, a mark. *A.*).
Kihneu, sharp, biting, harsh, jealous; (means sharp, only. *A.*)
Kihnhammen, to sharpen, to grind.
Kihnhanschikan, grindstone; (*kihnhican*, a sharpener. *A.*)
Kihnsu, sharp, biting, harsh, jealous.
Kikape, a single man; a bachelor.
Kikechum, the mother (of beasts); (properly, a female animal without a mate. *A.*)
Kikehuwet, physician.
Kiken, to mend in health, to grow better.
Kikewagan, cure, life; (*lit.*, the means of getting better in health. *A.*)
Kikey, old, aged; (*kikes*, adults, older people. *A.*)
Kikeyihen, to lend; *kigaihil*, *Z.* (not in use. *A.*)
Kikeyin, to be old, to be aged.
Kikeyjumhet, elder, chief man.
Kikeyochqueu, elderly woman.
Kikochques, a single woman.
Kiluna, we (including the party speaking and the party spoken to).
Kiluwa, ye or you.
Kimi, secretly.
Kiminachsin, to murder secretly.
Kiminachsoagan, murder, assassination.
Kiminachsu, a secret murderer.
Kiminalitten, to assassinate.

Kimiwipengeen, *Z.,* to commit adultery (*lit.,* to sleep secretly together. *A.*).
Kimixin, to go from some place secretly.
Kimochwen, to steal away privately.
Kinhican, *Z.,* a grindstone.
Kinhochkus, pike fish.
Kipachgiminschi, upland hickory; (species of oak. *A.*)
Kitschganinaquot, convenient.
Kitschgansowagan, convenience, commodiousness.
Kitschii, verily, truly; (great, very. *A.*)
Kitschikele, yes, it is true; (incorrect; *ele* is a superlative form, and could not be used with *kitschi*. *A.*)
Kitschinipen, summer, June.
Kitschitachquoak, autumn month, September.
Kitschiwi, certainly, truly, verily.
Kittachpanschi, spar, rafter; (any large piece of timber; from *pantschi*, timber. *A.*)
Kittahikan, great sea, ocean.
Kittakima, great king; (the word *sakima*, of which this is a compound, is no longer used. *A.*)
Kittan, great river; (arch., *kitscepu* would be used now. *A.*)
Kittapachki, thousand.
Kittaptonen, to affirm, to assure.
Kittelendam, to be in earnest.
Kittelendamwagan, earnest.
Kittelinsch, thumb.

Kitthukquewulinschawon, thumb.
Kittoaltewall, great ships.
Kittuteney, great city.
Kiwikaman, to visit somebody.
Kiwiken, to visit; (*lit.*, thy-house-going; not now used. *A.*)
Klahikan, trap.
Klakaptonaganall, *Z.*, an amusing tale.
Klakauchsowagan, divertisement, light-mindedness; (from *gluxsu*, he laughs.)
Klakelendam, to be rakish, to be extravagant, to be dissolute, to be a good-for-nothing fellow.
Klamachpin, to be quiet, to sit still.
Klamhattenamin, to be of a calm mind.
Klamhattenamoagan, calmness of mind.
Klammiechen, to be still, not to progress.
Klampeechen, still water.
Kloltin, to quarrel, to contend; (to use bad words to each other. *A.*)
Kloltowagan, quarrel, dispute.
Klunewagan, *Z.*, a lie, a falsehood.
Knattemihi, *Z.*, lend me.
Kolku, what, something; what?—*cet*, what may it be?—*tani?* what then?—*untschi*, for what reason, why;—*wuntschi*, why; (*queq! A.*)
Kombachquall, leaves, foliage.
Komelendam, to be free from trouble or care; (not in use. *A.*)

Kommot, to steal.
Kommotgen, stolen.
Kommothaken, to steal something out of a field.
Kopachkan, thick.
Kopachkisse, thick.
Kotschemunk, out of doors, out of this place; without; abroad; (*quotsch' mink.* *A.*)
Kpahasu, locked up, shut up, caught.
Kpahi, shut the door; (*kpah'hi'.* *A.*)
Kpahikan, stopper; a cover or lid.
Kpahon, door.
Kpahotink, prison; (*keh'pahotink.* *A.*)
Kpaskhasu, stopped.
Kpatten, frozen over; frozen shut.
Kpiktschehican, Z., a cover, a lid.
Kpitschchikan, breech of a gun.
Kpitscheu, unruly, foolish behaved.
Kpitschewagan, foolishness.
Ksakpatton, to make wet.
Kschachan, the wind blows hard.
Kschahepakandamen, to beat hard.
Kschamamquo, grievous, troublesome.
Kschamehhellan, to run fast.
Kschaptonalan, to use somebody ill, to abuse some one.
Kschatey, tobacco; *achwan Kschatey*, strong tobacco.
Kschatteechen, beaten road, path.
Kschiechanittowit, Holy God.

Kschiechauchsowagan, holiness, innocence.
Kschiechek, clean.
Kschiechelendam, to think one's self from stain; to think one's self sinless; to think that one is holy.
Kschiechelensin, to believe to be blameless, to believe to be holy.
Kschiechen, to wash.
Kschiechen, clean.
Kschiechgochgihillen, to bleed fast.
Kschiechhensin, to wash one's self.
Kschiechi, clear.
Kschiechihin, to make clean.
Kschiechpecat, clear water.
Kschiechsin, to be clean.
Kschiechton, to wash, to cleanse.
Kschihillen, to go fast, to go swiftly.
Kschikan, knife; (*pachschikan.* A.)
Kschilan, it rains hard.
Kschilandeke, summer.
Kschilandeu, very hot weather; (*lit.*, much sunshine. A.)
Kschipasques, green grasshopper.
Kschippehellen, the water flows rapidly; strong current.
Kschipsin, to have the itch.
Kschipsit, one that has the itch.
Kschite, broth; (*kschite*, the *i* long. A.)
Kschitten, warm, hot.

E

Kschiwineu, it snows very thick.
Kschochwen, to walk fast.
Kschuppan, blunt, dull.
Ksinachpin, to be at leisure.
Ksinelendam, to be easy, to be without care.
Ksinhattenamin, to be of an indifferent heart and mind.
Ksinhattenamoagan, indifference, calmness.
Ksukquamallsin, to be perplexed, to be in anguish of mind; (*ksakquelendam*, thou art perplexed. *A.*)
Ksukquamallsoagan, perplexity, mental anguish.
Ksukquinaquot, heavy in a manner.
Ksukquon, heavy; hard, difficult; hardly.
Ktakan, another; otherwise, in another manner.
Ktemakauchsoagan, poor, miserable life.
Ktemaki, poor, miserable, infirm.
Ktemakiechin, to lie sick in a poor condition.
Ktemaque, beaver; (*amochk.* *Z.*)
Ktemaxin, to be poor, to be miserable; to be poorly.
Ktschihillalan, to betray somebody.
Ktschillachton, to make known, to make manifest, to speak the truth.
Ktschimine, as soon as.
Ktschin, to go out; (*acktschin*, impers. *A.*)
Ktschinquehhellen, the sun rises.
Ktschiqwagan, gun drawer.
Ktscholtin, to come out of church.
Ktschukquihhilleu, it moves, it stirs.

Ktschukquilques, *Z.*, grasshopper (*lit.*, it moves in the grass. *A.*).
Ktukin, to turn back; (probably an error for *k'tokkin*, to wake up. *A.*)
Kulluppi, *Z.*, to convert (*lit.*, to turn. *A.*).
Kunhaffun, *Z.*, to polish, to grind, to sharpen.
Kutschin, to come out of the house.
Kuwe, pine; (see *Cuwe*.)
Kuweuchak, pine wood, pine logs.
Kuwewanik, red squirrel.

L.

Lachauweleman, to be concerned for somebody.
Lachauwelendam, to be concerned for something; to be troubled in mind.
Lachauwelendamen, to take care of, to be concerned for.
Lachauwelendamoagan, concern.
Lachauwiechen, to hinder.
Lachenendowagan, release, loosening.
Lachenummen, to untie, to loosen.
Lachgalaan, *Z.*, to anger.
Lachgaman, to treat somebody ill.
Lachkan, sharp tasted.
Lachpiechsin, to speak fast.
Lachpihhilleu, it goes fast, it moves swiftly.

Lachpikin, to grow fast.
Lachwegegquoakan, harrow.
Lachxowi'lenno, Z., captain (one experienced in war. A.).
Lachxu, Z., a fishing rod.
Lachxuagan, Z., anger.
Lakenindewagan, accusation.
Laktschehellan, to jump over, to leap over.
Lakusin, to climb up; *n'gendachgusi*, I climb up.
Lalchauchsitaja, fork of the toes; (*w'lhauchsitan*. A.)
Lalchauwulinschaja, fork of the fingers.
Lalenikan, scour grass; (*Equisetum hyemale*. B.)
Lalhan, to scrape something; (to rub, to polish. A.)
Lalhaquoakan, drawing knife.
Lalschin, to cut smooth, to make even.
Lamowo, downward, slanting.
Landawen, it runs up, it climbs up, it spins up; (not in use. A.)
Langan, easy, light, not heavy.
Langoma, Z., kinsman.
Langomuwinaxin, to look friendly.
Langundowagan, peace.
Langundowi, peaceable, peaceful; (without the prefixed *w'* this word means relationship. A.)
Langundowits'chik, Z., kindred, relatives.
Lapechikan, plough.
Lapeechton, to tune an instrument.
Laphaken, to replant.

Laphatton, to restore, to repair, to replace; (*lapachton*, to replace. *A.*)
Lappi, again, once more;—*tchen*, as much again.
Lappiechsin, to repeat, to say over.
Lappilennin, to come together again, to be together again.
Laptonachgat, meaning of the word, signification of the word.
Laptonasu, *Z.*, commanded (bridled, held by the mouth. *A.*).
Laschimuin, to dream; (not in use. *A.* Now *lungamen*.)
Laschinummen, *A.*, to see at a glance or for a moment.
Latschachken, to treat.
Latschessowagan, goods, merchandise.
Latschessowen, to enjoy riches; to possess.
Lattoniken, to search, to examine.
Lauchpoame, middle of the thigh.
Lauchsin, to live, to walk; (to live in a certain manner; to walk morally or otherwise, not literally. *A.*)
Lauchsohalid, he who makes me live.
Lauchsoheen, to make live, to make walk, to cause to be lively, to make happy.
Lauchsowagan, behavior, life.
Lauhakamike, middle of a piece of ground.
Lawachto, worth, value.
Lawachtohen, to set a price.
Lawachtowagan, price, value.
Lawantpe, crown of the head.

Lawasgoteu, Z., a wide plain (*lit.*, it is in the middle of a plain. *A.*).
Lawat, long ago; (*lawata. A.*)
Lawi, *A.*, the middle, midst.
Lawilowan, middle of winter; (*lawilowank. A.*)
Lawitpikat, midnight.
Lawochgalauwe, middle of the forehead.
Lawulinsch, middle finger.
Lechakquihhillen, it slackens.
Lechauhanne, fork of a river.
Lechauwak, fork; division, separation.
Lechauwaquot, a tree with a fork.
Lechauwiechen, fork of a road.
Lechewon, breath, air (from *awon*, mist. *A.*).
Lehellechemhaluwet, he who giveth life.
Lehellechen, to live, to breathe.
Lehellechewagan, breath, life; (*lehellachemhalgun*, Z., he saved my life.)
Lehellemattachpink, chair, stool, bench.
Lekau, sand, gravel.
Leke, true.
Lekhammen, to write.
Lekhammewagan, debt; (*lekhammawachtoagan*, an account. Z.)
Lekhasik, written.
Lekhasu, written.
Lekhikan, letter, epistle; book.
Lekhiken, to write.

Lekhiket, writer.
Lelawi, halfway, in the middle.
Lelemin, to let, to suffer, to permit, to grant.
Lelingen, to permit; to allow.
Lemachdappit, he who sits here.
Lemattachpin, to sit down.
Lenape, Indian; man.
Lenapeuhoxen, Indian shoes.
Lenhacki, *Z.*, upland (barren highlands. *A.*).
Lennahawanink, at the right hand, to the right.
Lennamek, chop fish.
Lenni, *Z.*, genuine, pure, real, original.
Lenni, hand it; (*linachke*, *Z.*, reach your hand.)
Lenniga'wan, *Z.*, a cabin (a common house, a temporary shelter, a store room. *A.*).
Lennikbi, linden tree (bark of the bass-wood tree. *A.*).
Lennitti, a little while.
Lenno, man; pl., *lennowak*.
Lennotit, little man.
Lennowasquall, fern; (*lit.*, male fern.)
Lennowechum, male of beasts.
Lennowehellen, male of birds and fowls.
Lennowinaquot, manfully.
Lepakgik, those who weep, weepers.
Lepakuwagan, weeping.
Lepoatschik, wise men.
Leppoewina, cunning man.
Leu, true; it is so.

Lewehhelleu, it sounds.
Li, to; thither.
Liechenan, to leave out.
Liechenummen, to take off, to take down.
Liechin, to lie down, to rest.
Liechsowagan, language.
Lihan, to do so to somebody.
Likhikqui, now, about that time; as soon as; as, so as.
Likhikquiechen, so as.
Lilchpin, to be willing; to be diligent.
Lileno, *A.*, an office, one holding an office.
Lilenowagan, custom, rule, law; (holding an office. *A.*)
Limattachpanschi, rafter on the roof of a house.
Linachgechtin, to lay hands to something.
Linachken, to reach forth the hand.
Linalittin, to fight; (refers to the extent of the fight. *A.*)
Linaquot, like unto; as this, that or the other; so, so as.
Linaxu, like unto.
Linchen, west wind.
Lingihhillen, it thaws, it melts.
Linhakamike, upland; (see *Lenhacki*.)
Linkteu, it melts.
Linnilenape, Indians of the same nation, Delawares.
Linquechin, to look, to behold.
Linschgan, finger.

Linxasu, melted.
Linxummen, to melt.
Lippoe, experienced; wise.
Lissin, to be so; to do so; to be so situated, to be so disposed; to act so.
Litchen, to think; to think so.
Litchewagan, thought, sentiment, opinion.
Littin, to say to each other, to say among themselves.
Littonhen, to preach in such a manner.
Liwamallsin, to mend, to grow better in health.
Liwasnosqueu, overgrown with weeds.
Liwasquall, weeds; (any kind of grass or weeds; generic. *A.*)
Liwi, toward.
Liwiechen, to rest.
Lo! see, behold!
Loaktschehellen, *Z.*, it leaps, it jumps.
Loamissowe, lately; (*lomisu. Z.*)
Loamoe, long ago, in olden times; (not now used in this form. *A.*)
Lochlogannechwin, to destroy.
Logahhellan, to be discouraged, to give up.
Logahhellen, discouraged; (broken up. *A.*)
Logahhellewagan, discouragement.
Loganechwin, to throw down, to destroy.
Logihilleu, it falls in.
Logillachton, to tear, to destroy, to stop, to cease.
Lohikan, forefinger; (*lit.*, the pointer. *A.*)

Lohumanwan, to show somebody.
Lokan, hip, thigh joint; (*w'lokan;* the possessive must be used. *A.*)
Lokat, flour; (something broken into bits; *loken,* flour. *A.*)
Lokenummen, to tear in pieces, to pull apart.
Lokhammen, bran, shorts.
Lokschummen, to cut loose; (arch., *pachschummen,* is to cut loose; *lokschummen,* to cut at the knot. *A.*)
Longachsiss, cousin; (error, a nephew. *A.*)
Lonquamwagan, a dream; (*lungwamen. Z.*)
Loquel! see!
Lowan, winter.
Lowanachen, north wind.
Lowaneu, northward, northerly, north; (*lowanewunk,* in the north; *lowanne Lenape, Z.,* northern Indians.)
Lowanneunk, northward.
Lowilaan, the rain is over.
Lowin, to pass by.
Lowunsuagan, *Z.,* a name. See *luwunsuagan.*
Lowulen, it burns in a flame.
Luchund, he is said to have said.
Luejun, said.
Luen, to say; (to give a definite sound of any kind. *A.*)
Luewagan, saying; (the giving a definite sound. *A.*)
Lungwamen, *Z.,* to dream.
Lunk, or, **Lunkus,** *Z.,* a cousin (error, a nephew. *A.*).

Luppoe, wisely.
Luppoëwagan, cunningness, wittiness.
Lusasin, to burn.
Lusasu, burnt.
Lussemen, to burn.
Lussin, to burn.
Luteu, it burns.
Lüwunsu, called, named.
Lüwunsuagan, the name; (*Kocu ktellünsi?* Z. What is thy name? *Kocu lowunsu wikimat?* What is thy wife's name?)

M.

Ma, here take it, there it is.
Maag, Z., female genitals.
Macheleman, to esteem somebody, to value some one, to honor some one, to praise somebody.
Machelemoachgeniman, to honor and praise somebody, to glorify some one.
Machelemoachgenimgussowagan, the receiving of honor and praise.
Machelemoachgenindewagan, praise, glory.
Machelemuwi, honorable, precious.
Machelemuxit, he that is honored.
Machelemuxowagan, honor.
Machelendam, to esteem, to value, to honor, to esteem it an honor.

Machelendamoagan, esteem, high value.
Machelensin, to be high minded, to be proud.
Machelensowagan, pride.
Macheli, much, many; (or, *cheli*. *A*.)
Macheu, great, large.
Machgachk, *Z*., a pumpkin.
Machgeuachgook, *Z*., copper snake.
Machiechsin, to speak loud.
Machkachsin, *Z*., copper.
Machkachtawunge, red bank of a river.
Machkachten, coal of fire.
Machkajappan, *Z*., the aurora, dawn (alludes to the redness of the morning sky. *A*.).
Machkalett, rusty.
Machkalingus, sunfish.
Machkametank, stream of a reddish color.
Machkanachkteu, twilight.
Machkasgachteyat, red-bellied snake.
Machkassin, brick.
Machkelechen, red looking.
Machkenummen, to pull off, to take off.
Machkeu, red; (*machkipachgihilleu*, *Z*., the leaves (of the trees) turn red (in the autumn). See *Combach*.)
Machkewehhellachtikan, flag, banner.
Machkhattachquall, red yarn, red thread.
Machkigen, *Z*., the white thorn.
Machkikeniminschi, thorn bush.
Machkipachgihhilleu, the leaves grow red.

Machkten, twilight; (redness of sky. *A.*)
Machque, bear.
Machquigen, plenty of bears.
Machquin, to swell.
Machquissin, to be swelled.
Machquissu, swelled.
Machtagen, to fight.
Machtageoagan, war, fighting.
Machtakeniman, to accuse somebody, to speak ill of some one.
Machtakenimgussin, to be ill spoken of.
Machtakenindewagan, bad accusation.
Machtalappajo, bad morning weather.
Machtalipachquall, bad shoes.
Machtallogagan, bad, wicked servant.
Machtallogasowagan, wicked act; sinful deed.
Machtalohumauwan, to direct somebody the wrong way.
Machtamallsin, to be sick.
Machtamellessuwi, indisposed, sick.
Machtando, devil; (*machtan'to*, a shortened form of machti-manitto. *A.*)
Machtandowagan, devilishness.
Machtandowinenk, *Z.*, hell; (*lit.*, among the devils. *A.*)
Machtapamukquot, dusky, dark.
Machtapan, bad, stormy weather; unpleasant morning.
Machtapeek, bad time, war time.
Machtapequonitto, evil spirit.

Machtaptonen, to speak uncivilly, to talk roughly, to use bad language.
Machtatenamen, to be unfortunate, to be unhappy, to be displeased; to be discontented, to be dissatisfied.
Machtatenamoagan, unhappiness, discontent.
Machtatenamohen, to make unhappy, to make dissatisfied.
Machtatenamuwi, unhappy, discontented.
Machtatschahen, to use somebody ill, to treat some one badly.
Machtauchsin, to sin; (*lit.*, bad life. *A.*)
Machtauchsowagan, sin.
Machtauchsuwi, sinful.
Machtenalittin, to fight, to fight with each other, to fight a battle.
Machtississu, bad, ugly; dirty looking.
Machtissu, bad, ugly.
Machtit, bad, ill.
Machtitso, bad, ill.
Machtittonhen, to abuse, to scold.
Machtiwitti, very little.
Machtonquoan, to have a bad dream.
Machtschihillen, spoiled, corrupted.
Machtschikamik, hole, grave.
Machtschikamikunk, *Z.*, a burial place.
Machtschikbiak, papaw tree; (*lit.*, red fruit tree. *A.*)
Machtschileu, bad action, troublesome time.

Machtschilissit, sinner.
Machtschilokes, leather-string.
Machtschiluppoat, hypocrite.
Machtschiluppoëwagan, hypocrisy.
Machtschimaquot, ill flavored, nasty smelled.
Machtschipak, shoe; (*machtsin*, whence moccasin. *A.*)
Machtschipoquot, ill tasted, of a disagreeable taste.
Machtschitehewagan, wickedness.
Machtu, bad.
Machtumbink, dung.
Machxitachpoan, bread mixed with beans.
Machxummen, to dye red.
Magami, early; (*majapowi. A.*)
Mahallamagen, to sell.
Mahellis, flint; (*mahales. Z.*)
Mahematschehellat, cock of a gun lock.
Mahonink, *H.*, at the deer-lick.
Majauchsin, to be of one mind.
Majauchsohen, to make of one mind.
Majauchsowagan, union, unity, agreement.
Majauchsu, one person, a certain one; (one alone. *A.*)
Majauchsuwi, of one mind, united.
Majauchsuwin, to be of one mind.
Majawat, one, only one.
Majawi, right, straight, proper; alone, simple;—wulit, best.
Majawiechen, it is right, it is as it should be; it agrees, it suits, it harmonizes, it corresponds.

Majawiechton, to do orderly, to do properly, to compare.

Majawihillen, it is right, it is as it should be.

Majewelendam, to be fixed in purpose, to be settled in mind.

Makesinnan, to shoe somebody; (see *machtschipak*.)

Makhaquoakan, grubbing hoe.

Maksaweek, Aaron root (*Rhus cotinus?* Z.)

Mallachsche, as if, as it were, like unto.

Mallachxit, bean; (the ordinary term. *A*.)

Mallaluns, iron wood (a sort of beech).

Malliku, witchcraft; (out of use at present; *machtanha*, one is bewitched. *A*.)

Mallikuwagan, witchcraft.

Mallsannuk, arrow, flint.

Mamachtachaweju, weakly.

Mamachtapewi, Z., naughty, bad.

Mamachtaptonagan, wicked language, vile talk; rough speaking.

Mamachtschiman, to revile somebody, to reproach some one, to insult somebody.

Mamachtschimgussowagan, the being insulted.

Mamalachgook, striped snake.

Mamalekhikan, writing, letter, book; (*lit.*, in crooked lines or stripes; applied to handwriting. *A*.)

Mamalis, fawn, young deer.

Mamalunquan, sort of stinging fly.

Mamawon, eyebrow.

Mamchachwelendam, to suffer, to endure pain.
Mamchachwelendamoagan, suffering, torment.
Mamelandamen, to vomit.
Mamguckcu, *Z.*, a plain without trees, a prairie (error; rather a plain with large trees. *A.*).
Mamiechanessin, to be ashamed.
Mamintschim, to praise.
Mamintschimgussowagan, the being praised.
Mamintschindewagan, praise.
Mamintschindin, to praise, to give glory.
Mamschalan, to remember somebody.
Mamschalgussowagan, the being remembered, remembrance.
Mamschaltin, to keep each other in remembrance.
Mamtschitsch, the last time, lastly.
Mamtschitschi, the last time, at last.
Mamukowagan, destruction, perdition; (refers especially to a fatal accident. *A.*)
Manachewagan, the cutting of fire wood.
Manask, second crop.
Manasuagan, *Z.*, jealousy (especially sexual jealousy. *A.*).
Mandoman, to blame somebody.
Mandomgussin, to be blamed.
Mandundewagan, blame, imputation.
Manejeu, it profits little, it contains but little.
Maniton, to make; *nin mattineto*, *Z.*, I make; *ki k'mallenito*, thou makest (arch., *nulitton*, I make, *kulitton*, etc. *A.*).

F

Manitto, maker, Creator, God; (properly, spirit, not maker. *A.*)
Manittowah'alaan, *Z.*, to bewitch.
Manittowihak, steel.
Mannachen, to chop wood.
Mannachet, wood cutter.
Manoquen, to scalp.
Manoquenasu, scalped (*manoquala*, one who is scalped. *A.*).
Manschasqueen, to mow, to reap.
Manschasquoakan, scythe.
Manschawileu, wonderful.
Mantowagan, spiritual power (from *manitto*).
Manungalan, to treat somebody badly.
Manunxin, to be cross, to be angry.
Manunxuagan, *Z.*, anger.
Manuppekhasu, skimmed.
Maqueleman, to be jealous of somebody; to envy some one.
Maschapi, bead.
Maschilamek, trout; (*lit.*, "like a fish," not now applied to a trout. *A.*)
Masgichteu, May apple.
Maskek, swamp.
Maskekhanne, muddy creek in a swamp.
Maskequimin, swamp huckleberry.
Maskik, grass, herb; (*maskequasq'*. *A.*)
Masktin, *Z.*, to ease one's self.

Massipook, the river drifts ice.
Matschachton, to carry away.
Matschalan, to bring somebody home.
Matschilissowagan, sinful behavior.
Matschin, to go home.
Matschinamen, to take ill; to be ill pleased.
Matschiton, to spoil something, to make mischief.
Matta, no, not;—*ta*, nowhere;—*tani*, in no way.
Mattago, no.
Mattalan, to come up with somebody.
Mattameechen, cross roads; (where one road enters another, not a cross road. *A.*)
Mattaptonaltin, to speak bad to one another; to scold each other, to abuse each other by words.
Mattaptonen, to speak uncivil, to talk roughly, to scold.
Matteleman, to despise somebody.
Mattelemuwi, despicable, contemptible.
Mattelemuxin, to be despised.
Mattelemuxowagan, the being despised.
Mattelendam, to be uneasy, to be troubled in mind; to despise.
Mattemigalan, to let somebody in.
Mattemigen, to enter in.
Mattochwen, to travel badly.
Mattonheen, *Z.*, to curse (to give bad words. *A.*).
Mauchsu, one living thing; one.
Mauwallauwin, to go hunting.
Mauwi, go and tell.

Mauwikhattoak, *Z.*, camped, encamped (collected together. *A.*).
Mawachpo, collector.
Mawachpoagan, tribute, tax.
Mawat, one, only one.
Mawemin, to meet, to assemble; (*mawewi, Z.*, an assembly.)
Mawenemen, to gather, to collect, to bring together.
Mawewigawan, meeting house.
Mawingewagan, reconciliation.
Mawinhaken, to go to war.
Mawinsin, to gather, to pick up.
Mawottakan, famine, scarcity of provision.
Mawunappin, to be assembled.
Mawuni, assembled, collectively.
Mbeson, *Z.*, brandy (spirits, from *mbi*. *A.*).
Mbi, water.
Mbiachgook, water snake.
Mbiachk, whale.
Mbidhitehemen, to cut one's self.
Mbil, *Z.*, beer; *mbilheen*, to brew beer.
Mbisis, *Z.*, a lake.
Mbison, *Z.*, bait; *tamaquei mbison*, beaver bait.
Mboagan, death.
Mboawikcham, hiccough.
Mboiwi, mortal, dead.
Mbokquasquihillan, to break in the ice.
Mechakgilik, great, big.

Mechakhokque, the month when cold makes the trees crack, December; (dub., *A*.)
Mechamek, wild rhubarb.
Mechaquiechen, high water, freshet.
Mechasktschat, thick bellied.
Mechateu, deep snow; (arch., *A*.)
Mechawachto, dear.
Mechek, great, large.
Mechelemuxit, the honored.
Mechelgik, great many; multitude.
Mecheli, much; (a great many. *A*.)
Mechelit, much.
Mechen, big, large.
Mechgilik, the great, the big.
Mechhanneck, large creek, large river.
Mechinkhakihakan, large field.
Mechinkhakihen, to plant a large piece of ground.
Mechinqui, great, large, big.
Mechinquinaquot, it appears large, it looks great.
Mechinquitehewagan, self pride.
Mechitquek, great depth.
Mechiwilawanit, great sarsaparilla.
Mechmauwikenk, *Z*., camp.
Mechmenahikeak, scum ladle.
Mechoak, old tree; (the *me*, prefix, in these and the following words would be omitted at present. *A*.)
Mechoammowi gischuch, shad month, March.
Mechohakihan, old field.

Mechouteney, old, dilapidated town.
Mechowasquall, old, dry grass.
Mechowi, old (in use); (*chowi.* *A.*)
Mechowijeyju, old from use.
Medhake, matter.
Medhapahin, to surprise.
Medhik, bad, wicked; evil.
Medsit, bad, wicked, evil one.
Meechgalanne, hawk.
Meechgalhukquot, red hair.
Meechgalowet, fish like a sucker; (red-finned sucker. *A.*)
Meechgapuek, ipecacuanha.
Meechxit, the red one.
Megucke, Z., a wide plain.
Megungi, wholly, entirely, purely, quite, alone.
Megutschi, wholly, entirely.
Mehakachtey, coal of fire.
Mehallamagen, to sell (error; to buy. *A.*).
Mehallamawachtowagan, merchandise.
Mehallamen, to buy, to purchase.
Mehamentschit, robber; (from *amentschiechten;* arch., *A.*)
Mehemendowan, to entreat somebody.
Mehemendowen, to ask pardon, to beg on.
Mehemetanglowagan, agony of death.
Mehihschiu, barren.
Mehittachpin, to be born.
Mehittachpit, begotten.

Mehittachpoagan, birth.
Mehittgus, twig.
Mehittschoak, barren tree.
Mehittschohawi, corporeal material.
Mehittuk, tree.
Mehokhokus, red cedar.
Mehokquami, ice.
Mehokquamileno, hail.
Mehokquik, bloody.
Mehokquiman, red bird.
Mehokquinewagan, bloody flux.
Mehokquitamen, to bleed at the nose.
Mehowimi, raspberry; (wild black raspberry. *A.*)
Mehuk, blood.
Mehukachgook, copper snake.
Mehukuwi, bloody.
Mejauchsit, one, a certain one.
Mejauchsoagan, *Z.*, an alliance, confederation.
Mejauchsu, one person.
Mejauchsuwin, *Z.*, to ally, to become one.
Meken, to give away, to surrender.
Mekeniechink, the end, the last day.
Mekih, corruption, matter; (error; giving it up; an error of the copyist for *melih*. *A.*)
Mekis, sheep; (*memekis*, imitative of bleating. *A.*)
Melandam, to vomit.
Melanschpen, to take a vomit.
Melanschpewagan, vomiting.

Melichgawan, pillow, cushion.
Melih, corruption, matter.
Melihasu, mattery, putrid.
Mellaam, to smell.
Memachtakeniman, to speak evil of somebody.
Memachtschilan, to speak evil to somebody.
Memachtschilissit, sinner; (of evil countenance. *A.*)
Memajauchsit, each one, every one.
Memakochkus, red-headed woodpecker.
Memanunxit, *Z.*, ill-natured, surly.
Memedhakemo, turtle dove; (*mowichleu*, the wild dove. *A.*)
Memeechxiteu, barefoot.
Memeechxitin, to be barefooted.
Memekis, sheep.
Memekschachey, sheep skin.
Memeu, woodcock.
Memgukek, plain; (not in use; *schingek*, level. *A.*)
Memhallamund, merchant, trader.
Memoschanigat, toothless.
Memsochet, traveller; (vagabond, idler. *A.*)
Men'achk, fence, fort; (*menachkhasu*, *Z.*, fortified place.)
Menachkah, fence rail.
Menachtin, to drink with each other, to tipple with one another.
Menachtin, *Z.*, to get drunk (*lit.*, to drink together, not necessarily intoxicants. *A.*).

Menantachk, swamp; (with trees meeting above. *A.*)
Menantak, pine swamp.
Menantschiwon, left hand; *menantschiwonunk*, to the left hand.
Menasowagan, jealousy, suspicion.
Menatehewagan, envy.
Menatey, island; (*menach'hen. A.*)
Menen, to drink.
Menenachkhasik, garden.
Menet, drunkard.
Meneton, to spend in drinking.
Menewagan, drinking.
Menewi, in some place; (all together in a place. *A.*)
Mengiechsu, a swan.
Mengwe, *H.*, an Iroquois; (lit., *glans penis. A.*)
Menhakehhamat, gardener.
Menhasik, skimmed; (scum. *A.*)
Menichink, congregation.
Menniwi, in some places, not everywhere.
Menpekhasik, skim milk.
Menuppek, lake, sea; (any enclosed body of water, great or small. *A.*)
Menutes, sack, bag; (generic. *A.*)
Mequik, bloody.
Mequit, bloody.
Mesak, building log; (*m'sagawon*, Z., a log house.)
Mesaquem, ear of corn.
Meschagen, to sit down; (out of use. *A.*)

Meschakan, wound; (out of use; *meschillawa*, wound. *A.*)
Meschandamen, to taste.
Meschatamen, to remember.
Mescheki, whole, entire, every bit.
Meschiechen, to slip, to fall.
Meschikaan, to come nigh to me, to draw near to somebody.
Meschuppalan, to sprinkle somebody.
Mesim, hickory nut.
Mesink, *Z.*, an idol.
Mesissachowak, large stinging flies.
Mesissu, whole; (the *me* in many of these words is not in use. *A.*)
Mesittewall, corn boiled whole; (out of use. *A.*)
Mesittschejeu, wholly, altogether.
Mesittschewi, quite, whole, entirely.
Messasquall, straw.
Messikanelan, to hail.
Messipook, the river drifts with ice.
Messixu, naked.
Mesukhoakan, glue.
Metachan, firewood.
Metachgelonen, to have told a ready lie.
Metakhammen, to cover.
Metakhan, to cover somebody.
Metapewit, wicked man; (a thievish fellow. *A.*)
Metaptonen, to break off speaking (he has said all he has to say. *A.*).

Metekenis, leather string.
Metelensit, humble being, low-minded person; (one who despises himself; *metauelensit*, humble person. *A.*)
Metellen, ten.
Metenaxin, to be ready.
Meteu, doctor; (out of use; it is derived from *meteohet*, to drum on a hollow body; a turkey cock is sometimes called *meteu*, from the drumming sound of his wings. The ancient medicine men used drums. *A.*)
Metimmeu, wolf; (arch. The word at present is *wiechcheu;* *lit.*, hairy dung, from the character of the excrement. *A.*)
Metschi, ready; already.
Metschiechgochgihillan, to bleed to death.
Metschihillan, to fall in; to vanish.
Metschihilleu, old, worn out..
Metschimhammen, to lock.
Metschimi, soon, presently.
Metschipachgihhilleu, fallen off.
Metschitehenemoalan, to design evil against somebody.
Metschitschank, soul, spirit.
Metschitschi, at last, the last time.
Mettachquohhemen, to cover.
Michalappotis, spider.
Michtquin'otees, *Z.*, a basket.
Miechakanak, ash; (white ash. *A.*)

Miechanatamen, to be ashamed.
Miechanelendam, to be ashamed of one's self.
Miechanelendamoagan, self shame.
Miechanessin, to be ashamed.
Miechanimgussin, to be made ashamed.
Miechaninaquot, shameful.
Miechanissowagan, shame.
Miechasquigamik, cabin covered with grass.
Miechbowe, plume of fowls; (the down, inner soft feathers. *A.*)
Miechhaquall, moss on trees.
Miechheken, hair.
Miechinquawon, eyebrow.
Miechponkthey, light white ashes.
Mietachsquall, hay.
Migihillan, to bow one's self down.
Migitamen, to bow toward.
Migomi, put me in mind.
Migopoquoak, taste.
Migun, quill; (*miquin*, a quill, *miquinuk*, feathers. *A.*)
Miguntin, to remind each other.
Mihillusin, to be aged, to be old.
Mihillusis, old man; (*mih'hillosis. A.*)
Mihn, huckleberry.
Mihnachpoan, huckleberry bread.
Mikemossin, to work, to labor; (out of use. *A.*)
Mikemossit, laborer.
Mikemossowagan, work, labor.

Mikindamen, to do, to make.
Milach, hair; pl., *milchall;* (*achtuch wiechewall, Z.,* deer's hairs; *allum miechegenall,* dog's hairs) (*wilach,* etc. *A.*)
Milan, to give to somebody (not expecting a return. *A.*).
Mileen, *H.,* the giving.
Milit, he who gives to me; (also, the thing given. *A.*)
Militak, father-in-law or mother-in-law; (error, aunt. *A.*)
Miltin, to give; (giving each other, mutually. *A.*)
Miltowagan, gift (without expectation of return. *A.*).
Minall, *Z.,* huckleberries, pl.
Mindawelendam, to be discontented, to be troubled; (expresses the feeling of discontent from unsatisfied hopes. *A.*)
Mindawewagan, discontentment.
Mingachsa, better, a little better.
Minschu, glad; (out of use. *A.*)
Minsi, one of the three tribes of the Linni Lenape, or Delawares; (from *min-achsin-ink,* where the stones are gathered together. *A.*)
Miqui, quite; far, far off;—*palliwi,* quite different;—*pili,* otherwise, by far otherwise.
Mis, elder sister; *n'mis, k'mis,* my, thy, etc.
Mischenahan, to touch somebody, to handle some one.
Mischenummen, to receive, to get.
Misseachpin, to be always abroad, to be seldom at home, to go a gadding.

Misseachpitschik, those who live scattered.
Misshakeuchet, frequent traveler, pilgrim.
Missochwen, to walk about, to travel about.
Mitachkaniechink, manifest.
Mitachkaniechton, to make manifest, to be revealed.
Mitachpin, *Z.,* to be born (*lit.,* to be seen in existence, in a place. *A.*).
Mitsuagan, *Z.,* food, aliment.
Miwelendam, to forgive.
Miwelendaman, to forgive somebody.
Miwelendamen, to forgive.
Miwelendamoagan, forgiveness.
Mizewagan, food, victuals, provision.
Mizin, to eat.
Mochgamen, to find.
Mochomsunga, *Z.,* forefathers, ancestors.
Moekaneu, dog; (see *Allum.*)
Mokdomus, lizard.
Mokum, blood; a vein (*moch'kum. A.*).
Monachgeu, ground hog; (from *monham. H.*)
Monhacaniminshi, *Z.,* dog wood (error, it is the black haw bush or tree. *A.*).
Monham, to dig; (*munhageen, Z.,* to dig a hole.)
Moochwes, worm; caterpillar (white grub. *A.*).
Moochwetit, little worm.
Mos, elk, cow; (applied only to deer and elk. *A.*)
Moschachgeu, bald, bare; clear, not turbid.
Moschakantpeu, bald headed.

Moschanigeu, toothless.
Moschhakquat, clear weather.
Moschiwi, clear, luminous, bare, naked; clearly, openly.
Moschpekat, clear water.
Mosigawan, cow stable.
Moskdonamen, to kiss; (from word for mouth, arch., at present *sissama* is used. *H.*)
Moskimŭs, *Z.*, a hare (the small gray rabbit. *A.*).
Motit, little calf; (dim. of *mos*. *A.*)
Muchigischgunemin, to keep holy day.
Muchomes, grandfather.
Muchwoapingus, opossum.
Mui, *Z.*, dung, excrement.
Muiminschi, wild cherry.
Muiúi, *Z.*, to beshit.
Mukoos, awl, nail.
Munhácke, *Z.*, a badger (see *monacque*).
Munschemen, to shave.
Muschgingus, rabbit.
Machtschilissowagan, sin.

N.

Na, the, that;—*eet,* perhaps;—*jupetschi,* until now, till here;—*shacki,* so far;—*tchi,* so much; *untschijey,* from thence.
Nacha, three.
Nachapachki, three hundred.
Nachawikan, three fathoms.
Nacheleney, three-fold.
Nacheleneyachgat, three different sorts.
Nachelii, together with.
Nachen, three times, thrice.
Nachenachke, thirty.
Nacheneyit, third.
Nachenol, three.
Nachenum, raccoon; (usually *espan. A.*)
Nachgiechen, contrary, against.
Nachgihhilleu, it stops.
Nachgohuman, to sing.
Nachgohumewagan, hymn.
Nachgoman, to answer somebody.
Nachgundin, to agree with one another.
Nachgundowagan, agreement, bargain; covenant.
Nachgutem, to answer.
Nachk, hand, my hand.
Nachkala, *Z.,* my forehead.
Nachogunak, three nights.
Nachohalemin, to be alone.

Nachohanneu, alone ; (*n'achoha*, I am alone. *A.*)
Nachoheteu, the house is empty, there is no one at home.
Nachpangoman, to salute somebody with a present.
Nachpauchsin, to possess, to have, to enjoy.
Nachpauchsowagan, conversation, familiarity, fellowship.
Nachpi, with, together with.
Nachpikin, to be by nature.
Nachquoawe, anything.
Nachwena, thereupon, after.
Nachxummawan, to enlighten somebody; to kindle a flame within one.
Nachxummen, to kindle, to light.
Nada, yonder to thither ; toward here.
Nadan, a float; *nadano amochol*, the canoe floats (*pithin*, afloat. *A.*).
Naga, according to.
Nagajek, by and bye, in a little while.
Nag'atamen, to trust, to confide in, to rely upon.
Nagelawendewagan, comfort.
Nageuchsin, to hope.
Nageuchsowagan, confidence, trust.
Nagewitti, in a little while.
Nagisgamen, to meet.
Nagisgauwan, to meet somebody.
Nagisgawachtin, to meet each other.
Nahanne, so, so it is.

Nahih, down stream.
Nahihillaan, to go down the water.
Nahimen, to sail down the stream.
Nahiwi, down the water.
Nahoochwen, to go down stream.
Najuman, to carry somebody.
Najundam, to carry a load.
Nakewi, a little while.
Nal, fetch.
Nalambeso, to gird.
Nalauchsin, to be fetched.
Nalauwi, heedless.
Nall, that, at last;—*nan*, that one; *netchi*, it is so much, that is all;—*tchen*, that is all.
Nallahhemen, to sail up the water.
Nallahih, up the stream.
Nallahiwi, up the river.
Nallahoochwen, to go up stream.
Nallowauchsowagan, heathenish life.
Names, fish.
Nan, that, that one, so;—*wtenk*, finally, at last; hereafter.
Nanachpauchsohen, to keep in fellowship.
Nanachxotawan, to mock somebody, to deride some one.
Nanatschitaquik, those that have the care of some business.
Nanhillowet, the one who takes care of the dead.

Naninga, a double plural termination denoting deceased persons.

Nanne, this one; that; so;—*leu*, that is the way of it, thus the matter stands; it is certainly true;—*talli*, through there, that way, even there;—*undachqui*, thitherward; toward where?—*untschi*, from thence, therefore;—*wentschi*, for this reason, therefore, because;—*woak*, as also.

Nanni, this, that.

Nanquon, heel.

Nanungihhillan, to tremble, to shake; (*ning'gihilla. A.*)

Napenallan, to seize somebody, to take some one prisoner.

Natachtu, he fetches wood.

Natasu, fetched.

Natchaquen, to fetch wood; (to go after wood. *A.*)

Natchen, it is all gone.

Naten, to fetch; (properly, to go after something. *A.*)

Natenan, to take somebody.

Natenummen, to take, to accept, to receive, to perceive, to discern, to know.

Natenuxowagan, fetching, reception.

Natenuxu, received.

Nathogen, to fetch over.

Natholan, to fetch somebody over in a canoe.

Natoochton, to inquire.

Natschiton, to engage in, to take care of, to be of opinion; (out of use. *A.*)

Natschuwallen, to fetch a load.
Nattawoapandamen, to look for, to seek.
Nattawoapin, to look for something; (to look around. *A.*)
Natto'namak, son-in-law (my).
Nattonamen, to seek for somebody.
Nauwaquepin, to hang down the head; (out of use; present form, *nimiquoquepu. A.*)
Nauweechinke, afternoon; (present form, *lauwauqueu. A.*)
Nawalan, to pursue somebody, to follow some one.
Nawalittin, to pursue each other.
Nawehhelleu, afternoon.
Nawochgen, to follow.
Nawotallauwin, to hunt by the way.
Ndappoanum, my bread.
Ndauwat, scarce, rare; rarely, seldom.
Ndelgiqui, etc., so as I, etc.
Ndellan, I tell somebody.
Ndelli, etc., that I, etc.
Ndoniken, to seek.
Ndoochtawachtin, to inquire of each other.
Ne, (pl., *nek*) the.
Nechasin, to be careful, to be watchful.
Nechink, the third time.
Nechit, third.
Nechnutschinget, nurse.
Nechochwen, to travel alone, to walk alone.

Nechoha, alone.
Nechohalennin, to be alone.
Nechohanne, to be alone.
Nechoheteu, the house is empty.
Nehellatank, the Lord; (*nehellalowit.* *A.*)
Neichgussin, to be seen, to be manifested.
Neichquot, apparent.
Neichtin, to see each other.
Neka, he, she, it.
Nekama, he, she, it.
Nekamawa, they.
Nekti, the only one, single.
Nektilennin, to be quite alone.
Nektinquot, one-eyed.
Nelema, not yet.
Nelemago, not yet.
Nelemata, not yet.
Nellnill, these.
Nelowauchsin, to lead a heathenish life, to be a heathen.
Nelowauchsit, unbeliever, heathen.
Nemen, to see.
Nemoagan, sight.
Nemochwitschet, the main sinew of the leg.
Nenachgistawachtin, to hearken to one another, to listen to each other.
Nenajunges, horse; (from *najundam*, to carry burdens on the back. *A.*)
Nenajungeshammen, to ride on horseback.

Nenapalek, unworthy, good for nothing.
Nendawagan, torch, lamp.
Nendawen, to carry a lamp, to go with a torch.
Nennachgallit, stammerer, stutterer; (*nachnachqueu. A.*)
Nennawipoquot, right tasted.
Nennemawahan, to find somebody out.
Nenostammoewagan, understanding.
Nentsitasin, to appear; (not in use. *A.*)
Nepe, I also; I too.
Nepene, we also; we too.
Nescalenk, or, Nesgessit Lenape, Z., black man, negro (*lit.*, black face. *A.*).
Ne schuk (used after negat.), but.
Ne shaki, so long as.
Nesquo, not yet.
Netami, first, the first.
Netamiechen, first, the first.
Netamiechink, first, in the first place.
Netopalis, warrior; (*menetopalis*, a scout or skirmisher. *A.*)
Netopalowewagan, war.
Neuchtin, to see each other.
Neweleney, fourfold.
Neweleneyit, fourth.
Newen, four times.
Newentschi, therefore.
Newinachke, forty.
Newo, four.

Newopachki, four hundred.
Newowikan, four fathoms.
Ngachkenumen, *Z.*, the break of day.
Ngagebinque, etc., I am blind, etc.
Ngagepchoa, etc., I am deaf, etc.
Ngagiguwe, etc., I am lively, etc.
Ngaginche, etc., I am.
Ngaltin, to quit each other.
Ngamuin, to keep a feast in Indian style.
Ngattummen, to leave behind, to bequeath; *nga'ttammen, Z.* (to abandon, *not* to bequeath. *A.*).
Ngemewi, always, constantly.
Nguttachtschessowen, to lay up one treasure only.
Nguttapachki, one hundred.
Nguttelendin, to be of one mind, to have one object.
Ngutteleneyachgat, a single one.
Ngutteli, one, single; singly.
Ngutti, one.
Nguttitehen, to be of one heart and mind, to agree.
Nguttitehewagan, the being of one mind; unanimity.
Nguttokuni, one night.
Nhakeuchsin, to hope, to trust.
Nhakeuchswochwen, to go in hope.
Nhakewelendamen, to hope, to trust.
Nhakewelendamoagan, hope.
Nhakey, myself.
Nhittami, at first, the first.
Ni, I.

Nianque, *Z.*, a wild cat.
Niechin, to come down.
Nieskeu, *Z.*, dirty.
Nigani, before, foremost, beforehand; (out of use; *nichala*, I outrun him. *A.*)
Niganigapawin, to stand foremost.
Niganit, the foremost.
Niganitawan, to run before somebody, to outrun some one; to come before somebody.
Nihillachquen, to kill a bear.
Nihillalatschik, subjects, people.
Nihillalgussin, to be dependent on another's command.
Nihillalquonk, Lord, master.
Nihillan, to strike somebody.
Nihil'lan, to kill somebody.
Nihillapejuwagan, redemption, ransom.
Nihillapeuhen, to make free, to liberate, to redeem.
Nihillapeuhoalid, my Redeemer.
Nihillapewi, free.
Nihillapewin, to be one's own master, to be free.
Nihillapewit, freeman.
Nihillasohen, to make free, to deliver.
Nihillasowagan, freedom, liberty.
Nihillatamen, to own, to be master of.
Nihillatammoewagan, right, privilege.
Nihillatschi, self, one's own person.
Nihillowen, to put to death, to murder.
Nihillowet, murderer.

Nihillowewi, murderous.
Nik, these, those.
Nikik, these, those.
Nil, these.
Nilchgussin, to be struck dead.
Nilchtin, to strike each other dead.
Nilum, my sister-in-law; (or brother-in-law, in opposite families. *A.*)
Niluna, we (including only the party speaking).
Nimat, my brother; (used also as friendly salutation between distant relatives. *A.*)
Nimawanachen, to make provision for a journey (from *nimawan*, a lunch. *A.*).
Nimenees, fish hawk.
Ninachtak, my brethren.
Ninutachpin, to be from the beginning.
Ninutschi, at the beginning, before now.
Nipachton, to raise, to set up.
Nipahwi, by night, at night.
Nipahwochwen, to go by night, to travel at night.
Nipawin, to stand, to stand up.
Nipen, summer.
Nipenachhen, summer hunt.
Nischa, two.
Nischapachki, two hundred.
Nischasch, seven.
Nischasch tcha pachki, seven hundred.
Nischasch tche nachke, seventy.

Nischekat, double.
Nischeleney, twofold, two sorts.
Nischen, twice.
Nischeneyit, second.
Nischinachke, twenty.
Nischink, in the second place.
Nischitquin, to kneel down; (*nishitquihin. A.*)
Nischitquitawan, to kneel to somebody.
Nischogunakat, two days ago, day before yesterday.
Nischogunakhake, two days hence, day after to-morrow.
Niskachgelunen, to lie abominably.
Niskachgelunewagan, an abominable lie.
Niskalamuin, to make an ugly noise, to cry.
Niskallogen, to do dirty work.
Niskallogewagan, nasty work.
Niskandamen, to taste nasty.
Niskassisku, muddy, miry.
Niskelan, ugly weather, rainy weather.
Niskelendam, to loathe.
Niskenolhand, miserably lazy.
Niskeu, nasty, dirty; (*niskaloje*, Z., it is dirty.)
Niskiton, to dirty; to bedaub.
Niskpatton, to make wet, to throw water.
Niskpeu, wet.
Nisktonhen, to be noisy, to talk nasty.
Nisktonhewagan, noisy, lying, nasty talk.
Nitaton, to be able to make something, to know how to do it; *n'nita*, I can.

Nitaus, sister-in-law (my brother's wife) (not in use. *A*.).
Nithuy, *Z*., the navel.
Nitis, friend, companion.
Nitsch! my child (exclamation of fondness).
Nitschan, my child, my friend; (my child) (not friend. *A*.)
Nitschantit, my little friend.
Noch, my father.
Nocha, my father.
Nochan, my father.
Nochgoatamen, to lick; (I lick. *A*.)
Nochnutemaliuwet, watchman, keeper; (*mechnotalixvet*. *A*.)
Nochnutemexetschik, shepherds.
Nodhittamen, to come into danger; (to meet by accident, lucky or unlucky. *A*.)
Nohenopenowagan, *Z*., the ague (*lit.*, the sickness that recurs again and again. *A*.).
Nohulentschik, those who give suck; (error; it means the infants who suck. *A*.)
Nolemelanden, sultry weather; (the word means something pleasing or agreeable, hence, warm weather. *A*.)
Nolemiwi, invisible, unseen; (properly means, not seeing, or not looking. *A*.)
Nolemutees, silk worm.
Nolhand, lazy; (out of use. See *gichtammen*. *A*.)
Nolhandewagan, laziness.
Nonagan, milk; (error; it means the nipple or mamma

of a woman; no native word for milk is known. The English *mellik* is used. *A.*)

Nonetschik, sucking babes.
Nonohellaan, *Z.*, to give suck.
Nonschetto, *Z.*, a doe.
Nosawoapamen, to gaze, to look steadfastly at something.
Noschhokquin, to go over the ice.
Nosogamen, to follow; (to imitate a person's conduct. *A.*)
Nostamoewagan, understanding.
Nostawachtin, to understand each other.
Notamaeishican, *H.*, a fishing spear.
Notchan, to come to somebody.
Notschingen, to nurse.
Nowahan, to know somebody; (dub., *n'nennawa*, I know him. *A.*)
Nowaton, to know.
Nowoaktschochwen, to go a crooked road.
Nowoawelendam, to be certain, to be sure of; (out of use; *m'majawelen'dam*, I am certain of it. *A.*)
Nquistook, my sons; an old form; modern form, *n'quisak*. (The syllable *to* is still inserted in certain formal addresses. *A.*)
N'schingi, etc., I do it unwillingly.
Ntiasohen, to feed, to pasture; (out of use. *A.*)
Ntite, for.
Ntite, I think; (*n'diteha*, I think. *A.*)

Ntitechquo, for, because.
Ntitechto, for, because.
Ntutemawachtin, to question each other.
Nukachtachemawachtowagan, last will, testament.
Nukachtummen, to forsake, to leave.
Nukalan, to forsake somebody, to leave some one.
Nukti, once more; only *one*.
Nuktogunak, one night.
Nuktoguni, only one night.
Nummahauwan, to perceive somebody, to be aware of some one.
Nuna'gan, Z., the breasts of a woman (see above).
Nundahemewagan, want, scarcity.
Nundajelensin, to be discouraged, to be low-spirited; (more exactly, I do not feel equal to it. *A*.)
Nundajelensowagan, humility.
Nundajelensuochwen, to go humbly.
Nundawi, wanting, less.
Nundehhellan, to want, to be in need.
Nundehhellewagan, want.
Nundejek, wanting, deficient, defective.
Nundewi, wanting, less.
Nungachtschin, to shake for cold, to shiver.
Nungihillan, to tremble, to shiver.
Nungiwi, trembling.
Nunscheach, she-bear.
Nunschetto, doe.

Nutachgamen, somebody calls from the other side of the river, he wants to be fetched across.
Nutamemensemin, to have children.
Nutamemenseu, child's nurse; (a companion of a child. *A.*)
Nutemalan, to watch somebody.
Nutemekiset, shepherd.
Nutemekschet, shepherd.
Nutiken, to keep watch; (rather, to mind a house. *A.*)
Nutiket, watchman, a guard.
Nutindam, to watch a place.
Nutschi, at the first, at the beginning.
Nutschihhillachsin, to be frightened.
Nutschihhowe, night walker, witch.
Nutschinallitin, *Z.,* to begin war.
Nutschingaat, *Z.,* a nurse.
Nutschisquandawet, doorkeeper.
Nutschque, in vain, to no purpose; (not in use. *A.*)
Nutschquehend, innocent sufferer, martyr.
Nuwingi, I like it, I am willing, etc.
N'wingi, etc., I do willingly, etc.

O.

Oapelukquon, white frost; (*wap-takpan. A.*)
Ochdomus, a woman's cousin; (dub., *A.*)
Ochquaso, belt of wampum.
Ochquechum, female of beasts.
Ochquehelleu, female of fowls and birds.
Ochquekangan, neck.
Ochquetit, little girl.
Ochquetschitsch, girl.
Ochqueu, woman.
Ochquewasquall, swamp fern.
Ochunk, at his or her father's.
Ochwall, his or her father.
Oh! exclamation used in answering.
Oho! exclamation used in answering.
Ohoh! exclamation of vociferation.
Ohum, grandmother.
Ojos, meat, flesh; a piece of meat.
Ojotit, a little piece of meat.
Ok, pl., *oquak*, Z., a moth (error; it means maggot. *A.*).
Olahellan, to have somebody, to possess some one.
Oleleu, bullfrog; (imitated from the croak. *A.*)
Olhatton, to have, to possess; to put up.
Olsittam, to believe.
Olsowagan, goodness; (out of use. *A.*)
Omen, to come from whence.

Oschummo, horn; (out of use; *wilawan. A.*)
Otchan, to somebody.
Otchuwewagan, his coming.
Otwebhassin, to become flesh.
Owoahan, to know somebody.
Owoaton, to know; (*weswaton*, to become conscious. *A.*)

P.

Paalochqueu, *Z.*, a coquettish girl.
Paan, to come.
Pabhaku, a pheasant; (*pachpachko. A.*)
Pachat, split; (*pachhaque*, to split. *A.*)
Pachelammen, to split wood.
Pachenikan, frow, splitting iron.
Pachgammak, black ash; (at present, *pechpohammen*, the pounded wood. Baskets were made from this, the strips being obtained by pounding. *A.*)
Pachgammakan, cutlass.
Pachgandhatteu, all is ready.
Pachgandikan, maul, hammer (*moquil*, maul, possibly a corruption of the English; *pachgandikan* is now confined to the flat piece of wood used in beating wash clothes. *A.*).
Pachganuntschi, white walnut; (at present, *quinokquim*, = oblong nut. *A.*)
Pachgeechen, where the road turns off.

Pachgelendam, *Z.*, to anger (*lit.*, to go from the right road. *A.*).
Pachgen, to turn out of the road.
Pachgihillan, to break, to break asunder; (*pachgeu*, one who leaves the road; *pachgihillan*, to leave the road at one side, to run off the road. *A.*)
Pachhakqueu, noon.
Pachhamawo, *Z.*, the wild red plum (*pochgama*. *A.*).
Pachhaquoakan, iron wedge.
Pachihillan, to split, to crack.
Pachkam'an, to beat somebody, to strike some one.
Pachkamen, to let blood.
Pachkenum, dark; (should be *pak'enum*, as below. *A.*)
Pachkschawen, to cut meat.
Pachkschikan, knife.
Pachkunummen, to break off.
Pachpanaloje, broad axe.
Pachsachenikan, tinder; (punk. *A.*)
Pachsa'jeek, *Z.*, a vale or valley; dim. *pachsajetit*, a gulley.
Pachschaquoacan, broad saw, board saw.
Pachsegink, *H.*, in the valley.
Pachsenummen, to halve.
Pachsilawe, half a fathom.
Pachsiwi, half.
Pachsukquin, to rise up.
Pachtenummen, to pull.
Pachtschukquilkees, grasshopper.

H

Pachtschuppeu, soft, mild; (doubtful; at present this word means tapering, pointed. *A.*)
Packcha'ck, *Z.*, a board.
Pagachtschateu, full, filled; (arch., *A.*)
Pagachtschaton, to fill; (*pagachtschuchpeen.* *Z.*)
Pagachtschiechen, filled.
Pagachtschuppen, to fill (used of liquids. *A.*).
Paiachkammen, to shoot, to fire off.
Paiachkhikan, gun, rifle.
Paihakquenaxin, to be glad to see somebody.
Pakachtechin, to fall to the ground; (to fall forward. *A.*)
Pakachtehellan, to prostrate.
Pakallohu, *Z.*, to halloo, to shout.
Pakandamen, to beat.
Pakandaptonen, to finish a discourse.
Pakandhatton, to repair, to make whole.
Pakantin, to box with each other; (to strike with anything. *A.*)
Pakantschi, complete, full; fully, entirely.
Pakantschiechen, accomplished.
Pakantschiechtasu, finished, completed.
Pakantschiechton, to fulfil, to complete.
Pakenum, dark.
Pakenummuihhilleu, it grows dark.
Pakihm, cranberries.
Pakitatamauwan, to forgive somebody.
Pakitatamawachtin, to forgive each other.

Pakitatamawachtowagan, forgiveness.
Pakiton, to throw away.
Pakquehellan, to desert.
Palaton, to earn, to acquire; (arch., *A.*)
Palenach, five.
Palenach tcha pachki, five hundred.
Palenachtchegit, fifth.
Palenach tche nachke, fifty.
Palippawe, buck.
Pallachpin, to be innocent.
Pallachpuwagan, innocence.
Pallalogasin, to sin.
Pallalogasowagan, crime, evil deed.
Pallatschimuin, to speak otherwise than the truth, to prevaricate.
Pallawewagan, transgression, guilt.
Pallelensin, to be innocent.
Pallenummen, to make wrong, to set about wrongly.
Pallhammen, to be unable to perform.
Pallhiken, to shoot amiss; (*pallakhiken. A.*)
Pallhittehemen, to strike amiss.
Palliaan, to go away.
Pallihillan, to miss the time.
Pallikteminak, unfortunate, unlucky.
Pallilennemen, to put elsewhere.
Pallilinaquot, otherwise.
Pallilisgawan, to drive somebody away.

Pallilissin, to do amiss; (now means, to look different from what was expected. *A.*)
Pallilissowagan, transgression.
Palliton, to spoil something, to do it wrong.
Palli undachqui, somewhere else; where else?
Palli untschi, from somewhere else.
Palliwi, elsewhere, otherwise; different.
Palliwochwen, to go elsewhere.
Palpateu, it boils over; (it overflows, from any cause; *pallikaminden*, water overflows because of a fire. *A.*)
Palsachtin, to be sickly.
Palsin, to be sick; (arch., *A.*)
Palsittamen, to disbelieve.
Palsowagan, sickness.
Pangepoantit, bit of bread.
Pangeschin, to cut a piece.
Pangewi, a piece; (anything broken off. *A.*)
Pankhanne, steep bank.
Pankpechen, drop.
Papabin, to play; (arch., *A.*)
Papaches, woodpecker; (*papachko. A.*)
Papachgillintsch, the flat of the hand.
Papallachwilsummen, to miss one's luck, to miss one's chance.
Papalligeen, *Z.*, to spoil; see *palliton*.
Papalsin, to be very sickly.
Papchakhitehasu, bruised.

Papeek, *Z.*, a pond.
Papenauwelendam, to pay attention to, to be concerned for.
Papen'damen, to hear by chance; (error; it is an iterative from *pendamen*, to hear, and means to continue to hear. The initial syllable *pa*, gives the iterative or continuing sense in this and most of the following words. *A.*)
Papesu, patient; (a person who waits. *A.*)
Papiluwulissin, to be otherwise disposed.
Papohhamen, to knock at the door.
Papommeuchtum, to go about weeping.
Papomminin, to go about idle.
Pasachtaje, wind in the belly.
Pasalanges, locusts.
Pasawinchikan, yeast.
Passenummen, to deny, to disown; (*pasuen. A.*)
Passihillachgechquiminschi, swamp oak.
Passikachk, board; also *packchack*.
Passikachkhen, to make boards.
Passitechin, to stumble.
Pasteu, it rises (bread).
Patachwilsin, to gain, to get; (*pachtachwilsin*, to gain by working. *A.*)
Patahowen, to overcome, to subdue.
Patahowewagan, *Z.*, wages, pay.
Pataman, to pray.
Patamauwan, to pray to somebody, to worship.

Patamawos, God.
Patamoelchan, to pray for somebody.
Patamoelchittewagan, supplication for each other.
Patamoelchittin, to pray for one another.
Patamoelchuwewagan, intercession.
Patamoewagan, prayer, worship.
Patamoewigawan, house of prayer, temple, church.
Patatammoewagan, merit.
Pawalin, the corn blossom falls off.
Pawallessin, to be rich.
Pawallessit, rich person.
Pawallessohen, to make rich.
Pawallsoagan, wealth, riches.
Pawinquehiken, to shell corn.
Pawunnen, to sieve,
Pawunnikan, sieve.
Pecho, soon, by and bye;—*linitti*, directly, in a little time.
Pechot, soon; near.
Pechotschi, very near, near by, close by.
Pechotschigalit, neighbor; (*pechwigalit*, he lives near me. *A.*)
Pechpommauchsohaluwet, Saviour.
Pechuwat, nigh, near.
Pechuwelendam, to think one's self near.
Pechuwigamen, to be near somebody.
Pechuwihhilleu, the time is near.
Pechuwiwi, near.

Pedhakquon, it thunders.
Peechgaugatase, knee, calf; (dub., refers to the joint or bend of the limb. *A.*)
Peechgawinachgaja, calf of the elbow.
Pegenawan, to dress somebody, to clothe some one.
Pegenind, dressed.
Pegenink, darkness.
Pege, *Z.*, by chance (error, it means to be tired of. *A.*).
Pegui, dressed, clothed; (*equit*, the clothing. *A.*)
Peguwoagan, clothing, dress, finery.
Pehachpamhangik, seafarers.
Pehawan, to wait for somebody.
Pehowen, to wait.
Pejat, he that cometh.
Pejeju, it comes.
Pejewike, it comes, it draweth nigh.
Pekandaptonen, to have finished speaking.
Pekandapanke, when it is quite daybreak.
Pekenink, *H.*, in the dark.
Peki, perhaps then.
Pelachpit, one that is innocent, a guiltless person.
Pelsittank, unbeliever.
Peltowak, they are coming.
Pemachpin, to be present.
Pemachtiewit, any creature that lives upon grass.
Pemapanik, the heavens, sky.
Pemapuchk, rock.
Pemauchsohaluwed, he who makes live; Saviour.

Pemauchsoheen, to make live, to cause to live.
Pemauchsowaptonamik, word of life.
Pemetonhen, to preach.
Pemhakamik, earth; (the landscape within the horizon. *A.*)
Pemhakamixit, man; the world, mankind; (it rather means all living creatures, not man only. *A.*)
Pemhakamixitschik, mankind.
Pemhallachpen, to hunt in company.
Pemi, until now; about this time, at present.
Pemmetonhen, to preach.
Pemsit, he that walketh; walker.
Pemuteneyik, the towns round about.
Pendamen, to hear; to understand.
Pendameuhen, to cause to hear, to make known.
Pendaquot, it is heard.
Pendaskitquehelleu, a rising river which swells the water of a creek.
Pendawachtin, to hear one another.
Peneawan, to hear somebody.
Pengelaku, dusk; (from *pange*, piece. *A.*)
Penihillan, to fall off, to fall down.
Penipachgihhilleu, it falls off.
Pennahum, to break off, to knock down.
Pennamen, to see, to behold.
Pennassiechen, downwards, down hill.
Pennassin, to come down; *penasse*, down hill (means now, to see, to look. *A.*).

Pennauwan, to look at somebody.
Pennauweleman, to consider about somebody, to be concerned for some one, to take care of somebody.
Pennauwelendam, to think, to consider.
Pennauwelendamoagan, consideration.
Pennawachtin, to look at each other.
Penquihilleu, dried.
Penquon, dry; (alludes to fabrics, clothes, skins, etc. *A.*)
Penundhiken, to testify, to bear witness, to show unto.
Penundhikewoagan, testimony, direction.
Penxummen, to dry.
Pepachgamgussowagan, beating, striking.
Pepachgank, calamus-root; sweet flag.
Pepachgekingil, branches; (twig, etc., anything that grows from the side; root, *pach.* *A.*)
Pepachgitschiminhis, manifold in the belly of animals.
Pepachkhamatunk, *Z.*, a lancet (or lance).
Pepalistank, unbeliever.
Pepalsittaamen, *Z.*, disobedient.
Pepenaus, looking-glass.
Pepetelan, showers of rain; it rains now and then.
Pepguschikan, anger.
Peptukquekhikenk, compass; circle.
Peschgonk, nine.
Peschgonktchapachki, nine hundred.
Peschgonk tchenachke, ninety.
Peschuwat, near.

Pesoop, he waited.
Petachdonamen, to come to seek.
Petachgussin, to climb hither.
Petapan, daybreak; dawn.
Petapaniwi, at break of day.
Petaquiechen, the water is rising.
Petaschowen, to swim hither.
Petasemowik, giving light, shining hither.
Petasummawan, to give light to somebody, to shine unto some one.
Petauchsin, to live until now.
Petauchsoheen, to cause to live until now; to preserve one's life until this time.
Petawoatamen, to expect.
Petekhamman, to write to somebody.
Petenumman, to be brought to somebody; (*pet'numa-wan*, to reach something to some one. *A.*)
Peteuchtummen, to come weeping.
Pethakwonn, Z., a thunder gust. See *pedhakwon*.
Pethinquechin, to look hither.
Petisgamen, to drive hither.
Petisgauwan, to chase or drive hither.
Peton, to bring.
Petschi, until, unto; until here, so far; (up to here. *A.*)
Petschihilleu, it draws near; he is coming on.
Petschimuin, to fly or escape hither; (error; it means to decoy animals, *lit.*, to draw them hither. *A.*)

Petschitehen, to think so far.
Petscholtin, to come hither.
Peuchtowagan, patience.
Pichpemmetonhet, preacher, minister.
Pichtaweu, double.
Pidhitehemen, to cut one's self.
Pihm, to sweat; (*n'dapi pihm, H.*, I come from sweating at the sweat house).
Pihmoakan, sweat house.
Pikihilleu, torn, rent in pieces.
Pikschummen, to cut fine.
Pilapeu, big boy; (a grown-up lad, not yet connected with a woman. *A.*)
Pilawessin, to be a boy.
Pilawetit, little boy.
Pilawetschitsch, boy; (the ordinary word for boy is *skahenso. A.*)
Pilewiechgussin, to be cleansed, to be made pure, to be sanctified.
Pilhik, clean, pure.
Pili, otherwise, another; *auwen*, some one else;—*keku*, something else.
Pililinaquot, it looks otherwise.
Pilkisch, peach.
Pilsin, to be clean, to be chaste.
Pilsit, chaste, pure.
Pilsohalgussowagan, holiness, purity.
Pilsuwi, clean, chaste.

Piluwi, clean, chaste.
Piluwinaquot, it looks cleanly.
Pimachtelinque, squint-eyed.
Pimenatan, thread; (*n'bimenate.* Z., I make thread.)
Pim'eu, slanting, oblique.
Pimiechen, slanting.
Pimiechton, to make slanting.
Pimihilleu, it is oblique.
Pimingus, red squirrel.
Pimoacun, Z., a sweat house. See *Pihm.*
Pimochkhasu, stirred, moved.
Pimochqueu, turned, twisted.
Pimochquikan, stirring-ladle.
Pindachsenacan, Z., tobacco pouch (cartridge pouch. *A.*).
Pindalanak, white pine.
Pindassenakan, a tobacco pouch.
Pindawan, to clothe somebody, to dress some one.
Pindham, to put in, to fill.
Pindhasu, loaded, charged.
Pindhewachton, to put in a bag; (means simply to put in, as in a room, etc. *A.*)
Pindhikan, ramrod; sausage.
Pindpehellachtikan, funnel.
Pintschihillachtauwan, to put clothes on somebody.
Pintschihillachton, to put on; to make slip in.
Pintschixin, to creep in.
Pipaan, to come awhile ago.

Pipinamen, to choose.
Pipinamoagan, an election (choosing of any kind. *A*.).
Pischk, night-hawk.
Piselid-tulpe, large sea-tortoise.
Piselisso, shrunken, wrinkled.
Pisgaje, it holds much.
Pisgapamoaquachtop, it was dusk.
Pisgapamukquot, dusky, somewhat dark.
Pisgeke, by night (last night. *A*); *pisgeep*, it was night.
Pisgenemen, to grow dark.
Pisgeu, dark, night; (*lit.*, it is dark. *A*.)
Pisgihilleu, it grows dark, night sets in.
Pishikamen, to go to meet somebody.
Pisikolis, snipe; large grey snipe.
Pit, perhaps.
Pitaptonen, to blunder in speaking.
Pitawegiechen, double.
Pitawigawan, porch in front of a house;—pent house.
Piteet, perhaps.
Pitelaweminschi, honey locust tree.
Pitenummen, to make a mistake.
Pi'tey, *Z*., foam, froth (*pichteu*, it foams. *A*.).
Pitkullentsch, the fist.
Pitschi, accidentally, by chance, inadvertently, unforeseen.
Piwitak, aunt; (*n'militak*. *A*.)
Pixu, ragged, rent; (torn, scratched in body. *A*.)
Pkindey, light ashes.

Pkuschikan, auger, gimlet.
Plipitehan, to knock somebody on the head.
Plitey, junk of fire, firebrand.
Poaktschehellan, to jump over a fence.
Poam, thigh; ham.
Poawin, to conceive; to be pregnant (*lit.*, to become swollen. *A.*).
Pochenikan, drum.
Pochquachpus, *Z.*, a mouse.
Pohonasin, *Z.*, to beat the drum (to beat; to pound; to lift up; *pochonummen*, he drums. *A.*)
Pokawachne, a creek between two hills.
Pokhakenikan, grave; (from *pokhawen*, a hole or hollow in the ground. *A.*)
Pokhammen, to knock out, to knock in, to break.
Pokqueu, clam, muscle.
Pomih', fat, oil, tallow.
Pomihen, to beat oil.
Pomillachtan, to go by water.
Pommauchsin, to live.
Pommauchsowagan, life.
Pommauchsowaganit, he who is the life.
Pommauchsuwi, living.
Pommenan, to beat somebody, to conquer somebody.
Pommihilleu, it flies away.
Pomminehiken, to dispute.
Pomminehotin, to dispute with one another.
Pommipeso, lath.

Pommisgen, to begin to walk.
Pommissin, to go afoot, to walk.
Pommitachpanschi, lath.
Pommixin, to creep.
Pomsin, to walk.
Ponelendam, to quit, to give up, to be no more concerned.
Ponemen, to let go, to leave off.
Pongus, sand fly.
Poniton, to let be, to remain; (*ponihil*, *H*., let me alone.)
Ponk, dust; (ashes, powder. *A*.)
Ponxu, full of sand flies.
Poochpsin, to be weakly.
Pooxit, the month of falling leaves; October.
Popachgandamen, to beat, to strike.
Popankpechen, it drops.
Popetelan, it rains now and then; it rains by showers.
Popohham, to knock.
Popokus, partridge.
Poquewachen, nigher road.
Poquewi, straightway.
Poquiechen, broken.
Poquiechton, to break.
Poquihhilleu, broken.
Poquihillachton, to break in two.
Potatikan, pumpkin-stem pipe.
Pottenin, to take off.
P'quitehican, *Z*., a chisel.

Psakquiechen, close together, tight.
Psakquietehasu, crucified.
Psakulinscheu, *Z.*, a squirrel.
Psattewoan, tinder.
Pschiki, *Z.*, fine, pretty. See *schigi*.
Psindamoakan, parched meal.
Psindhammen, to cover with earth.
Psindpeu, overflowed with water.
Ptukalluns, bullet; (*lit.*, round missile. *A.*
Ptukhanne, crooked river or creek.
Ptukhikan, round ball.
Ptukquim, walnut.
Ptukquiminschi, black walnut.
Ptukquinschu, bowl, dish.
Ptukschummen, to cut round.
Puchtschessu, hollow.
Pulpecat, *H.*, deep dead water (*walpecat*, very deep water. *A.*).
Pumoe, a boil.
Pundhen, to weigh.
Pundhikan, steelyards.
Punk, *Z.*, ashes, dust; gunpowder. See *Ponk*.
Pusihn, *Z.*, to enter a canoe (or any vehicle. *A.*).
Putam, to escape.
Putamohen, to cause to escape.
Putawen, to blow; (*puta'tamen*, to blow as in starting a fire. *A.*)
Putawoakan, bellows.

Putschek, corner of a room.
Putschisktey, poison vine; (*w'hatchiskey. A.*)

Q.

Quajaqui, still, yet, yet more, nevertheless, however.
Qualcheu, it smokes; (*qualchek*, smoke. *A.*)
Quallassin, to bathe; to sweat; (properly, to sweat. *A.*)
Quappalawan, to take somebody out of the water.
Quatsch, why;—*atta*, why not;—*eet*, why perhaps.
Quatschee! exclamation of surprise.
Queh! exclamation of joy.
Quekolis, whipper will; (*wekolis. A.*)
Quekulukquihilleu, lame.
Quekuluxit, he that is lame; (means rather, one who has joints. *A.*)
Quenek, length; (something long. *A.*)
Queneuhappachpoon, table.
Quenischquney, panther; (*lit.*, long-tailed. *A.*) *quenschukuney, Z.*
Quenschukuney, panther; (see above.)
Quequongalle, pike fish; (*lit.*, long-gilled; but the usual term is *günhonque*, tapering fish. *A.*)
Queschanigat, tooth holes.
Quesquelendam, to be out of humor; (usual term now is *nisquelendam. A.*)

Quetajaku, old tree; (applied to any plant or tree which has reached full age and the fibres hardened. *A*.)
Quetit, little girl.
Quidhikewagan, forbiddance, reproof.
Quilawelelendam, to be at a loss what to do.
Quilawelendamoagan, confusion, perplexity.
Quilawelensin, to be doubtful, to be uncertain.
Quilawelensitchewagan, distress, anguish.
Quilawelensowagan, concern, trouble.
Quilawelensu, doubtful, uncertain.
Quilutamen, to fall upon, to attack.
Quin, a long while; long.
Quiquingus, large wild duck.
Quis, son.
Quischgumowe, viper, snake.
Quischimawan, to appoint somebody to an office.
Quischktonhen, to whisper.
Quischoschemo, middle of the head; (out of use. *A*.)
Quitellitowoagan, *Z*., commandment.
Quitsut, *Z*., the great toe.
Quochoak, *Z*., he fears you.

S.

Sa! exclamation of indignation.
Sabbeleechen, sparkling, glittering.
Sabbeleu, it shines brightly; (refers to the reflection of light in the sky or water. *A*.)

DICTIONARY. 123

Sachapiwak, lightning afar off.
Sachgachtoon, *Z.*, to cook.
Sachgaguntin, to lead each other.
Sachgagunummen, to lead.
Sachkenachgen, to shake hands; (*lit.*, to take hold of; also and usually *wangundin*. *A.*)
Sachsapan, *Z.*, soup.
Sagachgutteje, top of a hill or mountain; (properly, "sloping upwards," applied to the upper slopes, not top of a mountain. *A.*)
Sagalachgat, so deep the hole.
Sajewi, at first, foremost.
Sakaweuhewi Gischuch, the month in which the deer begin to turn gray—August.
Saken, to shoot forth, to spring up.
Sakhaken, to stay out from home so long.
Sakima, chief, king.
Sakimauchheen, to make to a chief or king.
Sakimawagan, kingdom.
Sakime, mosquito.
Sakquachsoagan, troublesome life.
Sakquamallessin, to feel troubled.
Sakquamallsin, to feel troubled.
Sakquamallsoagan, trouble, uneasiness.
Sakquelendam, to be melancholy, to be sad.
Sakquelendamen, to be troubled in mind, to be disquieted.
Sakquelendamoagan, trouble, sorrow, disquietude.

Sakquipaan, to come in a troublesome time.
Saksak, pea vines, wild beans; (any kind of a bur. *A.*)
Sakuwit, mouth of a creek, mouth of a river; (more exactly *sakwihillak. A.*)
Salachgihillan, to be frightened, to be terrified.
Salamoagan, weeping, howling; (collective form, a number cry together. *A.*)
Salumbiechen, to ring the bell.
Salumbunikan, bell; (arch., *A.*)
Salumbuniken, to ring the bell.
Samumptan, to tie something (not in use. *A.*).
Samuttonen, to shut the mouth.
Saniqui, *Z.*, to blow the nose (*saniquin. A.*).
Sankhikan, gun lock.
Sanquen, weasel.
Sapiu, it lightens.
Sapiwagan, lightning; (not in use. *A.*)
Saputti, *Z.*, the arse-hole.
Sasappekhasu, spotted, speckled.
Sasappelehelleu, *Z.*, it flashes lightning.
Sasappeu, spotted, speckled.
Sasappis, lightning bug, fire fly.
Saschchuppawen, to gape, to yawn.
Sasehemen, to sow, to scatter.
Sasukhoalawan, to spit upon somebody.
Scaphackamigeu, *Z.*, wet ground.
Schaback, *Z.*, the box bush.
Schabuwihilleu, *Z.*, diarrhœa (*lit.,* running through, of liquids. *A.*).

Schachachgach'ne, a straight course in a river.
Schachachgageechen, straight road.
Schachachgameu, straight row.
Schachachgapewi, honest, righteous.
Schachachgapewin, to be just, to be upright, to be true, to be correct.
Schachachgapewit, an upright person.
Schachachgauchsowagan, righteousness.
Schachachgek, just so.
Schachachgekhasu, striped.
Schachachgelendam, to be sure of a thing, to have one's mind made up, to be determined.
Schachachgennemen, to make straight.
Schachachgeu, straight; right, exact, correct.
Schachachgiechen, straight road.
Schachachkaptonagan, upright saying.
Schachachkaptonen, to speak the exact truth, to tell a straight story.
Schachachkatschimuin, to speak the truth.
Schachachki, certain, certainly true, surely.
Schachachkoochwen, to go straight, to follow the straight road.
Schachamek, eel; (*w'schachamek*, *lit.*, it is a straight fish. *A.*)
Schachihilleu, it slips, it slides.
Schagaskat, grass wet with dew; (*sachgaskat*, green grass, or fresh young grass. *A.*)

Schagsüt, Z., covetous (out of use. A.).
Schahamuis, Z., a crawfish.
Schahowapewi, heartless, disheartened, desponding.
Schajahikan, seashore; (*w'shajahitcan*. A.)
Schajawonge, hill-side; (should have an initial *w'*. A.)
Schajelinquall, eyebrows; (error; properly, eyelid. A.)
Schakamon, food, nourishment; (anything put in the mouth, for food or otherwise. A.)
Schakhokquiwan, coat.
Schameu, Z., grease, fat (it is greasy. A.).
Schammenummen, to anoint, to grease.
Schapoalchasu, bored through, pierced through.
Schapulinsch, finger-ring; (out of use. A.)
Schaschiwilawechgussin, to be put to grief.
Schauchsin, to be tired, to be weak; (to be weak, *not* tired. A.)
Schauchsowagan, weakness, feebleness.
Schauwalamuin, to faint from hunger.
Schauwemi, beechwood.
Schauweminschi, red beech tree.
Schauwessin, to make haste; (*schauwesoagan*, Z., haste,) (*schauwelendam*, to be in a hurry. A.)
Schauwewi, tired, weak, weakly.
Schauwihilleu, it withers, it is weak, it faints.
Schauwinachk, weak hand.
Schauwinaxowagan, weakness, weakly look.

Schauwipachteu, withered, faded.
Schauwoppihilleu, it bends.
Schauwussu, weak.
Schauwutteu, withered, faded.
Schawanachen, southerly wind.
Schawanachgook, *Z.*, horned snake.
Schawanammek, shad (fish; *chwame gischuch*, *Z.*, the month of March, or of shad).
Schawaneu, southward, southerly.
Schawanewunk, southward.
Schawanochqueu, Shawano woman.
Schawek, weak.
Schawi, immediately, directly.
Schaxin, to be avaricious; (*schaxu*, *Z.*, greed.)
Schaxowagan, covetousness.
Sche! see there; lo!
Scheechganim, shelled corn coarse pounded; (chaff. *Z.*)
Schehelleu, it hangs; *wulli schehellak*, *Z.*, it hangs there (*w'eh'helleu. A.*).
Schejek, string of wampum; (*lit.*, edge or border. *A.*)
Schela! see there!
Schellachton, to hang up.
Schengiechen, it lies.
Schengiechin, to lie down.
Schepaje, this day early, this morning.
Schepella! see there!
Schesquim, bran, corn husk; (*schequasquim*, the hulls of the corn. *A.*)

Scheuchsit, weak.
Schewek, weak, tired.
Schewondikan, bag, tobacco pouch.
Schewongellikik, the lame.
Scheychellat, *Z.*, a forerunner; *scheyiachpitschik*, those who live on the border.
Scheyjunuppek, lake; (probably dialectic; not in use. *A.*)
Schi, either, or.
Schibhammen, to spread out; (with an initial *w'*. *A.*)
Schibhasu, spread out.
Schiechikiminschi, maple tree; (the soft maple. *A.*)
Schiess, *Z.*, an uncle (always with possess. prons. *A.*)
Schigi, fine, pretty; nice (generally applied to quality rather than appearance. *A.*).
Schikochqueu, widow.
Schikschasiki, shavings.
Schiku, widow; (error; it means an orphan. *A.*)
Schimuin, *Z.*, to flee; *noschimui*, I flee; *uchschimo*, he flees; *schimoagan*, flight.
Schind, spruce; (hemlock. *A.*)
Schindikeu, spruce forest; (hemlock woods. *A.*)
Schingachpin, to be somewhere unwillingly.
Schingachteyapuchk, flat rock.
Schingalan, to hate somebody.
Schingalgussowagan, the being taken.
Schingaltin, to hate each other; (*schinginawa altin*. *A.*)
Schingaltowagan, enmity, hatred.

Schingaluet, enemy, adversary.
Schingaskunk, bog meadow.
Schingattam, to be unwilling, to dislike, to disapprove.
Schingelendam, to dislike, to be against one's inclination, to be tired of.
Schin'geu, level; *schinghacki*, Z., a flat country.
Schingi, unwilling, disliking, unwillingly.
Schingihakihen, to plant unwillingly.
Schingimikemossin, to work unwillingly.
Schinginamen, to hate.
Schinginawachtin, to hate each other.
Schinginawachtowagan, enmity.
Schingiptikan, leather string, rope.
Schingochwen, to be unwilling to go.
Schingsittam, to dislike to hear.
Schingsittawan, to dislike to hear somebody.
Schingtschenamen, to hate excessively, to be unable to bear.
Schipaquitehasu, crucified, outstretched.
Schipenasu, stretched, spread out, extended.
Schiphammen, to spread, to extend.
Schiphasu, spread out, extended.
Schipihilleu, stretched.
Schipinachgen, to put forth the hand.
Schipinachk, outstretched arms.
Schiquineu, fatherless, motherless; (either one or the other. *A*.)
Schiquitehasik, chips.

Schiquitehasīd, *Z.*, booty (*schiquinitehasik*, booty obtained in war. *A.*).
Schita, either, or.
Schiwachpin, to be weary of staying.
Schiwamallessin, to feel grief, to feel sorrow.
Schiwamallsin, to feel grief and pain.
Schiwamallsoagan, sorrowful pain.
Schiwa'pew, *Z.*, blue (*wulih'ke*, blue, at present. *A.*).
Schiwelendam, to be sorry, to be sad, to be melancholy, to moan.
Schiwelendamowitehewagan, repentance.
Schiwilawechgun, to be put to grief.
Schkaa'k, a pole-cat, skunk.
Schkiwan, *Z.*, to piss.
Schohakan, glue.
Schquot, to abort, to miscarry, *Z.* (*lit.*, beat to a pulp, alludes to the pulpy afterbirth. *A.*)
Schuk, but, only; (used after negat.) but;—*atta*, but not, not only.
Schukquan, *Z.*, to chew; *schquanda*, thou chewest.
Schukund, only, but then.
Schukuney, the trail of an animal.
Schwewak, salt meat; (from *schewunk*, salt. *A.*)
Schwilawe, discouraged, disheartened.
Schwon, saltish, sour; (*schwoll*, *Z.* and *A.* A white man is called *schwonack*, from the salt ocean. *A.*)
Schwonnachquaxen, European shoes.
Schwonnachquinenk, among white people.

Schwonnihilla, snipe; (shore snipe, tilt birds. *A.*)
Sedpok, early in the morning; at daybreak (properly, part of the night, half of the night. *A.*).
Sedpokuniwi, early in the morning.
Segachpapachton, to make wet.
Segachtehikan, branch, twig.
Segachtek, ardent, fervent; (*segachteu*, it begins to burn. *A.*)
Segantpechink, overhead.
Segauchsin, to live so long.
Sehe, *H.*, hush, be quiet.
Sekentek, length; (refers to the length of a house, room, etc. *A.*)
Seki, so long, till.
Seksitechinan, at thy feet.
Seksitechink, at his feet.
Sesachquilawendam, to trouble.
Sesalassummoehund, frying pan; (*salasseu*, it is cooking or frying. *A.*)
Sesalumboink, bell.
Sesegauwihan, to whip somebody, to scourge some one.
Sesegauwihugewagan, scourging.
Sessuk, *Z.*, spittle.
Shaki, as long, so long, as far, so far as, until.
Shakochwen, to go so far.
Sigachgochgissin, to bleed.
Sigapehikan, strainer.

Sihhtanin, to run at the nose.
Sihilleu, the freshet abates, the river subsides.
Sihunasu, *Z.*, conquered (out of use. *A.*).
Sikey, salt (*sikheunk*, *H.*, at the salt spring), (out of use; see *schewewah*. *A.*)
Sikeyhasu, salted, pickled.
Sikunikan, scourgrass, rushes.
Sillikakhammen, to squeeze, to press, to beat.
Sillkitehemen, to press, to squeeze.
Simaquon, corn stalk; (arch., *A.*)
Singawikanawon, backbone; (refers to processes of the vertebræ, from *singek*. *A.*)
Singek, outside corner of a house; (corner, point, angle, in general. *A.*)
Singigamika, corner of a house.
Sipachgihhilleu, it buds, sprouts out.
Sipo, river.
Sipotit, small creek; (*siposis*. *A.*)
Sipuos, wild plum; (doubtful. *A.*)
Siquon, spring of the year; (*siequanke*. *Z.*, next spring.)
Siquonachen, spring hunt.
Siquonnatewinilleu, showers of snow and rain in the spring.
Sisawehak, oysters; (now called *e'sak* (pl.), referring to the shells. *A.*)
Sisi'lija, *Z.*, the buffalo (this means an animal that butts against and breaks in pieces. *A.*).
Sisinghos, iron pot; (out of use. *A.*)

Sisquahoasu, a plastered fireplace.
Sissummoek, bell.
Skaphakamigeu, wet ground.
Skaphakejeu, wet ground.
Skappeu, wet; (strictly, that which is wet partly, as toward the end. *A.*)
Skattek, burning, ardent, fervent, zealous, hot; (see *segachtek. A.*)
Skattelendam, to loathe, to hate.
Skattewi, burning.
Skattsin, to be loathsome.
Skin, to make water.
Skiquall, grass.
Skulin, to keep school; (English.)
Sogahellas, chain.
Sogahen, to spill.
Soganechin, to pour out.
Sokan, hind part of a church; (*lit.*, buttocks, arse, backside. *A.*)
Sokelan, it rains.
Sokenepaltowagan, baptism; (from *sogahen. A.*)
Sokenepasu, baptized.
Sokpehellak, cataract.
Sookpehelleu, the water tumbles down from a precipice.
Soopsu, naked; (out of use; *sohsexu*, at present. *A.*)
Sopenaxin, to be naked, to strip one's self.
Sophalan, to make one bare; to make somebody naked.
Soppinquen, to shut the eyes.

Spanquewagan, wink of an eye.
Spiechgejeu, member, joint; (out of use. *A.*)
Squandamen, to chew.
Squewachgitehen, to bruise one's self by accident.
Sukachgook, black snake.
Sukachqualles, negro.
Sukachsin, iron.
Sukachsinhet, smith.
Sukamek, black fish.
Sukanepil, black fish.
Sukelechen, it looks black.
Sukeu, black.
Sukhattaquall, black thread, black yarn.
Sukqui, spittle.
Suksit, black.
Sungi, eat thou.
Suppinquall, tears; (from the eyes) (always with a possessive. *A.*)

T.

Ta, no, not;—*am*, not at all;—*haschi*, never.
Ta, how;—*elgilen*, how large;—*elgiqui*, how soon;—*elinaxit*, what color;—*hatsch*, how will it be;—*linaquot*, what is it like;—*ne liechen*, how then, how is it;—*segek*, how long;—*shaki*, how long; *tchen*, how many; how many times;—*tchi*, how much.

Ta, where;—*talli*, whitherwards; *undachqui*, whereabouts, towards where;—*untschi*, whence, wherefrom;—*wo*, towards where.
Ta, then.
Ta keeche, some; a little;—*keechen*, so often.
Ta likhikqui, at what time.
Ta pemi, about, about this time.
Taan, where;—*a undachqui*, which then;—*ha*, how then.
Taat, as if, like.
Tachan, wood; piece of wood; (arch., *A*.)
Tachanigeu, woody, full of wood.
Tachpachaxu, little, mean, low, humble; (*tachpeachxu*, gives a general notion of condition, humble, exalted, etc. *A*.)
Tachpachelensuwi, low, little, humble.
Tachpachihilla, in the afternoon.
Tachpachiwi, humble, modest; little, low.
Tachpachsu, low; (indefinite term referring to condition. *A*.)
Tachpamsin, to be less, to be lower.
Tachpatamauwan, to keep or preserve unto somebody.
Tachpawewagan, advice, commandment.
Tachquahamoakan, parched meal.
Tachquahoakan, mortar, mill.
Tachquahoakaniminschi, gum tree.
Tachquahoaken, to pound, to grind.
Tachquallonikan, pair of scissors.
Tachquambeso, tied together.

Tachquatten, frozen; (frozen together. *A.*)
Tachquihilleu, it joins close together.
Tachquinschehikan, pair of pincers.
Tachquipoagan, feast.
Tachquipuin, to hold a feast;—*ahoaltuwi*, to hold a love feast.
Tachquiwi, together.
Tachquoak, fall; autumn; *tachquogike*, Z., next fall.
Tachquoakcheen, fall hunt.
Tachquoakches, fall skin.
Tachquoakike, in the fall.
Tachquoch, land turtle.
Tachquondikan, pair of pincers.
Tachsigiu, it hails.
Tachtakan, thick, stiff.
Tachtamse, now and then, often.
Tahakan, paddle oar; (always with the possessives, *n'*, *k'*, *w'*, etc. *A.*)
Tahunnan, to arrest somebody, to take some one prisoner.
Taiachquoan, bridge; *atta tajachgonewi?* Z., is there no bridge?
Takachquiminschi, white wood, linden tree.
Takachsin, lead.
Takan (pl., ik), another, other.
Takanilaku, moderately warm evening.
Takanitpikat, moderately warm night.
Takeet, perhaps, I don't know.

Takindamen, to count, to read.
Takomen, to come from some where.
Takpeu, wet, damp, soft, soaked; (*ta'hokpeu,* he is cold from wet. *A.*)
Takquak (pl., ik), other, second, the rest.
Taktani, I don't know, I don't know where; somewhere perhaps; be it where it may.
Takta undachqui, anywhere.
Takta untschi, from somewhere.
Talakat, cracked, split.
Talala, white cedar.
Talattauwoapin, to behold, to view.
Talawachto, how dear is it, what does it cost.
Taleka, crane.
Tallachpaje, cold morning.
Talli, there.
Tamse, sometimes, now and then, perhaps;—*nall,* once, finally;—*ta likhikqui,* once, sometime or other;—*tamse,* now and then.
Tandachgitechton, to shake off.
Taneek, perhaps, I don't know; (*takeet. Z.*)
Tangaman, *Z.,* to thrust, to stick.
Tangamikan, spear.
Tangandikan, spear.
Tangawachto, cheap, low-priced.
Tangawachtohen, to cheapen.
Tangeemhoantit, little spoon.
Tangelendam, to think little of one's self.

Tangelensin, to be lowly minded, to be humble.
Tangelensochwen, to walk humbly.
Tangelensowagan, lowliness of mind.
Tangelensuwi, humble, modest.
Tangenindin, to vouchsafe, to condescend.
Tangetto, short, small.
Tangitehen, to think little of one's self.
Tangitehewagan, humility.
Tangitehewi, humble, modest.
Tangitti, small, little; (*tanghotit,* Z., a little kettle.)
Tani, where; how; (used in questions) then;—*leu,* in what manner then.
Tanikaniminschi, white beech.
Tankalinschawontit, little finger.
Tankhakan, basket.
Tankhakanachen, to make baskets.
Tankhannen, little creek; (especially the narrows of a stream. *A.*)
Taquatschin, to freeze, to be cold.
Taquatten, frozen.
Taquiechen, joined together.
Tassenahamohen, to stone.
Tassenahamolan, to stone somebody.
Tatamse, often, sometimes;—*ne leep,* there was more done.
Tatandachgoquehellan, to shake the head.
Tatandachgoquehellewagan, shake of the head.
Tatask, sled.

Tatchen, little.
Tatchendo, but few, very little.
Tatchittu, very little.
Tatchuppekat, shallow water.
Tauchechin, to listen privately.
Tauchsittam, to hear privately.
Tauwachsin, to burn, to use for firewood.
Tauwatawik, an uninhabited place; (*achtawawek. A.*)
Tauwatawique, in the wilderness.
Tauwiechen, open.
Tauwinachgechi, open arms.
Tauwinipen, beginning of summer, May.
Tauwiquoakan, key.
Tauwunnasin, to be buried.
Tauwunummen, to open.
Tawonnalogewagan, labor in vain.
Tawonni, although.
Tawwunasin, Z., to bury; *tauwundin*, burial place (*lit.*, to put under, *i. e.*, the ground; it begins with *aq, q'tau. A.*).
Tchen, times.
Techi, quite;—*matta*, not at all, absolutely not, by no means (—*taku*).
Techthunnentschik, prisoners, captives.
Techtummischikan, candle snuffers.
Tehek, cold.
Tekauwontowit, the patient, meek, mild God, Lamb of God.

Tekauwussitawan, to show somebody favor.
Tekene, woods, an uninhabited place; (*tekenink*, *H.*, in the woods.)
Tellamasgeek, *Z.*, a cedar-swamp.
Tellen, ten.
Tellen tchen tchapachki, one thousand.
Temagehikan, water pail.
Temahikan, axe, hatchet.
Temiki, any; single; something;—*koeku*, anything, something, a single thing.
Temitehemen, to cut off.
Tengamend, pierced, stabbed.
Tengandasuwi, pierced through.
Tengettik, little.
Tenktitit, little.
Tenktschechen, open; (burst open, broken open. *A.*)
Tepalachgat, deep enough.
Tepawachto, reasonable, not too dear, fair price.
Tepelendam, to have enough, to be satisfied, to be content.
Tepelendamoagan, sufficiency.
Tepelook, enough of them.
Tepi, enough.
Tepihilleu, it is enough, it answers the purpose.
Tepiken, ripe, full grown.
Tepilawechgussin, to be satisfied, to have received satisfaction.
Tepilawehan, to satisfy somebody.

Tepilawen, to satisfy.
Tequipin, to hold a feast.
Tesquachtaminschi, shiver hickory.
Tesquoalintsch, the little finger.
Tetanktitit, little one.
Tetauwiwi, between.
Tetawonkhillentschik, those who have been deceived, misled; (out of use. *A*.)
Tetawonkhillowet, deceiver.
Tetpissin, to be in a like manner, to do in a like manner.
Tetschpihillen, split off, separated from one another.
Tetuppalachgat, rifle; (refers to the groove inside the bore; from *tuppen*, spiral, circular. *A*.)
Tetuptschehellak, wagon, cart; (from *tuppen*, referring to the wheel. *A*.)
Teu, it is cold.
Tgauchsin, to be good, to be kind, to be meek, to be friendly, to be good natured.
Tgauchsu, good, mild, gracious.
Tgauchsuwaptonen, to speak civil, to speak kind.
Tgauchsuwi, good, kind.
Tgauwitti, soft, mild; slowly, by little and little; also *tgaitte*.
Tgauwiwi, slowly, gently.
Thagitti, a very little while.
Thaquetto, short.
Thiechumin, *Z*., to bathe.
Thinaquot, *Z*., cool (anything that looks cold. *A*.).

Thitpan, bitter; (*ticcht'pan*, astringent, puckery. *A.*)

Thitpanihm, white hickory nut; (the root of an herb is called *ticcht'pan*. *A.*)

Thunnan, to arrest somebody; to take somebody prisoner; (*tach'hunnan*. *A.*)

Thuppeek, spring, well; (means simply cool water. *A.*)

Tigamikat, cold house; (cold room. *A.*)

Tihilleu, it is cold.

Tilaku, cool evening.

Timmeu, wolf; (out of use. *A.*)

Tinajappawe, cold morning.

Tindeuchen, to make fire.

Tindey, fire.

Tinnohagan, first finger.

Tipas, hen, fowl; (not in use; *kikipisch*, at present. *A.*)

Tipasigawan, hen coop; (*kikipshican*. *A.*)

Tipatit, little chicken.

Tiskemanis, little fisher bird.

Titpanunschi, bitter hickory tree; (*titpanim*, *Z.*, hickory nut.)

Titpikat, cold night.

Togenan, to waken somebody.

Togendowagan, wakening

Togihillan, to arise, to awake.

Tombikan, crab apple, wild apple.

Tonkdonechin, to open the mouth.

Tonktschechen, the door is open.

Tonktschechton, to open the door.

Tonktschenemen, to open.
Tonktschequoakan, key.
Tonquihilleu, open.
Topalowagan, war.
Topalowilenno, *Z.*, a warrior; pl., *netopallisak.*
Topalowoagan, *Z.*, war-time (scout, skirmisher. *A.*).
Topan, white frost.
Topi, *Z.*, the alder tree (*Alnus rubra ?*).
Towin, *Z.*, to wade, to ford (*towen,* he is walking in the water. *A.*).
Tpisgauwi, just alike, even.
Tpisgauwiechton, to do something just so, to make it alike, to make it even, to make it right.
Tpisgauwihhilleu, the time is at hand; it falls upon.
Tpisqui, just alike, even, just so; against, over, opposite; (*tipiskawi. A.*)
Tpisquihilleu, the time is at hand; it falls upon.
Tpittawe, altogether; all together.
Tpoku, last night; (arch., *A.*)
Tpoquik, by night; (*tipocuniwi gischuck,* *Z.*, the moon.)
Tschachgachtin, stump; (properly, a crooked limb torn off. *A.*)
Tschachgihilleu, torn off, broken, slipped off; (*niachgihilleu,* wrenched, violently torn; *tschachgillen* means straightened out, something crooked made straight. *A.*)
Tschachquochgamen, short day.
Tschallaan, *Z.*, an Indian bedstead.

Tschannauchsin, to be blamable, to sin, to transgress.
Tschannauchsowagan, misbehavior, fault, trespass.
Tschannelendam, to consider, to be in doubt, to scruple.
Tschannelendamoagan, doubt, scruple.
Tschannilissin, to do wrong, to make wrong.
Tschannindewagan, difference, disagreement.
Tschanninquanukgun, my eyes were kept from discerning.
Tschannistammen, to misunderstand.
Tschannistammoewagan, misunderstanding.
Tschansittamen, to hear wrong.
Tschansittamoewagan, hearing wrong.
Tschemamus, *Z.*, a hare.
Tschepsit, stranger.
Tschetschpat, otherwise, differently; it does not join together.
Tschetschpenammen, to separate.
Tschetschpi, different, unlike; asunder, apart.
Tschetschpiechen, asunder, to separate.
Tschetschpihilleu, split, split asunder, broken off, it cracks, it splits asunder.
Tschetschpissin, to disagree, to wrangle.
Tschibhattenamin, to be indisposed in mind.
Tschiechachpoakan, roasting spit.
Tschiechhammen, to comb; (out of use; now *wuliechquammen. A.*)
Tschigantschi, wholly, entirely, full, enough, all;—*likhiqui*, as soon as.

Tschihoapekelis, bluebird.
Tschikachpoochwe, sled.
Tschikenum, turkey; (arch., *A.*)
Tschikhammen, to sweep; (*tschik ik kammen. A.*)
Tschikhikan, broom.
Tschilchwehamen, *Z.*, to castrate.
Tschimakan, paddle, oar.
Tschimalus, bluebird.
Tschimamus, rabbit.
Tschimhammen, to row; to paddle.
Tschinga, pike fish.
Tschingalsu, stiff, unbending.
Tschinge, when.
Tschingteung, *Z.*, south side of a hill.
Tschinque, *Z.*, a wild cat (*nianque. A.*).
Tschipelendam, to think disagreeable; to be unpleasant.
Tschipelendamoagan, strangeness, oddness.
Tschipey, spirit, ghost; (also applied to the dead body. *A.*)
Tschipilek, strange, wonderful.
Tschipileu, strange, bad accident; awful.
Tschipinaquot, it looks strange, it looks disagreeable.
Tschipinaxu, he seems strange, uncommonly unpleasing.
Tschipisin, to have a fit, to get fits.
Tschipsoagan, uncommonness.
Tschiquoalale, a muscle; (a snail, refers to the spiral form of the shell. *A.*)

Tschiquoalaletit, little muscle; (a small snail, see above. *A.*)
Tschisgihilleu, wiped out, rubbed out; (scraped, applied to the skin when scratched, etc. *A.*)
Tschisgokus, robin.
Tschiskhammen, to wipe off, to blot out.
Tschitanambeso, tied fast.
Tschitanatten, hard frozen.
Tschitanek, fast, strong.
Tschitanennan, to hold somebody fast.
Tschitanessoagan, *Z.*, authority, power.
Tschitaneu, strong.
Tschitani, strong.
Tschitaniechton, to make fast, to make strong.
Tschitanigachen, established, firm, sure.
Tschitanissin, to be strong.
Tschitanigapawin, to stand fast.
Tschitanissohen, to strengthen.
Tschitanissowagan, power, capability; strength.
Tschitanissowaganit, he who is strength.
Tschitanitauwan, to strengthen somebody.
Tschitanitehen, to stand firm in mind; to persevere.
Tschitgussin, to be silent.
Tschitqui, silent.
Tschitquihilleu, he is silent.
Tschitsch, again, once more; yet, still; still more;— *tchen*, again as much.
Tscholens, bird; (not in use. See *Awehelleu*. *A.*)

Tscholentit, little bird.
Tschoskin, *Z.*, to ford, to wade.
Tschukquilques, *Z.*, a locust (insect).
Tschuppik, root; (*tschappik*, root generic; also medicine. *A.*)
Tschuppinamen, it seems odd, it looks strange.
Tschutti, *Z.*, a comrade, a friend; *n'tschu*, my friend.
Tsiheniken, to milk.
Tskennak, black bird; (now *tschukqualle*. *A.*)
Tspat, different, unlike, strange, unusual; separately.
Tspinaquot, it looks quite otherwise.
Tspinaxu, he looks strange.
Tspiwi, separately.
Tsquall, frog.
Tsqualli gischuch, the month in which the frogs begin to croak, February.
Tukauwussowagan, favor, kindness.
Tulpe, turtle, water turtle.
Tumb, brain; (always with the possessives, *n'*, *k'*, *w'*, etc. *A.*)
Tumhican, *Z.*, an axe; see *Temahican*.
Tuney, beard (*wiechtuney*, chin beard. *A.*).
Tunktonechin, *Z.*, to gape, to open the mouth.
Tuppehelleu, it flows out, it runs out; (*ktuppe'helleu*. *A.*)
Tuptschehelleu, it rolls; it revolves.
Tutaam, to set on, to set at; to incite one to do something.

U.

Uchtechsüt, Z., the sole of the foot (*pochsitawi*, the flat of the foot. *A.*).
Uchtehelinsch, palm of the hand.
Uchtscheyunque, within.
Uchtuchen, Z., a bough, a branch.
Ulakanahen, to make dishes; (wooden dishes. *A.*)
Ulakanahunschi, elm tree; *ulakanahemünschi*, Z.
Ulakanis, dish.
Ulakens, dish.
Ulakunipoagan, supper; (*lit.*, the evening meal. *A.*)
Ulaque, yesterday.
Ulepen, onion; (not in use; at present *wi'nonsch*. *A.*)
Unami, one of the 3 tribes of the Lenni Lenâpé or Delawares.
Undaaktschehellan, to jump hither.
Undach, here, this way.
Undachgamen, this side the water.
Undachlenni, hand it here.
Undachlitti, a little this way.
Undachqui, hither, this way, that way.
Undaptonen, to speak thereof.
Undauchsin, to live from, to live on.
Undauchsowagan, food to live upon.
Undenummen, to take from.
Undoochwen, to come or go for something.
Undsoagan, Z., an accident; *wundso*, he is unlucky.

Unitschaanin, *Z.*, to beget a child; to bring forth a child.
Unk, in, in the, on, out of.
Untschi, of, by, therefore; from; with; concerning.
Untschihilleu, to come from somewhere rapidly, to flow out of.
Uschewinaquot, painful.
Uschewinaxu, painful; (he looks weakly or in pain. *A.*)
Uschumallsin, to feel sorrowful, to feel painful.
Uschuwamallsin, to feel grief, to feel sorrow.
Uschuwauchsoagan, troublesome life, sorrowful life.
Uschuwelemuwi, miserable, painful, burthensome.
Uschuwelendam, to be grieved, to be troubled in mind, to be burthened with labor, sorrow or trouble.
Uschuwinaxowagan, sorrowful look, painful look.
Uteney, city, town; (*utaney. A.*)
Utsche, fly; (*utcheuwes. A.*)

W.

Wabiminschigeu, *Z.*, chestnut tree. See *Woak*.
Wachejeu, *Z.*, light, bright (*wacheyek*, light, brightness. *A.*).
Wachelachkey, fish scale; (*walachkey. A.*)
Wachganessu, *Z.*, lean (bony, from *wochgan. A.*).
Wachgutey, petticoat; (*wachgotey. A.*)

Wachschiechey, bird's nest; (*wisawi amoe wachschiechey*, a wasp's nest.)
Wachtanquall, his brother-in-law.
Wachteneu, he has the belly-ache.
Wachtey, stomach, belly.
Wachtschangussin, to be enslaved.
Wachtschu, hill, mountain.
Wachtschuhatteu, it is full; (*wa-chu-wateu.* A.)
Wachtschuwi, hilly.
Wachtschuwiketo, mountainous.
Wachtschuwikeu, hilly.
Wachtuchwepi, body, flesh.
Wachtuchwepiwi, bodily, personal.
Wagagapoak, Z., they stand in a circle.
Wahh, egg.
Wahhellemat, wide, far; (it is a great distance. A.)
Wahhellemelendam, to seem to be far.
Wajauwe, see *Wojauwe*.
Waktscheu, crooked; (bent, warped. A.)
Waktschiechen, the road is crooked.
Walak, hole; (*waleck,* a hollow or excavation, not a hole which penetrates. A.)
Walaxiall, Z., entrails, guts.
Waletittin, to advise one another, to inform each other.
Walha'ndi, Z., a ditch or trench.
Walhasu, buried; covered over with earth.
Walheu, he is digging a hole.
Waliechtschessu, a hollow tree.

Waloh, *Z.*, a cave.
Wanachkwim, *Z.*, an acorn.
Wanggwannelentsching, *Z.*, a span.
Wangundin, to salute one another; *wangomen, Z.*, to greet.
Wannessin, *Z.*, to forget; *n'wansi*, I forgot it; *wannessowoagan*, forgetfulness.
Wanquon, heel.
Wapahamink, back, backwards, behind; (at present *pachhammink* is used. *A.*)
Wapaleechen, white.
Wapanacheen, good morrow; (*lit.*, he has lived till morning. *A.*)
Wapaneu, easterly.
Wapanke, to-morrow.
Wapie'chquey, *Z.*, a bubble (a blown bladder. *A.*).
Wapielukquon, *Z.*, hail; a hail stone.
Wapintschachke, garfish, with a bill like a duck.
Wapsit, white person.
Wapsu, white.
Waputschies, *Z.*, a hornet (*wapotis*, from his hinder part being whitish. *A.*).
Wasachtehella, to lie on the back; (means to turn on the back and then turn again; to lie on the back is *wasachtehin. A.*)
Waselandeu, clear sunshine.
Waseleechen, clear, light.
Waselenemen, to lighten, to kindle.

Waselenikan, light, candle.
Waselenikanin, to burn.
Waseleu, clear, light.
Waskejek, thin ; (comp. *scheye.*)
Waskeu, thin.
Wassandeu, clear day.
Wattengim, milt, spleen.
Wattenkginem, colic.
Wauchtamsin, to tarry.
Wawangoman, to salute somebody.
Wawangomgussowagan, the being saluted; greeting.
Wawikan, the back.
Wawikanin, to have backache; (*wawikaninen. A.*)
Wawinuwen, to beg ; to ask for.
Wawoachepingus, lightning bug, firefly.
Wawulamallessin, to be always well.
Wawulauchsin, to live orderly, to live blameless.
Wdallachgummenanink, in our midst.
Wdallachpihewon, the net inside the belly; (the diaphragm. *A.*)
Wdallachquelendam, to grudge, to be unwilling to give ; (to give with hesitation. *A.*)
Wdallemuns, tame beast; (see *Dallemuns.*)
Wdallemunsin, to have cattle.
Wdallemunsit, the owner of cattle.
Wdallewussowagan, power, might.
Wdallowelemuwi, excellent, precious.
Wdallowilissowagan, glory.

Wdamemenshassin, to become a child.
Wdamemensuwi, childlike.
Wdanis, daughter.
Wdapandewagan, commandment.
Wdee, heart.
Wdehin, heart.
Wdehiwi, heartily, cordial.
Wdeleleman, to take some one to be, to consider somebody to be.
Wdelinamen, to imagine, to conjecture; (error; it means the mode of doing something. *A*.)
Wdellewunsowagan, name; (*w'liwünsowagan. A.*)
Wdelsowagan, behavior, conduct.
Wditehen, to think.
Wdoon, the mouth.
Wdulhe, the breast; (the thorax, not the mamma. *A*.)
Wdulhewinewagan, pain in the breast.
Wduschusowagan, grief, sorrow.
Wechwulammoehend, water pail.
Wechwulilawehuwet, comforter.
Wehemoalan, to mock at somebody, to make sport of some one.
Wehiwallahagan, horse gear.
Welanittowit, the good, gracious God.
Welapassigan, good physic.
Welapensit, the blessed; (the fortunate, the lucky. *A*.)
Welaquik, last evening, last night.
Welauchsit, an orderly, well-behaved person.

K

Welchos, stallion, boar.
Welemukquek, round hill; (arch., *welumqueu,* it is a knoll or mound. *A.*)
Welhik, good; (*wellihk'. A.*)
Welilissit, pious person.
Welsit, best;—*mtschitschank,* Holy Ghost.
Welsittank, believer in Christ.
Wemhundammen, to carry all.
Wemi, all;—*auwen,* everybody;—*ta li,* everywhere;—*ta untschi,* from everywhere.
Wemihan, to destroy somebody, to make an end of some one; (to destroy all. *A.*)
Wemihilleu, it is all gone, it is all spent.
Wemiten, to go all out.
Wemoltin, to go all away.
Wendachguttechen, where the road goes up the hill.
Wendachguttejek, up hill; (*lit.,* from below upwards. *A.*)
Wendamen, to fish with hook and line.
Wendaptonachga, of or from the word.
Wendasemowik, it shineth from thence.
Wendauchsin, by what to live.
Wendenuxowagan, reception, admittance.
Wengup, whence he came.
Wenhamma, almost, narrowly.
Wenigajek, trifle; (not in use. *A.*)
Wenigajekink, in small things, in trifles.
Wenitschanit, parent; (either father or mother or both; *lit.,* the one who has produced the child. *A.*)

Wentschi, because, therefore, for this reason.
Wentschijeyin, to belong to a place, to be from a place.
Wentschikin, to descend, to grow out of.
Wentschindewagan, call, invitation.
Wentschintin, to call each other.
Wentschipennassiechen, where the road goes down the hill.
Weschilematschil, his relation by marriage.
Weschilemuk, my relation in marriage; (used by either spouse with reference to the family of the other. *A.*)
Weschumais, cow, calf; (out of use.)
Weski, a little while ago; sometime to-day; (anew, again. *A.*)
Wetachguppachtak, he that watereth or moisteneth.
Wetegakil, his messengers; (out of use. *A.*)
Wetochemuxit, Father.
Wetochwink, Father; (one who is a father. *A.*)
Wetschitschauquit, man; (*i. e.*, one who has a soul. *A.*)
Weuchschummuis, horned cattle.
Weuchsin, to know.
Weuchsowagan, knowledge.
Weuhokeyit, man; (*i. e.*, one who has a body, from *hakey*, body. *A.*)
Wewidhiken, to testify; (something without doubt. *A.*)
Wewidhikewagan, testimony.
Wewiechgukil, his acquaintance.
Wewikit, master of the house.

Wewingtónheet, Z., a babbler (one who likes to talk. A.).
Wewitschi, perhaps.
Wewitschinaquot, it is likely; probable.
Wewoapisak, guard, watchmen.
Wewoatam, to be of good understanding, to be wise.
Wewoatamowi, wise, prudent.
Wewoatamowino, wise man.
Wewoatangik, wise men.
Wewulatenamohaluwet, Saviour.
Wewundachqui, on both sides; opposite; *wewundach-qui'wicu,* he lives opposite (*i. e.,* we live on both sides, he on one, I on the other. The word means "on both sides" and not opposite in the ordinary sense. A.)
Whittangan, neck (*lit.,* back of the head. A.).
Whittawak, ears.
Wiagasksin, to be unruly; (out of use. A.)
Wiagasksowagan, wantonness, unruly.
Wiakat, enough and to spare; plenty, abundance.
Wiaki, enough and to spare; plenty, abundance.
Wiakipuin, to have plenty; to have abundance to eat.
Wiamochki, among each other, mixed.
Wiaxowagan, plenty, sufficiency.
Widhoman, to go in a canoe with somebody.
Wiechenin, to boil, to cook, to prepare food; (not in use. A.)
Wiechgawotschi, unexpectedly; unawares.

Wiechpongus, nettle; (*wiechponganit*, the bitter weed. *A.*)
Wiechquelinschepi, gloves; (*lit.*, hands tied up; arch., *A.*)
Wiechquepiso, tied round; a bundle.
Wiechquepton, to tie around.
Wiguluk, bill of a fowl or bird.
Wigunacka, the point of an island.
Wihhinachk, birch tree.
Wi'hillaan, *Z.*, to name; *n'wihilluk*, he names one; root, *lunsi*.
Wihitawemguppanil, those that had been with him.
Wihoman, to make an offering to somebody.
Wihundewagan, sacrifice, offering.
Wihungemuin, to hold a feast.
Wihungen, to make an offering, to sacrifice.
Wijagaskau, fickle.
Wikasch, the nail on hand or foot; fingers; claws; *nikasch*, my nail.
Wikat, leg; *wi'ckaat*, *Z.* (*wihk'kaat; otenkhaat*, hind leg. *A.*)
Wikathoos, an iron pot with feet.
Wikbi, *Z.*, bast, the inner bark of trees.
Wikhakamik, end of the world.
Wikhetschik, builders.
Wikheu, to build; *gischuch wikheu*, *Z.*, halo of sun or moon; (*lit.*, the sun or moon builds a house.)
Wikiak, my house.

Wikian, thy house.
Wikimak, my wife; (out of use; *witawemak*, he or she who lives with me in the home, my house mate. *A.*)
Wikindewagan, marriage; (now, *witawendewagan. A.*)
Wikinditschik, married people.
Wikingen, to marry; *wiwu, Z.*, he is married (*lit.*, he copulates. *A.*).
Wikinget, married person.
Wikit, his house.
Wikiwon, nose.
Wiktschi, bottom of a keg, breech of a gun.
Wiktschiechak, butt end of a tree.
Wiku, he has a house.
Wikul, fat in an animal's belly.
Wikwahemunk, in the house.
Wikwam, house.
Wikwames, little house.
Wikwamhassin, to make an abode.
Wikwamtit, little room.
Wil, head.
Wilachkey, *Z.*, male genitals.
Wilano, tongue.
Wilanoall, pumpkin seeds; (any leguminous seeds. *A.*)
Wilawi, rich, valuable, precious; (from *wil*, head, with the idea as superior, royal. *A.*)
Wilawilihan, to treat somebody generously.
Wilawiochqueu, rich woman.
Wilawussall, his corn; his grain.

Wilinen, to have head ache.
Wilinewagan, head ache.
Wilooxi, warm thyself.
Wilsu, fat meat.
Wimachtendienk, *Z.*, brotherhood.
Wimb, heart of a tree; (any core or centre of a trunk, etc. *A.*)
Wimbeneman, to relieve somebody; (to sacrifice one's self for another; a strong expression. *A.*)
Winak, sassafras.
Winamallsachtin, to be a common sickness.
Winamallsachtowagan, sickness, distemper.
Winamallsin, to be sick, to feel pain.
Winamandamen, to feel pain.
Winamandamoagan, pain, sore.
Winamin, the corn is ripe; (when it is fit to eat. *A.*)
Winaminge, *Z.*, the month of August; (*lit.*, "time of roasting ears.")
Windamen, to mention.
Windasu, mentioned, named.
Wineu, it snows.
Wingachpin, to like to be in some place.
Wingachtochwilsit, lover of hunting.
Wingallauwin, to hunt willingly.
Wingan, sweet, savory; good tasted.
Wingandamen, it tastes good.
Wingapue, good, sweet broth.
Wingel, eatable.

Wingelawossi, it burns well.
Wingelendamoagan, approbation, liking.
Wingeleu, it burns well.
Wingelewemen, to do a pleasure.
Wingewochqueu, a raven; (out of use. *A.*)
Wingi, fain, gladly, willingly.
Wingilauchsin, to live willingly in a particular manner.
Wingilaweman, to do somebody a pleasure.
Wingimachtek, odoriferous.
Wingimaquot, it has a good pleasant smell.
Winginamen, to delight in, to be pleased with.
Wingipendam, to hear willingly.
Wingochwen, to go willingly, to travel with pleasure; to like to go.
Wingsittam, to like to hear.
Wingsittawan, to like to hear somebody.
Winhattak, bad accident; (not in use. *A.*)
Winhattakuwagan, danger.
Wini gischuch, snow month, November.
Winike, when it is ripe.
Winingus, mink.
Winktek, done, boiled.
Winkteu, done, boiled enough.
Winu, ripe; (ready to be eaten. *A.*)
Winunschi, *Z.*, an onion.
Winuwelchittewagan, supplication.
Winuwewagan, petition, request.
Winxu, ripe (fruit).

Wipachsoagan, fear; (out of use. *A.*)
Wipantin, to eat with each other.
Wipasin, to be in fear.
Wipelachteu, soot.
Wipentin, to lie with each other, to sleep with one another.
Wipiechkeu, rotten wood.
Wipit, tooth.
Wipochk, bush; grub; (a bushy place, a thicket. *A.*)
Wipochsoagan, *Z.*, fright.
Wipuelendam, to be fearful.
Wipundin, to keep a feast.
Wipungweu, *Z.*, brown.
Wipunquoak, white oak.
Wipunxit, gray; (*wapantpeu lenno*, *Z.*, a gray-headed man.)
Wiquajek or **Wiquek,** the head of a creek or run.
Wiquajeu, the head of a creek.
Wiquajungo, at the end.
Wiquajunquick, at the end.
Wiqualamo, to suffer hunger; (arch., *A.*)
Wiquenachk, the end of the fence.
Wiquey, box made of bark; bark trunk; (refers to birch bark, which is called *wiquey*. *A.*)
Wiquiechink, end, point; (*wiquajunquik*, *Z.*, to the end.)
Wiquihillau, to be tired.
Wiquimemguke, on the end of the plain.
Wiquon, dull, blunt.

Wiquonummen, to make dull.
Wisachgak, black oak; bark canoe.
Wisachgamallessin, to feel sore pain.
Wisachgamallsoagan, bitter pain.
Wisachgank, rum, brandy; (from the sharp, biting taste. *A*.)
Wisachgim, wild grapes.
Wisachgiminschi, wild vine.
Wisachgissi, it hurts me, it burns me; (means simply to hurt. *A*.)
Wisamek, catfish; (arch., at present *wahlheu*, mudfish; *wisamek* means " a fat fish." *A*.)
Wisaminschi, yellow-wood tree; (a species of oak, with a yellow bark used in dying. *A*.)
Wisawanik, red squirrel.
Wisawek, yellow; also, sulphur, etc.
Wisaweu, yellow.
Wischalau, frightened.
Wischalowe, rattlesnake; (the frightener. *A*.)
Wischassin, to fear; (*wischasnagan*, *Z*., fear.)
Wischiki, busily.
Wischixin, to be active, to be brisk, to be nimble; to exert one's self. (See Heckewelder, *History*, p. 439.)
Wiseu, scar.
Wishaque, to notch a tree; (*wis'haque*, to tap a maple tree. *A*.)
Wismi or Wiswi, *Z*., the gall.
Wisohen, to fatten.

Wisquon, elbow ; tobacco twist.
Wisu, fat, fleshy.
Wisuwagan, fatness.
Witachpin, to live with, to dwell with ; (to be with one at a place. *A.*)
Witaheman, to assist somebody, to relieve some one.
Witahentin, to help each other.
Witalamuin, to cry with ; to sing in company with.
Witalogen, to work with.
Witamehhellen, to walk with.
Witatschimolsin, to advise with, to hold council with.
Witauchsall, her brother's wife; (dub., it means living together. *A.*)
Witauchsoman, to be in fellowship with somebody.
Witauchsundin, to have fellowship with one another.
Witauchsundowagan, fellowship.
Witawematpanni, who was with him; *witawemat*, *Z.*, an aid, assistant (now used exclusively for man or wife. *A.*).
Witawentin, to be together, to live or dwell with each other.
Witchwi, *Z.*, the navel.
Witen, to go with.
Witgochquall, her sister.
Witisin, to esteem ; (not in use. *A.*)
Witochwen, to go with, to travel with.
Witonquoam, to lodge at one's house, to board with, to sleep with.

Witscheachgenimatpanni, one who helped to accuse him.
Witscheman, to help somebody; (*witsch'man. A.*)
Witschewan, to go with somebody.
Witschewot, he who goes with him.
Witschi, with, at the same time.
Witschindin, to help one another, to assist each other, to lend a hand.
Witschingen, to help along.
Witschu, calf of the leg; pl., *wak*.
Witschwochak, pine nuts; (out of use. *A.*)
Wiuchschachauwan, to load somebody with a burden.
Wiwasch, bundle, load.
Wiwaschin, to carry a load.
Wiwundhakamik, before now, in former time, very long ago.
Wiwunigagun, I am surrounded.
Wiwunigapawin, to stand all around.
Wiwuniwi, round about.
Wiwunochwen, to go all around; to go round about.
Wiwuntschi, before now, of old; (not in use. *A.*)
Wo! o! oh!
Woachejek, light.
Woachejekumin, to be light.
Woachejekumuit, he who is the light.
Woachejeu, clear, light.
Woagai, round about.

DICTIONARY. 165

Woak, and, also, as well as;—*atta*, neither, nor;—*lappi*, repeatedly, again.
Woakagapawin, to stand in a circle.
Woakawi, round about, anywhere around.
Woakhattimi, mulberry; (*mint'quakin. A.*)
Woakhattiminschi, mulberry tree.
Woakeu, crooked.
Woaktschachne, a bend in the river.
Woaktschaquot, crooked like.
Woaktschiechen, crooked road.
Woaktschiechton, to make crooked.
Woaktschinni, bend it.
Woaktschochwen, to go a crooked road.
Woakus, the gray fox.
Woalak, hole in the ground.
Woalhen, to dig a hole.
Woapachpoan, white bread.
Woapachsaney, white blanket.
Woapachsun, *Z.*, chalk.
Woapak, water beech; (not in use. *A.*)
Woapalanne, bald eagle.
Woapanacheen, good morning.
Woapaneu, morning.
Woapange, to-morrow.
Woapaniken, lime.
Woapank, to-morrow.
Woapaschapiall, white beads.
Woapassisku achsin, unburnt brick.

Woapasum, white sunshine.
Woapchwees, a marten.
Woapek, gensi root.
Woapelechen, it looks white.
Woapeu, white.
Woaphattaquall, white yarn, white thread.
Woaphokquawon, gray hair.
Woapim, chestnut.
Woapiminschi, chestnut tree.
Woapink, opossum, a wild beast.
Woapipen, wild white potato.
Woapsit, white person.
Woapsu, white.
Woaptigihilleu, pale.
Woaptiginquehelleu, broken eyes.
Woasgejeu, thin.
Woatasik, known; (*weuwistasik*. *A.*)
Woatauweju, it blossoms.
Woatawes, flower; (*wachawes*. *A.*)
Woaton, to know; (*weuwiton*. *A.*)
Woaxachey, fox skin.
Wochgalan, forehead.
Wochgan, bone.
Wochganihm, seed.
Wochganiponk, hard burnt ashes.
Wochganissin, to become lean, to grow meager.
Wochgidhakamik, on earth, upon the earth.
Wochgitachtenne, top of the hill.

Wochgitaque, on the top of the house.
Wochgitschi, above, on the top, on the surface.
Wochgitschik, above, on the top, up there.
Wochkunk, above, at the top.
Wochpahellan, to awake, to come to one's senses.
Wochpiechquey, bladder.
Wochtschuhatteu, full.
Woh! oh!
Wojauwe, *Z.*, a chief; (*wejjaweu*, he is a chief. This is the word now in use in place of the older word *sakema. A.*)
Wolanniall, feathers of a bird's tail.
Won, this, this one.
Wonachgulinschall, tips of the fingers.
Wonachquiwi, the top of anything.
Wonachxitall, tops of the toes.
Wonanno, cheek.
Wonatam, to be weak, to be impotent, to faint, to be out of one's senses; (*wonachq'ten. A.*)
Wonatammoagan, faintness.
Wonatamowi, weak, impotent, fanciful, out of one's senses.
Wonipakquihilleu, the leaves come out.
Wonnessin, to forget.
Wonnissowagan, forgetfulness.
Wonspi, *Z.*, sap of trees.
Wotsche anenk, by the way.
Wotschi, near by.

Wotschuwiechen, full.
Wottallauwin, to hunt by the way.
Wouchokquin, to cough; (*wohoch'quin.* A.)
Wowoatam, experienced, skilful.
Wowoatammoagan, wisdom.
Wowoatammowino, wise man.
Wsamgigun, too big.
Wsami, too much.
Wsamiechen, too much.
Wschachan, smooth, glossy.
Wschacheu, slippery; smooth, glossy.
Wschachihillan, to slip.
Wschappan, thin.
Wscheechachquall, chips, shavings.
Wscheton, lip; (*w'schej'ton.* A.)
Wschewinaxu, painful.
Wschimuin, to fly, to run off, to escape.
Wschummo, horn; pl., *wschumowall* (arch., the usual word is *wilawan*, from *wil*, head, headgear. A.).
Wsigau, sunset; (*w'si'gau.* A.)
Wsihotewagan, gain, profit.
Wsihotin, to gain a wager.
Wsihuwen, to gain, to win.
Wsit, foot.
Wsitak, handle.
Wsuppi, sap of trees; (see *wonspi.*)
Wtakanachen, moderately warm wind.
Wtakaneu, mild weather.

Wtakaquenimo, tough tree.
Wtakeu, soft, tender; (pliable. *A.*)
Wtakhammen, to divide.
Wtakhattenamoagan, softness, mildness.
Wtakigachen, it lies, soft.
Wtakolsin, to save, to preserve.
Wtaksu, soft, tender, supple.
Wtankhitton, to loose.
Wtappandewagan, advice, counsel, information.
Wtaspiwagan, ascension.
Wtauwachtojummenanink, in our midst.
Wtawongellowagan, loss, damnation.
Wtegauwan, to follow somebody.
Wtehim, strawberries.
Wtelgiqui, likewise, in like manner, so much so.
Wtelgixin, to be worthy; (not in use. *A.*)
Wtelgixowagan, worthiness, merit.
Wtellenahawanink, on the right hand;—*li*, towards the right hand.
Wtellewunsowagan, name.
Wtelli, thus, so.
Wtellsin, to be so, to do so.
Wteltschenemen, to roll.
Wtenk, after, behind; thereon, thereafter; lastly, at last; afterward;—*untschi*, thereupon, afterward.
Wtitehan, to think, to conjecture; (now *telitchan*. *A.*)
Wtschagamique, in the earth.
Wtscheet, sinew; (*u'tsch-het*. *A.*)

Wtscheyunque, within, inwardly.
Wtschitschank, spirit.
Wtschitschanquiwi, spiritual.
Wtukauwatschachtowagan, kind treatment, kind usage.
Wuhhala, *Z.*, to protect.
Wulacans, *Z.*, a basin (a bowl. *A.*).
Wulachen, to give up; (this word means "a fair wind;" probably an error for *wulachnummen*, to loosen, to untie. *A.*)
Wulachneu, a stream without falls; (a pleasant, smooth stream; from *anne*, stream, and *wulit*. *A.*)
Wuladhakawanik, good physic.
Wulaha, better.
Wulahellan, to have somebody, to possess some one; (to put a person or thing in safe keeping. *A.*)
Wulakamike, *Z.*, bottom land (*lit.*, fine land, good land. *A.*).
Wulakenimgussin, to be spoken well of, to be praised.
Wulakenimgussowagan, the being praised.
Wulakenindewagan, good report of somebody.
Wulakhelan, to take somebody in care.
Wulāku, evening.
Wulakuniwi, in the evening.
Wulalogewagan, good work.
Wulalowe, black fox; (*lit.*, beautiful tail; this may be an error for *w'halowes*, bushy tail, which is the present name of the animal. *A.*)

Wulamallessin, to be well, to be happy.
Wulamallessohalid, he who makes me happy.
Wulamallessohaluwed, he who makes one happy.
Wulamallessohen, to make well, to cause to be happy.
Wulamallessuwi, well, happy.
Wulamallsin, to be well, to be happy.
Wulämat, fine ground.
Wulamehelleu, it goes well, it goes gently.
Wulamhittamen, to believe.
Wulamhittamoewagan, faith, belief; (rather, the proof or testimony. *A.*)
Wulamissowe, a little while ago; (out of use. *A.*)
Wulamoc, he speaks truly ; true.
Wulamocan, *Z.*, a calabash, a gourd (formerly used for the rattles in ceremonies. *A.*).
Wulamoe, long ago; (out of use; *chiihn'ne* is the present term. *A.*)
Wulamoehen, to convince of the truth.
Wulamoeii, truly.
Wulamoeju, true, right.
Wulamoen, to keep one's promise.
Wulamoewagan, truth.
Wulamoewaganit, he who is truth.
Wulamoewaptonamik, true word, true saying.
Wulampton, to tie well.
Wulamquoam, *Z.*, to dream; *n'delungwam*, I dream, etc. (to dream good things. *A.*)
Wulamsittamen, to believe what is said.

Wulandeu, fine day, warm weather, fine, clear weather.
Wulangundin, to be at peace with one another.
Wulantowagan, grace; (having a good spirit; *wulit* and *manitto*. *A*.)
Wulapamukquot, clear, well to be seen.
Wulapan, fine morning.
Wulapeju, just, upright, honorable.
Wulapejuwagan, uprightness.
Wulapendamen, to enjoy a benefit.
Wulapensohalan, to bless somebody.
Wulapensowagan, blessing; (*lit.*, the things which we enjoy, prosperity, blessings. *A*.)
Wulaptonachgat, fine word, good news.
Wulaptonaelchukquonk, he speaks a good word for us, he advocates our cause.
Wulaptonaltin, to speak good to each other, to be reconciled to one another.
Wulaptonamik, good tiding.
Wulaptonen, to speak favorably.
Wulaque, yesterday.
Wulaquik, evening.
Wulaquike, this evening.
Wulaskat, good pasture.
Wulatachkat, fine linen.
Wulatenamen, to be happy; (*wulah'tenamin*. *A*.)
Wulatenamoagan, happiness.
Wulatenamuwi, happy.
Wulaton, to save, to put up.

Wulatschahan, to use somebody well.
Wulatschimolsin, to treat friendly, to discourse in a friendly manner.
Wulatschimolsowagan, treaty of peace.
Wulattauwoapin, to have good sight.
Wulattauwoapuwagan, good sight.
Wulauchsowagan, good conduct, good behavior.
Wuleleman, to take or consider somebody to be.
Wulelemelendam, to wonder, to admire.
Wulelemi, wonderful; (not in use. *A.*)
Wulelemileu, it is wonderful.
Wuleleminaquot, it seems wonderful.
Wulelendam, to be glad, to rejoice, to be joyful, to be merry.
Wulelendamoagan, joy.
Wulelendamowaptonamik, word of rejoicing, glad tiding, gospel.
Wulelendamuwi, joyful, merry.
Wulelensin, to be proud, to be haughty, to be high-minded (*welelensin. A.*).
Wulelensowagan, pride, high-mindedness.
Wulenensin, to dress; (not in use; *wulak'ko*, to have a handsome dress; *waweesho*, to dress carefully. *A.*)
Wulenschgansit, toe; (*wules'hawesit. A.*)
Wulensin, *Z.*, attire, dress, ornament (decoration rather than dress. *A.*).
Wulhallan, to keep somebody, to take care of some one.

Wuli, there, yonder; (out of use; at present *nellak*. *A.*)
Wuliachpin, to be in a good place.
Wuliechen, it is good, it is well done.
Wuliechenummen, to take down; (this means to split into splinters; the proper form *wuniechenummen*. *A.*)
Wuliechsin, to speak plainly, to pronounce well.
Wuliechtagun, he makes good again.
Wuliechtschessu, hollow, rotten; (out of use. *A.*)
Wuligatschis, pretty little paw.
Wuligischgu, fine day.
Wulihan, to do somebody good.
Wulihilleu, it is good; (more exactly, it functions properly, it works well. *A.*)
Wulik, the good; handsome, pretty.
Wuliken, it grows well, it thrives well.
Wulilaweman, to comfort, to give satisfaction.
Wulilawemkewagan, our comfort.
Wulilawendewagan, comfort.
Wulileu, good news, it is a good time.
Wulilissin, to be good, to behave well.
Wulilissowagan, goodness, kindness.
Wulilissu, good, kind.
Wulinamen, he likes it, it pleases him; (arch., *A.*)
Wulinaquot, it looks well.
Wulinaxin, to appear well, to look fine.
Wulineichquot, it is plainly visible.
Wulinemen, to see very well.
Wulipendamen, to hear well, to understand well.

Wulipommissin, good walking.
Wulipoquot, it has a fine taste.
Wulisso, good, handsome, fine, pretty.
Wulissowagan, fineness, prettiness, beauty.
Wulistammen, to believe.
Wulistammoewagan, faith, belief.
Wulit, good, right, handsome, pretty; well.
Wulitehasu, well hewn, well cut, well squared; (*wulih' tehasu. A.*)
Wulitehemen, to hew well.
Wuliton, to make well.
Wuliweuchsin, to know well.
Wuliwiechinen, to rest well.
Wuliwoatam, to know well, to be of good understanding.
Wullamoe, *Z.*, ancient.
Wuloamisowe, lately, some days ago.
Wulongachsis, a man's cousin; (out of use; it is from *wulonquan*, wing. *A.*)
Wulonquan, wing.
Wulonquoam, to dream something good.
Wulowachtauwoapin, to look over, to look beyond.
Wulowinquehellan, to overlook, to take no notice of.
Wulumhigiechen, to squat down.
Wulummachdappin, to sit; (especially on the ground with the legs in front. *A.*)
Wulumqueu or Wulumquot, a round hill.
Wunachgin, thou hand!

Wunachk, his hand; his arm; (it means either. *A.*)
Wunachqualoje, a sharp point; (the extreme end. *A.*)
Wunachquim, an acorn.
Wunajumawall, he carries him.
Wunalan, to fetch somebody; (not in use; at present *peschwan*, means to bring some one. *A.*)
Wunattochton, to inquire, to search after.
Wunattonamak, his son-in-law; (or her; proper form is *wunattonomakwall*. *A.*)
Wundaman, to show to somebody; to declare unto some one.
Wundanglen, to die for some cause.
Wundangunsin, to pray for.
Wundanunxin, to be angry at, to be angry for something.
Wundaptonen, to speak of.
Wundchen, the wind comes from thence.
Wundchenneu, west, westerly; (out of use; the present word is *clochsichgat*, when the sun disappears. *A.*)
Wundchennewunk, westward.
Wundelemuin, to boast, to look upon as an honor; (rather, to put trust or confidence; it is from *wuntschi*, from; to rely upon what we expect *from* another. *A.*)
Wundelendamoagan, boasting, glorying in.
Wundenasik, where it is to be got from.
Wundeu, it boils.
Wundpeu, it leaks, it drops, it boils over; (*kündpeu*, it oozes out; *wüngiku*, it leaks. *A.*)

DICTIONARY. 177

Wundsowagan, misfortune; (not now used. *A.*)
Wundschun, the wind comes from a particular quarter.
Wundsummen, *Z.*, to cook (properly, to boil something. *A.*).
Wunenachgistawan, to hearken to somebody.
Wunentsitawoaganit, his appearing.
Wunipachgihilleu, it buds, it sprouts.
Wunipak, leaf; (see *Combach.*)
Wunita, he can, he is able; (he knows how. *A.*)
Wunitaton, he can do it; (he knows how to do it. *A.*)
Wunspak, *Z.*, juice (juice extracted by pressure; from *wuntschi, i. e.,* that which comes *from. A.*).
Wuntschi, of, on account of, from, therefore.
Wuntschijeyju, where he belongs to, from whence he is.
Wuntschiman, to call somebody hither.
Wunutschi, he began.
Wuschgink, eye, face, sight.
Wuschginquiwi, face to face.
Wuskamamquot, new feeling.
Wuskchum, young creature, young beast.
Wuskelenape, young person.
Wusken, anew, latterly.
Wuskhaxen, a new shoe.
Wuski, new.
Wuskijeyju, it is new.
Wuskiochqueu, young woman.
Wuttoney, beard.

M

Wundamawachtowagan, declaration, message.
Wewoatamoewagan, wisdom.
Wawangundowagan, salutation.

Y.

Yabtschi, *Z.*, yet.
Yanewi, *Z.*, always.
Yapeechen, *H.*, along the bank (rather, along the edge of the water. *A.*).
Yapewi, *Z.*, on the river bank (on the edge of the water. *A.*).
Yucke, *Z.*, now; *gischquik*, to-day;—*untschi*, here; *petschi*, till now; (*yuch. A.*)
Yukella, O that!
Yuni, *H.*, this, this one.
Yu undach, *Z.*, on this side (*yuh windach. A.*).

Z.

Zelozelos, cricket; (*tschelo'tschelos*, an imitative word. *A.*)

INDEX.

The figures in broad-faced type indicate the page, those that follow, the line.

Aaron root, **72**, 6.
Abandon, to, **95**, 10.
Abates, the freshet, **132**, 2—the water, **48**, 12.
Abide in somebody, **12**, 12.
Able, he is, **177**, 8.
Abode, **12**, 8—to make an, **158**, 16.
Abominably, to lie, **98**, 11.
Abort, to, **130**, 14.
About, **12**, 1; **45**, 7—the present time, **51**, 13—this time, **112**, 8 —to turn, **44**, 17—to walk, **12**, 2; **86**, 3—turned, **44**, 18.
Above, **24**, 5; **49**, 4; **167**, 2, 3, 4 —from, **49**, 4—the earth, **49**, 4.
Abridgment, **31**, 20.
Abroad, **56**, 6—to be always, **85**, 19 —to carry, **17**, 5.
Absolutely not, **139**, 20.
Abundance, **156**, 15, 16.
Abuse to, **70**, 15—each other by words to, **75**, 12—some one, to, **56**, 23.
Accept, to, **91**, 13.
Accident, an, **148**, 24—bad, **145**, 20; **160**, 16—to meet by, **99**, 13.
Accidentally, **117**, 24.
Accomplished, **106**, 18.
According to, **89**, 14.
Account of, on, **177**, 11.
Accusation, **10**, 15; **13**, 3; **42**, 5; **60**, 6—bad, **69**, 11.
Accuse him, one who helped to, **164**, 1—somebody, to, **69**, 9.
Acorn, an, **151**, 2; **176**, 3.

Acquaintance, his, **155**, 22.
Acquainted with, to be, **52**, 20.
Acquire, to, **107**, 4.
Act, so, to, **65**, 4—strangely, to, **13**, 24—wicked, **69**, 15.
Action, bad, **37**, 8; **70**, 22.
Active, to be, **162**, 18.
Activity, **17**, 2.
Admire, to, **173**, 8.
Admittance, **154**, 19.
Admonish, to, **41**, 20; **46**, 14— somebody, to, **41**, 21.
Admonition, **46**, 15.
Adultery, to commit, **54**, 1.
Adults, **53**, 11.
Advantage, to desire to give one an, **49**, 19.
Adversary, **129**, 1.
Advice, **24**, 3; **135**, 17; **169**, 9.
Advise one another, to, **150**, 22—. with, to, **163**, 10.
Advocates our cause, he, **172**, 12.
Affirm, to, **54**, 19.
Afflicted to death, to be, **9**, 7.
Afloat, **89**, 13.
Afoot, to go, **119**, 2.
After, **89**, 9; **169**, 23—a little while, **22**, 14—Sunday, **15**, 20.
Afternoon, **92**, 7, 10—in the, **135**, 12.
Afterward, **169**, 23.
Again, **52**, 5; **61**, 2; **146**, 24; **155**, 10; **165**, 1.
Against, **88**, 13; **143**, 13—one's inclination, to be, **129**, 4.

INDEX.

Aged, 53, 11—to be, 53, 13; 84, 21.
Ago, a little while, 40, 3; 41, 24; 171, 11—long, 62, 2; 65, 17; 171, 14—not long, 40, 3.
Agony of death, 78, 24.
Agree to, 95, 18—with one another, to, 88, 18.
Agreement, 71, 20; 88, 19.
Agrees, it, 71, 26.
Aground, it is, 28, 9.
Ague, the, 99, 14.
Ah! 51, 14.
Aid, an, 163, 15.
Air, 62, 13.
Alder tree, the, 143, 8.
Alike, just, 143, 10, 13—to make it, 143, 11.
Aliment, 86, 7.
All, 144, 23; 154, 8—for good and, 15, 11—is ready, 104, 15—over the country, 32, 9—the world round, 33, 1—to carry, 154, 7—together, 143, 15.
Alliance, an, 79, 18.
Allow, to, 63, 4.
Ally, to, 79, 20.
Almighty, the, 34, 6.
Almost, 36, 18; 38, 4; 154, 21—nearly, 36, 10—too much, 36, 10.
Alone, 71, 25; 78, 15; 89, 1; 93, 1—let, 50, 11—let it, 52, 4—to be, 88, 24; 93, 2, 3—to be quite, 93, 13.
Along shore, 50, 18—the bank, 50, 18; 178, 6—the road, 32, 11—to roll, 17, 9—to take, 39, 10.
Aloud, to cry, 46, 27.
Already, 16, 14; 83, 7.
Also, 33, 11; 141, 18; 165, 1.
Also, they, 52, 16—thou, 52, 13—we, 52, 14—ye, 52, 15.
Although, 82, 13; 139, 17; 143, 15.
Always, 9, 3; 50, 17; 95, 11; 178, 5—well, to be, 152, 16.

Am, as I, 33, 20.
Amiss, to do, 108, 1—to shoot, 107, 19.
Among each other, 156, 18.
Amusing tale, an, 55, 7.
Ancestors, 12, 13; 86, 15.
Ancient, 175, 14.
And, 165, 1.
Anew, 155, 10; 177, 20.
Anger, 24, 9; 60, 5; 74, 14; 113, 20—to, 59, 16; 105, 1.
Angle, to, 20, 16.
Angry, to be, 74, 13—at, to be, 176, 11—for something, to be, 176, 11.
Anguish, 122, 7—mental, 58, 9—of mind, to be in, 58, 8.
Animal, any domesticated, 18, 9—domestic, 29, 6—the trail of an, 130, 18—to skin an, 26, 14.
Animate, 25, 23.
Anoint, to, 126, 10.
Another, 58, 12; 115, 17; 136, 21—manner, 58, 12—to pay one, 30, 1.
Answer, to, 88, 20—somebody, to, 88, 17.
Answering, exclamation used in, 103, 13, 14.
Answers the purpose, it, 140, 21.
Ant, 33, 8.
Anvil, 22, 15.
Any, 140, 8.
Anything, 89, 8; 140, 8.
Anywhere, 137, 6—around, 165, 3.
Apart, 144, 16—to pull, 66, 4.
Apparent, 93, 7.
Appear, to, 94, 8—well, to, 174, 23.
Appearance, his, 33, 12.
Appearing, his, 177, 5.
Appears, as he, 33, 12—large, it, 77, 18.
Apple, 22, 4—crab, 142, 22—May, 74, 19—wild, 142, 22.

INDEX. 181

Appoint somebody to an office, to, 122, 15.
Apprehension, 16, 10.
Approbation, 160, 2—exclamation of, 30, 8.
Approval, exclamation of, 45, 2; 52, 11.
Ardent, 131, 6; 133, 6.
Ardently, to desire, 29, 3.
Arise, to, 20, 18; 142, 21.
Arm, his, 176, 1; the thick part of the, 29, 13.
Arms, open, 139, 11—outstretched, 129, 23.
Around, anywhere, 165, 3—to go all, 164, 17—to stand all, 164, 15.
Arrest somebody, to, 136, 17; 142, 3.
Arrow, 18, 19; 72, 12.
Arse, 133, 16—-hole, the, 124, 16.
As, 32, 18; 33, 5; 64, 8—also, 91, 2—big, 32, 19—far, 131, 20—he appears, 33, 12—he does, 33, 21—he is minded, 33, 21—he saith, 33, 22—he thinks, 33, 14—I am, 33, 20—I do, 33, 20; if, 72, 7; 135, 7—is customary, 33, 9—is usual with one, 33, 9—it is, 32, 4—it were, 71, 7—long, 131, 20—many as, 34, 12—many as are here, 34, 9—much again, 61, 2—much as, 34, 12—much as one owes, 34, 10—much so, 32, 18—often as, 32, 18; 34, 11—soon as, 58, 20; 64, 8; 144, 23—that, 33, 10—the other, 33, 10—this, 33, 10; 64, 17—well as, 32, 18; 165, 1—wide as, 32, 19.
Ascend, to, 23, 17, 19.
Ascension, 169, 10.
Ash, 83, 20—black, 104, 13.
Ashamed, to be, 73, 5; 84, 1, 2, 4—to be made, 84, 5—of one's self, to be, 84, 2.

Ashes, 119, 10; 120, 21—hard burnt, 166, 25—light, 117, 27—light white, 84, 13.
Ask for, to, 152, 14—pardon, to, 78, 23.
Assassinate, to, 53, 23.
Assassination, 53, 21.
Assemble, to, 76, 5.
Assembled, 76, 13—to be, 76, 12.
Assist each other, to, 164, 6—somebody, to, 163, 5.
Assistant, 163, 15.
Assure, to, 54, 19.
Astringent, 142, 1.
Asunder, 144, 16, 17—it splits, 144, 18—split, 144, 18—to break, 105, 3—to go, 16, 8.
At all times, 9, 3; 50, 17—first, 95, 26—last, 83, 16; 90, 13, 20—what time, 135, 4.
Attach one's self to, 21, 20.
Attack, to, 122, 10.
Attention to, to pay, 109, 2.
Attire, 173, 20.
Auger, 118, 1.
August, the month of, 123, 10; 159, 15.
Aunt, 117, 25.
Aurora, the, 68, 12.
Authority, 146, 9.
Autumn, 136, 7—month, 54, 12.
Avaricious, 24, 8—to be, 127, 13.
Avert, to, 45, 10.
Awake, 167, 5—to, 142, 21.
Aware of some one, to be, 101, 10.
Away, he that is going, 32, 15—to be cast, 23, 2—to bring somebody, 18, 16—to carry, 18, 15; 75, 2—to go, 18, 17; 107, 21—to go all, 154, 12—to throw, 107, 2—weeping, to go, 18, 14.
Awful, 145, 20.
Awhile, 45, 25.
Awl, 87, 15.

182   INDEX.

Axe, 140, 7—an, 147, 18—broad, 105, 14—to cut with an, 44, 3.
Ay! 31, 12.
Aye! 31, 9.

Babbler, a, 156, 1.
Babe, 19, 23.
Babes, sucking, 100, 1.
Bachelor, a, 53, 6.
Back, 151, 7—the, 152, 12—to come, 22, 3; to drive, 46, 17—to give, 46, 26—to lie on the, 151, 18—to look, 44, 16; 45, 16—to push, 45, 10.
Backache, to have, 152, 13.
Backbone, 132, 10.
Backside, 133, 16.
Backwards, 151, 7.
Bad, 69, 14, 23; 70, 11, 12, 13, 14; 71, 9; 72, 14; 78, 7, 8—action, 37, 8; 70, 22—accusation, 69, 11—behavior, 37, 8—it is too, 17, 17—morning weather, 69, 12—report, 10, 15—shoes, 69, 13—times, 69, 24—travelling, to have, 11, 22.
Badger, a, 87, 16.
Badly, to travel, 75, 21.
Bag, 81, 21; 128, 3—saddle, 27, 12—shot, 18, 21.
Bait, 76, 21.
Baking, the bread is done, 42, 8.
Bald, 86, 25—eagle, 165, 20—headed, 86, 26.
Ball of the foot, 39, 27; 40, 1—round, 120, 11.
Band for carrying burdens, a, 47, 22.
Bank, a high, 51, 1—along the, 50, 18; 178, 6, of a river, high, 14, 11—on the 51, 1—on the river, 178, 7—steep, 108, 16.
Banner, 68, 22.

Baptism, 133, 18.
Baptized, 133, 19.
Bare, 86, 25; 87, 3—to make one, 133, 24.
Barefoot, 80, 12.
Barefooted, to be, 80, 13.
Bargain, 88, 19—in the, 47, 21.
Bark, 20, 25—canoe, 20, 24; 162, 2—of a tree, 49, 1—of trees, the inner, 157, 18—trunk, 161, 21.
Barrel, 47, 15.
Barren, 78, 25—tree, 79, 3.
Basin, a, 170, 6.
Basket, 138, 14—a, 83, 19—wood, 25, 15.
Baskets, to make, 138, 15.
Bast, 157, 18.
Bath, sweat by a, 29, 15.
Bathe, to, 121, 5; 141, 22.
Battery of a gun lock, 30, 17.
Battle, to die in, 9, 8.
Bay, wild, 35, 18.
Be in somebody, to, 12, 12—it where it may, 137, 5—of opinion, to, 39, 7—so good, 15, 12—willing, 38, 3.
Bead, 74, 17.
Beads, white, 165, 26.
Beam, 12, 3.
Bean, 47, 8; 72, 8.
Beans, 47, 3—earth, 47, 3—wild, 124, 2.
Bear, 69, 2—she, 101, 24—to kill a, 96, 8.
Beard, 147, 19; 177, 25.
Bears, plenty of, 69, 3.
Beast, 25, 4—a wild, 166, 10—tame, 152, 21—young, 177, 18.
Beasts, female of, 103, 4—male of, 63, 20.
Beat, to, 106, 13; 118, 9; 119, 14; 132, 7—hard, to, 56, 20—oil, to, 118, 15—somebody, to, 105, 8; 118, 21—the drum, to, 118, 9.

INDEX. 183

Beaten road, 56, 25.
Beating, 113, 11.
Beauty, 175, 4.
Beaver, 58, 16—bait, 76, 21.
Because, 33, 5; 91, 2; 101, 1, 2; 155, 1.
Become a child, to, 153, 1—flesh, to, 104, 4; one, to, 79, 20.
Bed, 38, 21; a, 12, 9; 38, 15.
Bedaub, to, 98, 22.
Bedstead, 27, 6—an Indian, 143, 21.
Bee, 20, 12—hive, 20, 13.
Beech tree, red, 126, 18—white, 138, 12.
Beechwood, 126, 17.
Beer, 76, 19—to brew, 76, 19.
Before, 33, 13; 96, 4—now, 97, 14; 164, 13, 18.
Beforehand, 96, 4.
Beg, to, 152, 14—on, to, 78, 23.
Began, he, 177, 14.
Beget a child, to, 149, 1.
Beggar, 23, 8.
Begin war, to, 102, 13.
Beginning, at the, 97, 14; 102, 10 —of summer, 139, 12—to be from the, 97, 13.
Begotten, 78, 27.
Behave well, to, 174, 18—wonderfully, to, 13, 24.
Behaved, foolish, 56, 16.
Behavior, 61, 17; 153, 11; bad, 37, 8—good, 173, 6—sinful, 75, 4.
Behind, 25, 14, 15; 151, 7; 169, 23 —the fence, 25, 12—the house, 25, 8—to leave, 95, 10.
Behold, 65, 14—to, 10, 12; 64, 24; 112, 22; 137, 10.
Belief, 171, 10; 175, 6.
Believe, to, 103, 23; 171, 9; 175, 5—to be blameless or holy, to, 57, 4—what is said, to, 171, 24.
Believer in Christ, 154, 6.

Bell, 124, 7; 131, 16; 133, 2—to ring the, 124, 6, 8.
Bellied, thick, 77, 4.
Bellows, 120, 26.
Belly, 150, 4; fat in an animal's, 158, 12—the net inside the, 152, 19—ache, he has the, 150, 3.
Belong to a place, to, 155, 2.
Belongs to, where he, 177, 12.
Beloved, 14, 25; 31, 5—above all things, the, 33, 26—best, 33, 26 —the, 14, 17; 31, 6.
Below, from, 47, 12.
Belt, a, 39, 1—of wampum, 103, 3.
Bench, 47, 19; 62, 17.
Bend in the river, a, 165, 7—it, 165, 11—of the river, in the, 32, 14.
Bends, it, 127, 2.
Beneath, 34, 18.
Benefit, to enjoy a, 172, 8.
Bent, 150, 18.
Bequeath, to, 95, 10.
Beshit, to, 87, 14.
Besides, 52, 5.
Best, 71, 25; 154, 5—beloved, 33, 26—the, 34, 3—the very, 34, 5.
Betray each other, to, 40, 15—somebody to, 40, 14; 58, 18.
Better, 85, 12; 170, 10—a little, 85, 12—to grow, 53, 9—to love, 51, 3.
Between, 141, 6—to step or stand, 35, 9.
Bewitch, to, 74, 2.
Bewitched, one is, 72, 10.
Beyond, 24, 5; 25, 14, 15—to look, 175, 19.
Big, 19, 13; 76, 26; 77, 12—as, 32, 19—and wide as the world is, as, 33, 1—as, as, 33, 2—rock, 37, 10—too, 168, 7—trough, 28, 1.
Bill of a fowl or bird, 157, 5.
Bind up into sheaves, to, 21, 17— up or dress a wound, to, 11, 18.

Binding, 36, 4.
Birch bark, 161, 21—tree, 157, 7.
Bird, 146, 25—a, 24, 11, 12—bill of a fowl or, 157, 5—black, 147, 8—little, 147, 1—red, 79, 10—the young of a, 21, 9.
Birds and fowls, male of, 63, 21.
Bird's nest, 150, 1.
Birth, 79, 1.
Biting, 53, 2, 5.
Bitter, 142, 1—weed, the, 157, 1.
Black, 134, 12, 14—ash, 104, 13—bird, 147, 8—cloth, 15, 15—fish, 134, 9, 10—fox, 170, 20—it looks, 134, 11—man, 94, 11—oak, 162, 2—or broad cloth, 13, 5—snake, 134, 5—snakeroot, 26, 11—thread, 134, 13—yarn, 134, 13.
Blackberries, 13, 6.
Bladder, 167, 6—a blown, 151, 12.
Blamable, to be, 144, 1.
Blame, 73, 21—one another, to, 10, 16—somebody, to, 73, 19.
Blamed, to be, 73, 20.
Blameless, to believe to be, 57, 4—to live, 152, 17.
Blanket, 13, 5; 15, 15—white, 165, 17.
Bleed, to, 131, 22—at the nose, to, 79, 12—fast, to, 57, 7—to death, to, 9, 4; 83, 8.
Bless somebody, to, 172, 9.
Blessed, the, 153, 23.
Blessing, 172, 10.
Blind, 10, 19; 38, 25—I am, 95, 4—person, a, 38, 25—to be, 10, 18.
Blood, 79, 9, 14; 86, 18—to let, 105, 9.
Bloody, 79, 9, 16; 81, 22, 23—flux, 79, 11.
Blossoms, it, 166, 18.
Blot out, to, 146, 4.
Blow, to, 120, 25—the nose, to, 124, 11.

Blows hard, the wind, 56, 19.
Blue, 130, 7—bird, 145, 1, 8.
Blunder in speaking, to, 117, 6.
Blunt, 58, 3; 161, 25.
Boar, 154, 1.
Board, 109, 14—a, 106, 2—a thick, 28, 18—saw, 105, 17—with, to, 163, 22.
Boards, to make, 109, 15.
Boast, to, 176, 16.
Boasting, 176, 17.
Boat, 20, 9—line, 44, 22—wood, the, 20, 11.
Bodily, 47, 6; 150, 12.
Body, 47, 5; 150, 11—the, 27, 11.
Bog meadow, 129, 2.
Boil, a, 120, 18—to, 156, 21—water in till dry, to, 48, 14.
Boiled, 160, 21—enough, 160, 22.
Boils, it, 176, 19—over, 176, 20—over, it, 108, 8.
Bone, 166, 23.
Bony, 149, 18.
Book, 26, 1; 62, 24; 72, 19.
Booty, 130, 1.
Border, those who live on the, 128, 5.
Bored through, 126, 11.
Born, 43, 6—to be, 43, 5; 78, 26; 86, 6.
Borrowed, 41, 16.
Bosom, the, 29, 18.
Both, 33, 16—sides, on, 156, 10.
Bottle, a, 31, 4.
Bottom land, 170, 12—of a keg, 158, 9.
Bough, a, 148, 4.
Boulder, a, 37, 10.
Bound, 42, 14.
Boundary, a, 53, 1.
Bow, 48, 2—one's self down, to, 84, 15—toward, to, 84, 16.
Bowl, 120, 14—a, 170, 6—large, 28, 1.

INDEX.

Box bush, the, 124, 25—made of bark, 161, 21—with each other, to, 106, 16.
Boy, 115, 14—big, 115, 11—little, 115, 13—to be a, 115, 12.
Brace one's self for a jump, to, 10, 20.
Brain, 147, 17.
Bran, 66, 5; 127, 25.
Branch, 131, 5—a, 148, 4.
Branches, 113, 13.
Brandy, 76, 14; 162, 5.
Bread, 12, 17—bit of, 108, 13—huckleberry, 84, 24—is done baking, the, 42, 8—mixed with beans, 71, 11—my, 92, 13—piece of, 12, 18—white, 165, 16.
Break, to, 105, 3, 13; 118, 12; 119, 22—in two, 119, 24—off, 112, 21—in the ice, to, 76, 25—of day, the, 95, 3—off, to, 35, 17—off in speaking, to, 15, 16—off speaking, to, 82, 25.
Breast, pain in the, 153, 15—the, 29, 18; 153, 14.
Breasts of a woman, the, 101, 11.
Breath, 62, 13, 16.
Breathe, to, 62, 15.
Breathing, to cease, 15, 25.
Breech of a gun, 56, 15; 158, 9.
Breeches, leather, 27, 17.
Brethren, 97, 12.
Brew beer, to, 76, 19.
Briars, 38, 12.
Brick, 68, 18—unburnt, 165, 27.
Bridge, 136, 18.
Bridle, 44, 14—bit, 38, 16.
Bridled, 61, 6.
Bright, 149, 16.
Brightly, it shines, 122, 23.
Brightness, 149, 16.
Bring, to, 114, 20—somebody away, to, 18, 15—somebody home, to, 75, 3—together, to, 76, 6.

Brisk, to be, 162, 18.
Broad, 10, 6; 31, 11—axe, 105, 14—saw, 105, 17.
Broadness, 31, 10.
Broil, to, 12, 21.
Broken, 119, 21, 23; 143, 19—off, 144, 18—up, 65, 20.
Brokenly, to speak, 19, 15.
Broom, 145, 5.
Broth, 57, 23—sweet, 159, 24.
Brother, elder, 27, 5—in-law, his, 150, 2—my, 97, 9—or sister, younger, 27, 16.
Brotherhood, 159, 5.
Brother's wife, his, 163, 11.
Brought to somebody, to be, 114, 14.
Brown, 161, 12.
Bruise one's self by accident, to, 134, 4—the finger nail, to, 20, 14—the hand, to, 26, 17.
Bruised, 108, 24.
Bubble, a, 151, 12.
Buck, 15, 9; 107, 9—great, 27, 20—young, 24, 18.
Bud, to, 22, 11.
Buds, it, 132, 13; 177, 6.
Buffalo, the, 132, 21.
Build, to, 157, 21.
Builders, 157, 20.
Building log, 81, 24.
Bullet, 18, 19; 120, 9—mould, 18, 20.
Bullfrog, 20, 23; 103, 21.
Bundle, 164, 11—a, 157, 3.
Burden, to load somebody with a, 164, 10.
Burdens, a band for carrying, 47, 22.
Burial, 139, 18—place, a, 70, 20.
Buried, 150, 24—to be, 139, 14.
Burn, to, 67, 3, 5, 6; 139, 7; 152, 2—it begins to, 131, 6—the kettle, 11, 17.
Burning, 133, 6, 8.

186 INDEX.

Burns, it, 67, 7—in a flame, it, 66, 17—me, it, 162, 8—well, it, 160, 1, 3.
Burnt, 67, 4.
Burst open, to fall and, 29, 5.
Burthensome, 149, 10.
Bury, to, 139, 18.
Bush, 161, 8—a, 9, 11—thorn, 68, 25.
Bushnet, 13, 9—for fishing, 12, 22—to fish with, a, 13, 8.
Bushy, 9, 11.
Bushy place, a, 161, 8.
Busily, 162, 17.
Business, those that have the care of some, 90, 23.
But, 94, 12; 130, 15—few, 139, 2—if, 15, 12—then, 130, 17.
Butt end of a tree, 158, 10.
Buttocks, 133, 16.
Buttonwood, the, 20, 11.
Buy, to, 15, 14; 78, 18, 20.
Buzzard, turkey, 19, 16.
By, 149, 3—and bye, 22, 14; 89, 14; 110, 17—close, 36, 10—degrees, 20, 26; 21, 1—little and little, 20, 26; 21, 1; 141, 18—to pass, 17, 7—the way, 22, 12; 32, 12.

Cabin, a, 63, 14—covered with grass, 84, 8.
Calabash, a, 171, 13.
Calamus-root, 113, 12.
Calf, 111, 2; 155, 9—little, 87, 8—of the elbow, 111, 3—of the leg, 164, 8.
Call, 155, 4—each other, to, 155, 5—somebody hither, to, 177, 13.
Called, 67, 8—as he is, 32, 17.
Calling, exclamation used in, 51, 11.
Calm mind, to be of a, 55, 11.

Calmness, 58, 7—of mind, 15, 8; 55, 12.
Came, whence he, 154, 20.
Camp, 77, 22.
Camped, 76, 1.
Can, he, 177, 8—he, do it, 177, 9—I, 98, 27.
Candle, 152, 1.
Candle snuffers, 139, 22.
Canoe, 20, 9—bark, 20, 24; 162, 2—floats, the, 89, 13—little, 20, 10—is finished, the, 42, 15—rope, 44, 22—to enter a, 120, 22—with somebody, to go in a, 156, 20.
Cap, 17, 21.
Capability, 146, 17.
Captain, 60, 3.
Captives, 139, 21.
Care, 20, 21—of somebody, to take, 39, 12; 113, 2—of, to take, 39, 14; 59, 11; 91, 19—to be free from trouble or, 55, 21—to be without, 58, 5—to take, 20, 22—to take somebody in, 170, 16.
Careful, to be, 92, 21.
Carries him, he, 176, 4.
Carry, abroad, to, 17, 5—all, to, 154, 7—a load, to, 90, 7; 164, 12—away, to, 18, 15; 75, 2—somebody, to, 90, 6—some one through, to, 34, 23.
Cart, 141, 12.
Cask, 47, 15.
Cast away, to be, 23, 2.
Castrate, to, 145, 6.
Cat, a wild, 96, 1; 145, 15.
Cataract, 133, 20.
Catch something with a net, 13, 7.
Caterpillar, 86, 22.
Catfish, 162, 9.
Cattle, 24, 10—horned, 155, 16—the owner of, 152, 23—to have, 152, 22.

INDEX. 187

Caught, 56, 7.
Cause, he advocates our, 172, 12—to, 42, 21—to hear, to, 112, 13—to live until now, to, 114, 11.
Cautiousness, 20, 21.
Cave, a, 151, 1.
Cease, to, 65, 24.
Cease breathing, to, 15, 28.
Ceases, the wind, 15, 24.
Cedar, red, 79, 6—swamp, 140, 3—white, 137, 9.
Cellar, a, 47, 2.
Certain, 125, 17—of it, I am, 100, 15—one, a, 71, 21; 79, 17—to be, 24, 19; 100, 15.
Certainly, 54, 13—true, 125, 17.
Chain, a, 49, 3; 133, 13.
Chair, 47, 19; 62, 17.
Chalk, 165, 18.
Chance, by, 111, 7; 117, 24—to hear by, 109, 3—to miss one's, 108, 21.
Chapter, 22, 18.
Charge, 13, 3.
Charged, 116, 19.
Chase or drive hither, to, 114, 19.
Chaste, 115, 21, 23; 116, 1—to be, 115, 20.
Chastisement, 19, 19.
Cheap, 22, 24; 137, 21.
Cheapen, to, 137, 22.
Cheat, to, 11, 9.
Cheek, 167, 15.
Cherry, wild, 87, 13.
Chestnut, 166, 8—tree, 149, 15; 166, 9.
Chew, to, 130, 16; 134, 3.
Chicken, little, 142, 15.
Chief, 123, 13—a, 167, 9—man, 53, 14—to make to a, 123, 14.
Child, 19, 21—my, 99, 4, 5—to become a, 153, 1—to beget or bring forth a, 149, 1.

Child's nurse, 102, 3.
Childish, 19, 22.
Childlike, 19, 22; 153, 2.
Children, to have, 102, 2.
Chin, 49, 12.
Chips, 129, 25; 168, 14.
Chisel, a, 119, 27.
Choose, to, 10, 7; 117, 1.
Chop fish, 63, 11—to, 44, 2, 3—wood, to, 74, 4.
Chosen, the, 38, 23—thy, 38, 22.
Christ, believer in, 154, 6.
Church, 110, 7—hind part of a, 133, 16—to come out of, 58, 24.
Circle, 113, 21—they stand in a, 150, 13—to stand in a, 165, 2.
Circular, 141, 11.
City, 149, 13—great, 55, 3.
Civil, to speak, 141, 16.
Clam, 31, 2; 118, 13.
Claws, 157, 15.
Clay, 23, 21—daubed with, 23, 24—to mix, 23, 25.
Clean, 57, 2, 6; 115, 16—to be, 57, 12; 115, 19, 23; 116, 1—to make, 57, 10.
Cleanly, it looks, 116, 2.
Cleanse, to, 57, 13.
Cleansed, to be, 115, 14.
Clear, 42, 11; 57, 9; 86, 25; 87, 3; 151, 20; 164, 23; 172, 4—day, 152, 6—it is, 42, 12—sunshine, 151, 19; 152, 3—water, 57, 11—weather, 87, 2; 172, 1.
Clearly, 87, 3.
Cleft of a rock, in the, 29, 12.
Climb hither, to, 114, 3—up, 1, 60, 3—up, to, 39, 18; 60, 8.
Climbs up, it, 60, 16.
Close by, 36, 10; 41, 14; 110, 19.
Close, to shut, 45, 8—together, 120, 1.
Cloth, black, 13, 5; 15, 15—his, 30, 14.

o

INDEX.

Clothe somebody, to, 11, 16; 116, 17—some one, to, 111, 4.
Clothed, 111, 8.
Clothes-lice, 27, 2.
Clothes, to put on, 13, 2—to put on somebody, 116, 23.
Clothing, 13, 2; 30, 13; 111, 9.
Cloud, 11, 14.
Cloudy, 11, 13, 15.
Clown, 38, 14.
Coal, 47, 4—of fire, 68, 11; 78, 17.
Coarse linen, 19, 12.
Coat, 126, 8.
Cock, a turkey, 26, 12—of a gun-lock, 71, 16.
Cold, 139, 23—it is, 141, 13; 142, 6—morning, 137, 13—to be, 138, 17—to shake for, 101, 21.
Colic, 152, 8.
Collect, to, 76, 6.
Collectively, 76, 13.
Collector, 76, 2.
Color, what, 134, 19.
Colt's foot, the herb, 19, 17.
Comb, to, 144, 22.
Come, 38, 3—to, 104, 8—awhile ago, to, 116, 26—back, to, 22, 3—before somebody, to, 96, 7—down, to, 96, 2; 112, 24—from cutting wood, to, 22, 2—from hunting, to, 21, 23—from planting, to, 21, 21—from somewhere, to, 137, 2—from somewhere rapidly, to, 149, 4—from whence, to, 103, 25—from work, to, 21, 24—hither, to, 115, 2—in a troublesome time, to, 124, 1—into danger, to, 99, 13—nigh to me, to, 82, 6—or go for something, to, 148, 23—out of church, to, 58, 24—out of the house, to, 59, 5—together again, to, 61, 4—to one's senses, to, 167, 5—to seek, to, 114, 2—to somebody, to, 98, 10—up with somebody, to, 75, 10.
Comes, it, 111, 14, 15.
Cometh, he that, 111, 13.
Comfort, 89, 17; 174, 16—our, 174, 15—to, 174, 14.
Comforter, 153, 18.
Coming, his, 104, 3—on, he is, 114, 22—they are, 111, 22.
Commanded, 61, 6.
Commandment, 122, 18; 135, 17; 153, 4.
Commit adultery, to, 54, 1.
Commodiousness, 54, 8.
Commonly, 48, 15.
Companion, 99, 3.
Comparative form, 17, 10; 17, 16.
Compare, to, 72, 1.
Compass, 113, 21.
Compassionate some person, to, 40, 17.
Complete, 106, 17—to, 106, 20.
Completed, 106, 19.
Comrade, a, 147, 6.
Conceal, to, 37, 6, 23.
Conceive, to, 118, 6.
Concern, 59, 12; 122, 8—to wait for with much, 29, 3.
Concerned for, to be, 59, 11; 109, 2—for somebody, to be, 59, 9—for some one, to be, 113, 2—for something, to be, 59, 10—to be no more, 119, 6.
Concerning, 149, 3.
Conclude, to, 42, 7.
Concluded, 42, 6.
Condemn, to, 39, 22.
Condemnation, 39, 21.
Condemned, to be, 39, 20.
Condemneth, he that, 39, 23.
Condescend, to, 138, 5.
Conduct, 153, 11—good, 173, 6.
Confederation, 79, 18.
Confide in, to, 89, 16.

INDEX.   189

Confidence, 89, 19.
Confusion, 122, 5.
Congregation, 81, 17.
Conjecture, to, 153, 9; 169, 24.
Conquer somebody, to, 118, 21.
Conquered, 132, 3.
Conscious, to become, 104, 6.
Consider, to, 113, 3; 144, 3—about somebody, to, 113, 2—somebody to be, to, 153, 8; 173, 7.
Consideration, 113, 4.
Considered, to have, 43, 12.
Conspiracy, a, 26, 19.
Constantly, 95, 11.
Consult, to, 24, 2.
Contains but little, it, 73, 22.
Contemptible, 75, 15.
Contend, to, 55, 15.
Content, to be, 140, 17.
Contrary, 88, 13—mind, 22, 13.
Convenience, 54, 8.
Convenient, 54, 7.
Conversation, 89, 5.
Convert, to, 59, 3.
Convince of the truth, to, 171, 15.
Cook, to, 123, 2; 156, 21; 177, 3.
Cooked, 40, 8.
Cool, 141, 23.
Copper, 68, 9—snake, 68, 7; 79, 15.
Coquettish girl, a, 104, 7.
Cord, 19, 3.
Cordial, 153, 7.
Corn blossom falls off, the, 110, 9.
Corn, boiled whole, 82, 12—coarse pounded, shelled, 127, 16—ear of, 81, 25—his, 158, 25—husk, 127, 25—Indian, 27, 7—is ripe, the, 159, 14—roasted, 12, 19; 35, 15—stalk, 132, 9.
Corner of a house, outside, 132, 11.
Corners, many, 47, 23.
Corporeal, 47, 6—material, 79, 4.
Correct, 125, 12—to be, 125, 5.
Corresponds, it, 71, 26.

Corrupted, 70, 18.
Corruption, 79, 23; 80, 2,
Cost, what does it, 137, 11.
Cough, 27, 26—to, 27, 24; 168, 3 —whooping, 9, 5—to have the, 9, 6.
Coughing, he has a disease with, 27, 25.
Council with, to hold, 163, 10.
Counsel, 24, 3; 169, 9—to hold, 24, 2.
Count, to, 11, 5; 137, 1.
Country, a flat, 129, 5—all over the, 32, 9.
Cousin, 66, 7, 23—a man's, 175, 16 —a woman's, 103, 2.
Covenant, 88, 19.
Cover, a, 56, 9, 14—to, 82, 22; 83, 17—somebody, to, 82, 23—with earth, to, 120, 7.
Covered over with earth, 150, 24.
Covetous, 126, 1.
Covetousness, 127, 14.
Cow, 86, 24; 155, 9.
Cow stable, 87, 5.
Crab apple, 142, 22.
Crack, to, 105, 7.
Cracked, 137, 8.
Cracks, it, 144, 18.
Cradle, an Indian, 19, 18.
Cranberries, 106, 23.
Crane, 137, 12.
Crawfish, a, 126, 2.
Create with the hands, to, 43, 7— with the mind, to, 42, 18.
Creator, 74, 1—Great, 40, 11.
Creature, 24, 10; 42, 19—tame, 29, 6—that lives upon grass, any, 111, 24—young, 177, 18.
Creep, to, 119, 4—in, to, 116, 25.
Creek between two hills, a, 118, 10 —crooked, 120, 10—large, 77, 14—little, 138, 16—mouth of a, 124, 3—or run, the head of a,

161, 15—small, 132, 15—the head of a, 161, 15.
Cricket, 178, 12.
Crime, 107, 13.
Crooked, 150, 18; 165, 6; like, 165, 8—road, 165, 9—road, to go a, 100, 14; 165, 12—the road is, 150, 19—to make, 165, 10.
Crop, second, 73, 17.
Cross, roads, 75, 11—the, 23, 7—to be, 74, 13.
Crow, a, 14, 13—to, 42, 1.
Crown, 21, 19—of the head, 61, 22.
Crucified, 120, 2 ;. 129, 17.
Cry, to, 98, 13—aloud, to, 46, 27—out, to, 19, 14; 37, 9—with, to, 163, 7.
Cunning man, 63, 26.
Cunningness, 67, 2.
Cup, a, 30, 15.
Cure, 53, 10.
Current, strong, 57, 20.
Curse, to, 75, 22.
Cushion, 80, 1.
Custom, 29, 14; 64, 12.
Customary, as is, 33, 9.
Cut a piece, to, 108, 14—fine, to, 115, 10—loose, to, 66, 6—meat, to, 105, 11—off, to, 19, 1; 140, 9—one's self, to, 76, 18; 115, 6—round, to, 120, 15—smooth, to, 60, 14—with a knife, to, 43, 18—with an axe, to, 44, 3.
Cutlass, 104, 14.
Cutting of firewood, the, 73, 16—wood, to come from, 22, 2.

Daily, 46, 9.
Dam, a fish, 11, 10.
Damnation, 39, 21; 169, 12.
Damp, 137, 3.
Dance, to, 40, 2.

Danger, 180, 17—to come into, 99, 13.
Dangerous, 11, 24.
Dark, 69, 22; 105, 10; 106, 21; 117, 11—in the, 111, 18—it grows, 106, 22; 117, 12—pitch, 14, 9—somewhat, 117, 8—to grow, 117, 10.
Darkness, 111, 6.
Daubed with clay, 23, 24.
Daughter, 153, 3.
Daughter-in law, 28, 3.
Dawn, 68, 12; 114, 4.
Day, 42, 24; 43, 19—after to-morrow, 98, 10; at break of, 114, 5—before yesterday, 98, 9—by, 42, 25; 43, 20—clear, 152, 6—early, this, 127, 23—fine, 172, 1; 174, 9—is spent, 15, 21—past, this, 41, 17—short, 143, 20—the break of, 95, 3—the last, 79, 22.
Daybreak, 42, 16; 114, 4—at, 131, 2—when it is quite, 111, 17.
Daylight, 42, 16.
Days ago, some, 175, 15—ago, two, 98, 9—hence, two, 98, 10—in a few, 32, 10—one of these, 32, 13.
Daytime, in the, 42, 25.
Dead, 76, 24—the, 30, 18—the one who takes care of the, 90, 24—to be struck, 97, 5—to strike each other, 97, 6.
Deadly, 21, 6.
Deaf, I am, 95, 5—person, a, 38, 24—the, 38, 24—to be, 10, 17.
Deal, a great, 27, 14—to be hard to, 24, 7—with, difficult to, 24, 8.
Dear, 14, 25; 27, 10; 31, 5; 77, 6—is it, how, 137, 11—so, 32, 3.
Death, 21, 5; 76, 22—agony of, 78, 24—painful, 25, 2—to be afflicted to, 9, 7—to bleed to, 9, 4; 83, 8—to freeze to, 22, 16—to grieve to, 22, 17—to put to, 96, 25.

INDEX. 191

Debt, 62, 21.
Debts, our, 32, 5.
Decay, to, 37, 20—going to, 21, 4.
Deceit, 11, 8; 36, 19.
Deceive, to, 11, 9—somebody, to, 11, 7.
Deceived, those who have been, 141, 7.
Deceiver, 141, 8.
December, 77, 1.
Declaration, 178, 1
Declare unto some one, to, 176, 8.
Decoy animals, to, 114, 23.
Decrease, to, 17, 6.
Decreed, to have, 42, 17,
Deed, evil, 107, 13—sinful, 69, 15.
Deep, 28, 4; 45, 22—enough, 140, 15—mire, 46, 5—mud, 46, 5—the hole, so, 123, 8—water, 27, 22.
Deeply marshy, 46, 6.
Deer, 14, 1—lick, at the, 71, 17—plenty of, 14, 14—tracks, a great many, 28, 6—young, 72, 20.
Deer's hair, 14, 2.
Defective, 101, 19.
Deficient, 101, 19.
Degrees, by, 20, 26; 21, 1—more by, 21, 15.
Delawares, 64, 23; 148, 12—one of the three tribes of the, 85, 14.
Delight in, to, 160, 11.
Deliver, to, 96, 20.
Deny, to, 109, 12.
Depart this life, to, 34, 19.
Dependent on another's command, to be, 96, 10.
Depth, great, 77, 20.
Deride some one, to, 90, 22.
Descend, to, 155, 3.
Descended from, 14, 12.
Desert, to, 107, 3.
Design evil against somebody, to, 83, 14.

Desirable, it is, 15, 3; 36, 7.
Desire, 15, 4; 36, 13—to, 36, 15; 37, 22; 38, 2—ardently, to, 29, 3—to give one an advantage, 49, 19.
Desired, 15, 5.
Despicable, 75, 15.
Despise, to, 75, 18—somebody, to, 75, 14.
Despised, the being, 75, 17—to be, 75, 16.
Desponding, 126, 3.
Destined, for what we are, 32, 7.
Destroy, to, 65, 18, 22, 24—somebody, to, 154, 9.
Destruction, 73, 15.
Determined, 42, 6—to be, 43, 12, 13; 125, 10.
Devil, 69, 19.
Devilishness, 69, 20.
Dew, grass wet with, 125, 21.
Diaphragm, the, 152, 19.
Diarrhœa, 124, 26.
Die, to, 15, 25; 21, 4; 34, 19—easily, to, 22, 22—for some cause, to, 176, 9—in battle, to, 9, 8—quickly, to, 22, 22.
Difference, 144, 6.
Different, 108, 6; 144, 16; 147, 9.
Differently, 144, 14.
Difficult, 11, 24; 58, 11—to deal with, 24, 8—to think, 11, 25—traveling, 14, 24.
Dig, 86, 21—a hole, to, 165, 14.
Digging a hole, he is, 150, 25.
Dilapidated town, 78, 1.
Diligent, to be, 64, 10.
Diminish, to, 31, 19.
Direct somebody the wrong way, to, 69, 16.
Direction, 113, 9.
Directly, 41, 24, 110, 17, 127, 12.
Dirty, 23, 22; 96, 3; 98, 21—look-

ing, 70, 11—to, 98, 22—work, to do, 98, 14.
Disagree, to, 144, 19.
Disagreeable, it looks, 145, 21—to, think, 145, 16.
Disagreement, 144, 6.
Disapprove, to, 129, 3.
Disbelieve, to, 39, 11; 108, 11.
Discern, to, 91, 13.
Discerning, my eyes were kept from, 144, 7.
Discontent, 70, 3.
Discontented, 70, 5—to be, 70, 2; 85, 10.
Discontentment, 85, 11.
Discouraged, 65, 20; 130, 20—to be, 65, 19; 101, 13.
Discouragement, 65, 21.
Discourse in a friendly manner, to, 173, 2—to finish a, 106, 14.
Disease with coughing, he has a, 27, 25.
Disesteem, to, 31, 19.
Dish, 120, 14; 148, 7, 8.
Dishclout, 37, 19.
Disheartened, 126, 3; 130, 20.
Dishes, to make, 148, 5.
Dislike, to, 129, 3, 4—to hear, to, 129, 14—to hear somebody, to, 129, 15.
Disliking, 129, 6.
Disobedience, 13, 22; 20, 1, 8.
Disobedient, 113, 17.
Disobey, to, 20, 7.
Disown, to, 109, 12.
Disperse, to, 13, 13.
Display, to, 21, 20.
Displeased, to be, 70, 2.
Disposed, to be otherwise, 109, 5—to be so, 65, 4.
Dispute, 37, 2; 55, 16—to, 118, 23—with one another, 118, 24.
Disquieted, to be, 11, 20; 123, 22.
Disquietude, 123, 23.

Dissatisfied, to be, 70, 2—to make, 70, 4.
Dissolute, to be, 55, 9.
Distemper, 159, 10.
Distress, 122, 7.
Distribute to somebody, to, 10, 4.
Distributer, 30, 9.
Distribution, 10, 5.
Ditch, a, 150, 23.
Divertisement, 55, 8.
Divide, to, 169, 3.
Divider, 30, 9.
Division, 10, 5; 62, 10.
Dizzy, to be, 36, 20.
Do, as I, 33, 20—to, 85, 1—great wonders, to, 37, 12—so to somebody, to, 64, 7—something just so, to, 143, 11—what to, 31, 24.
Doctor, 83, 5.
Doe, 101, 25—a, 100, 3.
Does, as he, 33, 21.
Dog, 18, 9; 86, 16—little, 18, 11.
Dogwood, 48, 3; 86, 20.
Doing, to be incapable of, 16, 9.
Domesticated animal, any, 18, 9, 11.
Done, 40, 8; 160, 21, 22—it is well, 174, 3—to be, 43, 3—planting, to be, 42, 26—there was more, 20, 3; 138, 22.
Don't, 52, 4.
Door, 35, 2; 56, 10—is open, the, 143, 24—shut the, 56, 8—to knock at the, 109, 6—to open the, 142, 25.
Doorkeeper, 102, 15.
Doors, out of, 56, 6.
Double, 98, 1; 115, 5; 117, 17.
Doubt, 144, 4—something without, 155, 20—to be in, 144, 3.
Doubtful, 122, 9—to be, 122, 6.
Dove, a, 20, 5.
Down hill, 112, 23—stream, 90, 1 —to come, 96, 2; 112, 24—to

INDEX.

lie, 64, 5; 127, 22—to sit, 81, 26—to take, 64, 4; 174, 4—to throw, 65, 22.
Downward, 60, 15.
Downwards, 112, 23.
Draw near to somebody, to, 82, 6—them hither, to, 114, 23.
Draweth nigh, it, 111, 15.
Drawing knife, 60, 13.
Draws near, it, 114, 22.
Dream, a, 66, 8—I, 171, 23—to, 61, 7; 66, 22; 171, 23—something good, to, 175, 18—to have a bad, 70, 17.
Dress, 111, 9; 173, 20—to, 173, 18—a wound, to, 11, 18—carefully, to, 173, 18—somebody, to, 111, 4—some one, to, 116, 17
Dressed, 111, 5, 8.
Dried, 36, 5; 113, 6.
Drink, to, 81, 7—with each other, to, 80, 23.
Drinking, 81, 11—to spend in, 81, 10.
Drive back, to, 46, 17—hither, to, 114, 18—in a nail, to, 39, 19—out, to, 40, 12—somebody away, to, 107, 26—through, to, 34, 24.
Drop, 108, 17.
Drops, it, 119, 15; 176, 20.
Drowned, 22, 21.
Drowsy, 38, 8.
Drum, 118, 7—to beat the, 118, 9.
Drums, he, 118, 9.
Drunk, to get, 80, 24.
Drunkard, 81, 9.
Drunkenness, 11, 6.
Dry, 36, 9; 113, 7—grass, 78, 2—to, 36, 6; 113, 10—to be, for thirst, 36, 8.
Duck, large wild, 122, 12.
Dull, 11, 13; 58, 3; 161, 25—to make, 162, 1.
Dung, 71, 10; 87, 12.

Dusk, 112, 18—it was, 117, 7.
Dusky, 69, 22; 117, 8.
Dust, 119, 10; 120, 21.
Dwell with, to, 163, 4—with each other, to, 163, 16.
Dye red, to, 71, 12.
Dying, the, 16, 1.

Each one, 80, 8.
Eagle, bald, 165, 20—fork-tailed, 27, 9.
Ear of corn, 81, 25.
Early, 35, 19; 71, 13—in the morning, 15, 10; 16, 6.
Earn, to, 107, 4.
Earnest, 54, 21—to be in, 54, 20.
Ears, 156, 12.
Earth, 47, 7; 112, 4—above the, 49, 4—bears, 47, 3—covered over with, 150, 24—I hide myself in the, 37, 6—in the, 16, 18; 169, 25—on, 166, 27—to cover with, 120, 7—upon, 13, 1—166, 27.
Earthen pot, 23, 23.
Ease one's self, to, 74, 24.
Easily, 22, 23—to die, 22, 22.
East wind, the, 12, 4.
Easterly, 151, 10.
Easy, 22, 23; 60, 17—to be, 58, 5—to make, 22, 26—to think, 22, 25.
Eat, thou, 134, 16—to, 86, 13—to have abundance to, 156, 17—with each other, 161, 2.
Eatable, 159, 25.
Eaten enough, to have, 44, 4.
Ebb tide, 48, 13.
Edge, at the, 51, 1.
Eel, 125, 19.
Egg, 150, 14.
Eight, 26, 20—hundred, 26, 21.
Eighty, 27, 1.
Either, 128, 7; 130, 2.

Elated by praise, the being, 19, 8.
Elbow, 163, 1—calf of the, 111, 3.
Elder, 53, 14—brother, 27, 5—sister, 85, 16.
Elderly woman, 53, 15.
Elect, the, 38, 23—thy, 38, 22.
Election, an, 117, 2.
Elk, 86, 24.
Elm, 11, 3—tree, 11, 3, 12; 148, 6.
Else, some one, 115, 17.
Elsewhere, 108, 6—to go, 108, 7—to put, 107, 24.
Empty, the house is, 89, 2; 93, 4.
Encamped, 76, 1.
Encourage, to, 41, 20.
End, 161, 22—at the, 161, 17, 18—of the plain, on the, 161, 24—of the world, 31, 14; 157, 19—the, 79, 22—the extreme, 176, 2.
Endurance, power of, 15, 2.
Endure pain, to, 73, 1.
Enemy, 129, 1.
Engage in, to, 91, 19.
Enjoy, to, 22, 6; 89, 4—a benefit, to, 172, 8—riches, to, 61, 11.
Enjoyable, 22, 10.
Enjoyment, 22, 9.
Enlighten, to, 42, 10.
Enlighten somebody, to, 89, 10.
Enlightening, 42, 9.
Enmity, 128, 24; 129, 11.
Enough, 140, 20; 144, 23—and to spare, 156, 15, 16—it is, 140, 21—of them, 140, 19—to have, 140, 17—to have eaten, 44, 4.
Enslaved, to be, 150, 5.
Enter a canoe, to, 120, 22—in, to, 75, 20.
Entire, 27, 11; 82, 4.
Entirely, 78, 15, 16; 82, 14; 106, 17; 144, 23.
Entrails, 150, 21.
Entrance, 35, 2.
Entreat somebody, to, 78, 22.

Envy, 81, 5—some one, to, 74, 16.
Epistle, 62, 24.
Escape to, 120, 23; 168, 17—hither, to fly or, 114, 23—to cause to, 120, 23.
Established, 146, 13.
Esteem, 68, 1; 163, 20—great, 18, 4—to, 14, 23; 67, 19—highly, to, 18, 3—it an honor, to 67, 19—somebody, to, 67, 12.
Estimation, high, 18, 4.
Eternal, 47, 14.
Eternally, 47, 14.
European shoes, 130, 22.
Even, 143, 10, 13—not, 50, 11—there, 91, 2—to make, 60, 14; 143, 11.
Evening, 170, 17; 172, 17—cool, 142, 7—good, 45, 16—in the, 170, 18—last. 153, 24—moderately warm, 136, 22—this, 172, 18.
Ever, 48, 1.
Every bit, 82, 4.
Everybody, 154, 8.
Every one, 80, 8.
Everything, that which is above, 18, 7—to prize above, 18, 3.
Everywhere, 32, 8—154, 8—from, 154, 8—not, 81, 18.
Evil, 78, 7—against somebody, to design, 83, 14—deed, 107, 13—of somebody, to speak, 80, 5—one, 78, 8—spirit, 69, 25—to speak, to somebody, 80, 6.
Exact, 125, 12.
Examine, to, 61, 12.
Excavation, 150, 20.
Excellent, 152, 25.
Except, 41, 24.
Excited, to be, 44, 7.
Exclamation of approbation, 30, 8—of approval, 45, 2; 52, 11—of grief, 50, 3, 9, 13—of indignant surprise, 31, 16—of indig-

nation, 44, 5, 6; 122, 21—of joy, 48, 23, 24; 51, 4; 121, 9—of laughter, 47, 1; 48, 8—of pain, 31, 15; 52, 23—of surprise, 31, 9, 12; 48, 22; 121, 8—of vociferation, 48, 19; 49, 11; 103, 15—of wonder, 52, 2—used in answering, 103, 13, 14—used in calling, 51, 11.
Excrement, 87, 12.
Exert one's self, to, 162, 18.
Exhort, to, 46, 14—some one, to, 41, 21.
Exhortation, 46, 15.
Expect, to, 114, 12.
Experienced, 65, 3; 168, 4.
Expression, a strong, 159, 7.
Extend, to, 129, 19.
Extended, 129, 18, 20.
Extravagant, to be, 55, 9.
Eye, 177, 15—pupil of the, the, 26, 6—to raise the, 23, 20—wink of an, 134, 1.
Eyebrow, 72, 22; 84, 12.
Eyebrows, 126, 6.
Eyelid, 126, 6.
Eyes, broken, 166, 15—to shut the, 133, 25.

Face, 177, 15—to, 177, 16.
Fade, to, 37, 20.
Faded, 127, 1, 4.
Fain, 160, 6.
Faint, to, 167, 16—from hunger, to, 126, 16.
Faintness, 167, 17.
Faints, it, 126, 21.
Faith, 171, 10; 175, 6.
Fall, 136, 7—hunt, 136, 8—in the next, 136, 7, 10—skin, 136, 9—to, 82, 5; 83, 9—and burst open, to, 29, 5—down, to, 112, 19—off
P

to, 112, 19—to the ground, to, 106, 10—upon, to, 122, 10.
Fallen off, 83, 13.
Falls in, it, 65, 23—in price, 17, 6—off, it, 112, 20—the water, 48, 12—upon, it, 143, 12, 14.
Falsehood, a, 55, 17.
Familiarity, 89, 5.
Famine, 76, 11.
Fanciful, 167, 18.
Far, 85, 15; 150, 15—as, 131, 20 off—85, 15—so, as, 131, 20—to go so, 131, 21—to seem to be, 150, 16.
Farm, to, 47, 10.
Farmer, 47, 11.
Fast, 146, 7—it goes, 59, 20—to go, 57, 14—to grow, 60, 1—to make, 146, 12—to run, 56, 22—to speak, 16, 7; 59, 19—to stand, 146, 15—to walk, 58, 2.
Fat, 118, 14; 126, 9; 163, 2—in an animal's belly, 158, 12—meat, 159, 4.
Fatness, 163, 3.
Father, 155, 13, 14—his or her, 103, 12—my, 99, 7, 8, 9.
Father-in-law, 85, 6.
Fatherless, 129, 24.
Father's, at his or her, 103, 11.
Fathom, half a, 105, 20.
Fathoms, four, 95, 2.
Fatten, to, 162, 22.
Fault, 144, 2.
Favor, 40, 18; 147, 15—to show somebody, 140, 1.
Favorably, to speak, 172, 15.
Fawn, 72, 20.
Fear, 16, 10; 161, 1—to, 162, 16—to be in, 161, 3.
Fearful, to be, 161, 10.
Fears you, he, 122, 20.
Feast, 136, 4—to hold a, 136, 5; 141, 2; 157, 12—to hold a love,

136, 5—to keep a, 95, 9; 161, 11.
Feathers, 84, 19—of a bird's tail, 167, 10.
February, 147, 14.
Fed, 27, 4.
Feebleness, 126, 15.
Feed, to, 100, 18.
Feel, to, 19, 5; 100, 18—as, to, 31, 25—better, to, 31, 18—equal to it, I do not, 101, 13—great pain, to, 14, 5—grief and pain, 130, 5—grief or sorrow, 130, 4; 149, 8—less pain, to, 31, 18—love, to, 14, 21—painful, to, 149, 7—sore pain, to, 162, 3—sorrowful, to, 149, 7—troubled, to, 123, 18, 19.
Feeling, 19, 6—new, 177, 17.
Feet, at his, 131, 13—at thy, 131, 12.
Felicity, 41, 10.
Fellow, foolish, 38, 14—to be a good-for-nothing, 55, 9.
Fellowship, 89, 5; 163, 14—to keep in, 90, 21—with one another, to have, 163, 13—with somebody, to be in, 163, 12.
Female genitals, 67, 11—of beasts, 103, 4—of fowls and birds, 103, 5.
Fence, 80, 21—is finished, the, 42, 22—over or behind the, 25, 12—rail, 80, 22—the end of the, 161, 20—to jump over the, 10, 20; 118, 4.
Fern, 13, 12; 63, 19—swamp, 103, 10.
Fervent, 131, 6; 133, 6.
Fetch, 90, 9—to, 91, 11—a load, to, 92, 1—over, to, 91, 16—somebody, to, 176, 5—somebody over in a canoe, to, 91, 17—wood, to, 91, 9.

Fetched, 91, 8—to be, 90, 11—across, he wants to be, 102, 1.
Fetches wood, he, 91, 7.
Fetching, 91, 14.
Few, but, 139, 2—times, a, 52, 7.
Fickle, 157, 14.
Fiddle, 12, 11.
Field, 47, 9—large, 77, 15—old, 77, 26.
Fifth, 107, 7.
Fifty, 107, 8.
Fight, to, 64, 16; 69, 7; 70, 10—a battle, to, 70, 10—with each other, to, 70, 10.
Fighting, 69, 8—to stop, 16, 2.
Figure, 33, 12.
File, a, 29, 15.
Fill, to, 106, 4, 6; 116, 18.
Filled, 106, 3, 5.
Finally, 90, 20; 137, 15.
Find, to, 86, 14—somebody out, to, 94, 6.
Fine, 25, 23; 120, 5; 128, 12; 172, 1; 175, 3—day, 172, 1; 174, 9—morning, 172, 5; to look, 174, 23—word, 172, 11.
Fineness, 175, 4.
Finery, 111, 9.
Finger, 64, 25—first, 142, 12—little, 138, 13; 141, 4—middle, 62, 7—nail, to bruise the, 20, 14—-ring, 126, 12.
Fingers, 157, 15—fork of the, 60, 10—tips of the, 167, 12.
Finish, to, 43, 14—a discourse, to, 106, 14—a work, to, 42, 13.
Finished, 106, 19—the canoe is, 42, 15—the fence is, 42, 22—to be, 43, 3.
Fire, 142, 11—coal of, 68, 11; 78, 17—off, to, 106, 7—to make, 142, 10—to quench, 23, 26.
Firebrand, 118, 3.
Firefly, 124, 20; 152, 15.

Fireplace, a plastered, 133, 1.
Firewood, 82, 20—the cutting of, 73, 16—to use for, 139, 7.
Firm, 146, 13.
First, 94, 15, 16, 17—at, 95, 26; 102, 10; 123, 9—place, in the, 94, 17—the, 94, 15, 16; 95, 26.
Fish, 90, 19; 127, 7—black, 134, 9, 10.
Fish-chop, 63, 11—dam, a, 11, 10 —hawk, 97, 11—large, 19, 10— like a sucker, 78, 11—pike, 54, 5; 121, 17; 145, 11—scale, 149, 17—with a bushnet to, 13, 8— with hook and line, to, 154, 15.
Fisher bird, little, 142, 16.
Fishing, bushnet for, 12, 22—line, 19, 3, 4—rod, a, 60, 4—spear, a, 100, 9.
Fist, the, 117, 23.
Fit, to have a, 145, 23.
Fits, to get, 145, 23.
Five, 107, 5—hundred, 107, 6.
Fix, to, 48, 7—upon, to, 21, 20.
Flag, 68, 22.
Flame, it burns in a, 66, 17.
Flashes lightning, it, 124, 18.
Flat country, a, 129, 5—rock, 128, 20.
Flea, 12, 10.
Fleas, full of, 12, 15.
Flee, to, 128, 16.
Flesh, 103, 17; 150, 11—to become, 104, 4.
Fleshy, 163, 2.
Flies away, it, 118, 22
Flies, large stinging, 82, 10.
Flight, 128, 16.
Flint, 71, 15; 72, 12.
Flinty, 35, 5.
Float, a, 89, 13.
Flour, 66, 3.
Flow out of, to, 149, 4.
Flower, 166, 19.

Flows out, it, 147, 21.
Flute, 12, 11.
Flux, bloody, 79, 11.
Fly, 149, 14—to, 17, 7; 168, 17— or escape hither, to, 114, 23—sort of stinging, 72, 21.
Flying squirrel, 26, 10.
Foam, 117, 22.
Fog, 25, 5.
Foliage, 55, 20.
Follow, to, 92, 11; 100, 6—somebody, to, 169, 13—some one, to, 92, 8—the straight road, to, 125, 18.
Food, 86, 7, 12; 126, 7—to live upon, 156, 21—to prepare, 148, 21.
Fool, a, 37, 3; 40, 4.
Foolish, behaved, 56, 16—fellow, 38, 14.
Foolishness, 56, 17.
Foot, 168, 23—ball of the, 39, 27; 40, 1—joint of the foot, 26, 13— sole of the, 148, 1—to tread under, 29, 7.
For, 16, 14; 18, 22; 100, 19; 101, 1, 2—good and all, 15, 11—that reason, 51, 6—the most part, 45, 3.
Forbiddance, 122, 3.
Force somebody, to, 13, 21.
Forcible, 14, 10.
Ford, to, 143, 9; 147, 2.
Forefathers, 86, 15.
Forefinger, 65, 25.
Forehead, 166, 22—middle of the, 62, 6—my, 88, 22.
Foremost, 96, 4; 123, 9—the, 96, 6—to stand, 96, 5.
Forerunner, a, 128, 5.
Foreshoulder, 49, 8.
Forget, to, 151, 5; 167, 20.
Forgetfulness, 151, 5; 167, 21.
Forgive, to, 86, 8, 10—each other,

INDEX.

to, 105, 25—somebody, to, 86, 9; 106, 24.
Forgiveness, 86, 11; 107, 1.
Forgot, it, I, 150, 5.
Fork, 62, 10—a tree with a, 62, 11—of a river, 62, 9—of a road, 62, 12—of the fingers, 60, 10—of the toes, 60, 9.
Form, an old, 100, 16—modern, 100, 16.
Forsake, to, 101, 5—somebody, to, 101, 6.
Fort, 80, 21.
Forth the hand, to put, 129, 22.
Fortunate, 41, 9—the, 153, 23.
Forty, 94, 25.
Foundation, 34, 16.
Fountain, 30, 24.
Four, 94, 26—fathoms, 95, 2—hundred, 95, 1—times, 94, 23.
Fourfold, 94, 21.
Fourth, 94, 22.
Fowl, 24, 12; 142, 13—or bird, bill of a, 157, 5—the young of a bird or, 21, 9—with young ones. a, 41, 12.
Fowls and birds, female of, 103, 5—plume of, 84, 9.
Fox, black, 170, 20—skin, 166, 21—the gray, 165, 13.
Fraud, 11, 8.
Free, 96, 17—to be, 96, 18—from trouble, to be, 55, 21—to make, 96, 15, 20.
Freedom, 96, 21.
Freeman, 96, 19.
Freeze, to, 138, 17—to death, to, 22, 16.
Frequent traveler, 86, 2.
Freshet, 77, 3—abates, the, 132, 2.
Friend, 31, 27; 99, 3; 147, 6—my, 32, 1; 99, 5; 147, 6—my little, 99, 6.
Friendly, to be, 141, 14—to look, 60, 19—to treat, 173, 2.

Fright, 161, 9.
Frightened, 162, 14—to be, 102, 11; 124, 4.
Frog, 147, 13.
From, 149, 3; 177, 11—a place, to be, 155, 2—descended or sprung, 14, 12—hence, 5, 16—thence, 88, 1; 91, 2.
Frost, white, 103, 1; 143, 7.
Froth, 117, 22.
Frow, 104, 12.
Frozen, 44, 8; 136, 1; 138, 18—hard, 146, 6—over, 56, 13—shut, 56, 13.
Fruit, to produce, 43, 8.
Fruition, 22, 9.
Frying pan, 131, 15.
Full, 106, 3, 17; 144, 23; 167, 7; 168, 1—grown, 140, 22—it is, 150, 7—of fleas, 12, 15—of holes, 12, 6—of rocks, 37, 11.
Fully, 106, 17.
Fulfil, to, 106, 20.
Funnel, 116, 22.
Further, 50, 7; 52, 5—a little, 50, 8—still, 50, 7.
Fury, 24, 9.

Gadding, to go a, 85, 19.
Gain, 168, 20—to, 109, 18; 168, 22—a wager, to, 168, 21.
Gall, the, 162, 21.
Gape, to, 124, 21; 147, 20.
Garden, 81, 8.
Gardener, 81, 15.
Garfish, 151, 14.
Gather, to, 76, 6, 10.
Gaze, to, 100, 4.
Gear, horse, 153, 20.
Generously, to treat somebody, 158, 23.
Genitals, male, 158, 19.
Gensi, root, 166, 3.

INDEX. 199

Gently, 141, 19—it goes, 171, 8.
Genuine, 63, 12.
Get, to, 85, 18; 109, 18.
Ghost, 145, 18.
Giddy in the head, to be, 36, 20.
Gift, 85, 8.
Gimlet, 118, 1.
Gird, to, 90, 10.
Girdle, a, 39, 1.
Girl, 103, 8—a coquettish, 104, 7—little, 103, 7; 122, 2.
Girth of a saddle, 44, 10.
Give, to, 85, 7—away, to, 79, 21—back, to, 46, 26—honor, to, 20, 2—suck, to, 100, 2—to be unwilling to, 152, 20—to somebody, to, 85, 3—up, to, 16, 4; 65, 19; 170, 7.
Gives to me, he who, 85, 5.
Giving the, 85, 4.
Glad, 85, 13—to be, 173, 12—to see somebody, to be, 106, 9.
Gladly, 160, 6.
Gladness, 41, 10.
Glittering, 122, 22.
Glorify some one, to, 67, 13.
Glory, 67, 15; 152, 26—to give, 73, 9.
Glorying in, 176, 17.
Glossy, 168, 10, 11.
Gloves, 157, 2.
Glue, 82, 19; 130, 13.
Go, to, 9, 2—all around, to, 164, 17—all away, to, 154, 12—all out, to, 154, 11—and tell, 75, 25—asunder, to, 16, 8—away, to, 18, 17—away weeping, to, 18, 14—by water, to, 118, 16 - from some place secretly, to, 54, 2—home, to, 75, 5—hunting, to, 75, 24—in a canoe with somebody, to, 156, 20—or cross over one another, to, 23, 6—out, to, 58, 21—so far to, 131, 21—to let, 119,

7—to like to, 160, 13—through, to, 34, 24—to venture to, 13, 20—to war, to, 76, 9—wherever or whither I, 31, 8—with, to, 163, 18, 21—with somebody, to, 164, 3—up, to, 23, 19.
God, 40, 11; 74, 1; 110, 1—above all, 33, 24—Holy, 56, 26—Lamb of, 139, 24—mild, 139, 24—the good, gracious, 153, 21.
Goes fast, it, 59, 20—with him, he who, 164, 4.
Going, hard, 14, 24.
Gone, it is all, 91, 10; 154, 10.
Good, 25, 23; 141, 15; 141, 17; 154, 3; 159, 24; 174, 20; 175, 3, 7—again, he makes, 174, 6—and all, for, 15, 11—be so, 15, 12—evening, 45, 16—for nothing, 94, 1—for-nothing fellow, to be a, 55, 9—gracious God, 153, 21—it is, 174, 3, 11—morning, 165, 21—morrow, 151, 9—natured, to be, 141, 14—physic, 153, 22—tasted, 159, 23—the, 174, 12—the supremely, 34, 35, —to be, 141, 14; 174, 18—to do somebody, 174, 10—very, 49, 16.
Goodness, 103, 24; 174, 19.
Goods, 61, 10.
Goose, wild, 52, 1.
Gooseberries, 38, 13.
Gospel, 173, 14.
Gourd, a, 171, 13.
Government, 38, 28.
Governor, 38, 27.
Grace, 172, 3.
Gracious, 141, 15—one, the most, 34, 2.
Grain, his, 158, 28.
Grandfather, 87, 10.
Grandmother, 103, 16.
Grant, to, 63, 3.

INDEX.

Grapes, wild, 162, 6.
Grass, 23, 13; 74, 23; 133, 11—any creature that lives upon, 111, 24—cabin covered with, 84, 8—dry, 78, 2—old dry, 28, 2—scour, 60, 11—wet with dew, 125, 21.
Grasshopper, 59, 1; 105, 24—green, 52, 22; 57, 19.
Grateful, 39, 17.
Grave, 70, 19; 118, 11.
Gravel, 62, 18.
Gray, 161, 14—fox, the, 165, 13—hair, 166, 7—-headed man, 161, 14.
Grease, 126, 9, 10.
Great, 19, 13; 54, 9; 68, 5; 76, 26; 77, 7—buck, 27, 20—city, 55, 3—deal, a, 27, 14—depth, 77, 20—esteem, 18, 4—it looks, 77, 18—king, 54, 16—many, 77, 9, 10—river, 54, 17—sea, 54, 15—ships, 55, 2—the, 77, 13, 17.
Greater, 18, 8—power, 17, 10.
Greed, 127, 13.
Green, 23, 9, 14—it is, 23, 9—grasshopper, 52, 22; 57, 19—snake, 23, 10.
Greeting, 152, 11.
Gridiron, 30, 12.
Grief, 153, 16—exclamation of, 50, 3, 9, 13—to be put to, 126, 13; 130, 10—to feel, 130, 4, 5; 149, 8.
Grieve to death, to, 22, 17.
Grieved, to be, 149, 11.
Grievous, 56, 21.
Grind, to, 53, 3; 59, 4; 135, 21.
Grindstone, 53, 4; 54, 4.
Ground, 47, 7—fine, 171, 7—hog, 86, 19—hole in the, 165, 14—middle of a piece of, 61, 18—squirrel, 21, 8; 47, 16—to fall to the, 106, 10—to plant a large piece of, 77, 16—wet, 124, 24; 133, 3, 4.

Grounded, 43, 4.
Grow better, to, 53, 9—better in health, to, 65, 9—dark, to, 117, 10—fast, to, 60, 1—out of, to, 155, 3.
Grows dark, it, 106, 22; 117, 12—well, it, 174, 13.
Grub, 161, 8.
Grubbing hoe, 72, 5.
Grudge, to, 152, 20.
Guard, 156, 4—a, 102, 8.
Guide, a, 52, 19.
Guilt, 107, 15.
Guiltless person, a, 111, 20.
Gulley, a, 105, 16.
Gum tree, 135, 20.
Gun, 106, 8—breech of a, 56, 15; 158, 9—drawer, 58, 23—lock, 124, 12—lock, battery of a, 30, 17—lock, cock of a, 71, 16—the hind sight of a, 34, 7.
Gunpowder, 120, 21.
Guts, 150, 21.

Habit, 29, 14.
Habitation, his, 30, 11.
Hail, 49, 13; 79, 8; 151, 13—stone, a, 151, 13—to, 82, 16.
Hails, it, 136, 13.
Hair, 84, 11; 85, 2—deer's, 14, 2 gray, 166, 7—red, 78, 10.
Half, 105, 21—a fathom, 105, 20.
Halfway, 63, 2.
Hallow, to, 106, 12.
Halo of sun or moon, 157, 21.
Halve, to, 105, 19.
Ham, 118, 5.
Hammer, 104, 16—a, 19, 20.
Hand, 88, 21—at the right, 63, 10—his, 176, 1—it, 63, 13—it here, 148, 16—left, 81, 3—my, 88, 21—on the right, 169, 18—palm of the, 148, 2—the flat of the, 108,

20—the time is at, 143, 12, 14—thou, 175, 24—to bruise the, 26, 17—to lend a, 164, 6—to lift up the, 23, 18—to put forth the, 129, 22—to reach forth the, 64, 15—to the, 81, 3—towards the, 169, 8—weak, 126, 22.
Handle, 168, 24—some one, to, 85, 17.
Hands tied up, 157, 2—to create with the, 43, 7—to shake, 123, 5—to something, to lay, 64, 14—to warm the, 21, 18.
Handsome, 174, 12; 175, 3, 7.
Hang down the head, to, 92, 6—up, to, 127, 20.
Hangs, it, 127, 17—there, 127, 17.
Happens, as it, 32, 4.
Happiness, 41, 10; 172, 22.
Happy, 41, 9; 172, 23—he who makes me, 171, 2, 3—to be, 171, 1, 6; 172, 21—to cause to be, 171, 4—to make, 61, 16—to rest, 15, 18.
Hard, 11, 24; 14, 8; 58, 11—going, 14, 24—to beat, 56, 20—to deal with, to be, 24, 7—to labor, 11, 23.
Hardly, 13, 19; 58, 11.
Hare, a, 87, 7; 144, 12.
Harmonizes, it, 71, 26.
Harrow, 60, 2.
Harsh, 53, 2, 5.
Haste, to make, 126, 19.
Hat, 17, 21.
Hatch or meditate something good or bad, to, 42, 20.
Hatchet, 140, 7.
Hate, to, 129, 9; 133, 7—each other, to, 128, 23; 129, 10—excessively, to, 129, 16—somebody, to, 128, 21.
Hatred, 128, 24.
Haughty, to be, 173, 16.

Have, to, 89, 4; 103, 22—a bad dream, to, 70, 17—bad travelling, to, 11, 22—one object, to, 95, 14.
Having, 48, 5.
Hawk, 78, 9.
Hay, 84, 14.
Hazel nut, the, 40, 10.
He, 93, 9, 10—has, 48, 6—is said to have said, 66, 18—that is love, 14, 20—who gives to me, 85, 5—who is merciful, 41, 4—who is there, 34, 17—who sits here, 63, 5.
Head, 158, 18—at his, 33, 4—chief, 38, 27—crown of the, 61, 22—lice, 49, 14—middle of the, 122, 17—of a creek, the, 161, 16—tied about the, 39, 6—to be giddy in the, 36, 20—to hang down the, 92, 6—to knock somebody on the, 118, 2—to shake the, 138, 23.
Headache, 159, 2—to have, 159, 1.
Health, to grow better in, 65, 9—to mend in, 53, 9.
Hear, to, 112, 12—by chance, to, 109, 3—one another, to, 112, 16—privately, to, 139, 6—somebody, to, 112, 17—somebody, to dislike, to, 129, 15—to cause to, 112, 13—to dislike to, 129, 14—to like to, 160, 14—somebody, 160, 15—well, to, 174, 26—willingly, to, 160, 12—wrong, to, 144, 10.
Heard, it is, 112, 14.
Hearing, to be quick of, 11, 4—wrong, 144, 11.
Hearken to, 44, 13—to one another, to, 93, 24—to somebody, to, 177, 4.
Heart, 153, 5, 6—and mind, to be of an indifferent, 58, 6—it pene-

trates my, 34, 25—of a tree, 159, 6—to be of one, 95, 18.
Heartily, 153, 7.
Heartless, 126, 3.
Heathen, 93, 20—to be a, 93, 19.
Heathenish life, 90, 18—life, to lead a, 93, 19.
Heaven, 25, 7.
Heavens, the, 111, 25.
Heavy, 58, 11—in a manner, 58, 10—not, 60, 17.
Hedgehog, the, 38, 11.
Heedless, 90, 12.
Heel, 91, 4; 151, 6.
Hell, 69, 21.
Help along, to, 164, 7—each other, to, 163, 6—one another, to, 164, 6—somebody to, 40, 17; 164, 2—somebody through, to, 34, 23.
Helped to accuse him, one who, 164, 1.
Helplessness, 21, 2.
Hemp, wild, 47, 13.
Hen, 142, 13.
Hencoop, 142, 14.
Hence, from, 51, 6.
Henceforth, 51, 13.
Herb, 74, 23—"colt's foot," the, 19, 17.
Herbs, 23, 13.
Here, 17, 1; 51, 6, 19; 148, 14; 178, 8—as many as are, 34, 9—take it, 67, 10—till, 88, 1.
Hereafter, 90, 20.
Hew well, to, 175, 9.
Hiccough, 76, 23.
Hickory nut, 82, 8—nut, white, 142, 2—shiver, 141, 3—tree, bitter, 142, 17—upland, 54, 6.
Hide. myself in the earth, I, 37, 6—to, 37, 6, 23.
High, 45, 24; 46, 2—bank, a, 51, 1—bank of a river, 14, 11—estimation, 18, 4—minded, to be, 68,
2; 173, 16—mindedness, 173, 17—priced, 27, 10—to be, 46, 1—value, 68, 1—water, 27, 22; 28, 4 ; 77, 3.
Highly, to esteem, 18, 3.
Hill, 150, 6—a round, 175, 23—on the north side of a, 17, 4—or mountain, top of, 123, 7—over or beyond the, 25, 6—round, 154, 2—side, 126, 5—south side of a, 145, 14—top of the 166, 28—under the, 16, 17—up, 154, 14—where the road goes down the, 155, 6—where the road goes up, 154, 13.
Hills, a creek between two, 118, 10.
Hilly, 150, 8, 10.
Himself, 49, 2.
Hinder, to, 59, 13.
Hip, 66, 2.
Hit somebody, to, 43, 2.
Hither, 51, 6, 8, 13; 148, 18—to come, 115, 2.
Hoarse, to be, 26, 4.
Hobble, 44, 10.
Hobbled, 44, 11.
Hoe, 13, 4—grubbing, 72, 5.
Hog, 45, 11—ground, 86, 19—sty, 45, 12.
Hold a feast, to, 141, 2; 157, 12—somebody fast, to, 146, 8—to take, 39, 8.
Holds much, it, 117, 6.
Hole, 70, 19; 150, 20—a, 118, 11—he is digging a, 150, 25—in the ground, 165, 14—so deep the, 123, 8—to dig a, 165, 15.
Holes, full of, 12, 6.
Holiest, 34, 1.
Holiness, 57, 1; 115, 22.
Hollow, 120, 16; 174, 7—in the ground, a, 118, 11—tree, a, 150, 26.
Holy, 40, 5, 6—Ghost, 154, 5—

God, 56, 26—the most, 34, 1—to
believe to be, 57, 4—to think that
one is, 57, 3.
Home, there is no one at, 89, 2—
to be at, 12, 7—to be seldom at,
85, 19—to bring somebody, 75,
3—to go, 75, 5.
Honest, 125, 4.
Honey locust tree, 117, 20.
Honor, 67, 18—some one, to, 67,
12—the receiving of, 67, 14—to,
67, 19—to give, 20, 2—to look
upon as an, 176, 16.
Honorable, 67, 16; 172, 6.
Honored, he that is, 67, 17—the,
77, 8.
Hoop-ash, 35, 16.
Hope, 95, 24—to, 89, 18; 95, 21,
23—to give in, 95, 22.
Horn, 104, 1; 168, 18.
Horned cattle, 155, 16—snake,
127, 6.
Hornet, a, 151, 17.
Horse, 93, 25—gear, 153, 20.
Horseback, to ride on, 93, 26.
Hot, 38, 19; 57, 24; 133, 6—
weather, 57, 18.
House, 50, 15; 158, 14—behind
the, 25, 8—cold, 142, 5—he has
a, 158, 11—his, 158, 7—in order,
to put a, 43, 10—in the little,
158, 15—is empty, the, 89, 2;
93, 4—log for a, 12, 3—master
of the, 155, 23—my, 157, 22—of
prayer, 110, 7—on the top of
the, 167, 1—outside corner of a,
132, 12—rafter on the roof of a,
64, 3—ready, to make a, 43, 10
—thy, 158, 1—to come out of
the, 59, 5—to finish a, 43, 10—
warm, 44, 1.
How, 134, 19; 138, 11—is it, 134,
19—large, 134, 19—long, 52, 10
—many, 134, 19—much, 52, 6, 8;
134, 19—soon, 134, 19—then,
134, 19; 135, 6—to feel, 31, 25
will it be, 134, 19.
However, 16, 14; 24, 17; 50, 4,
11; 121, 3.
Howling, 124, 5.
Huckleberry, 84, 23—bread, 84, 24
—swamp, 74, 22.
Huckleberries, 85, 9.
Hulls of the corn, the, 127, 25.
Humble, 40, 22; 135, 10, 11, 13;
138, 4, 9—being, 83, 2—one's
self before somebody, to, 40, 21
—one that is, 40, 20—to be, 40,
19; 138, 1.
Humbly, to go, 101, 15—to walk,
138, 2.
Humility, 101, 14; 138, 8.
Humor, to be out of, 121, 19.
Hundred, five, 107, 6—four, 95, 1
—one, 46, 21; 95, 13—seven,
97, 24—six, 46, 23—two, 97, 22.
Hunger, to, 38, 6—to faint from,
126, 16—to suffer, 161, 19.
Hungry, to be, 38, 6.
Hunt, to, 17, 3—by the way, to, 92,
12; 168, 2—in company, to, 112,
7—willingly, to, 159, 21.
Hunter, 32, 2.
Hunting, lover of, 159, 20—to come
from, 21, 23—to go, 75, 24.
Hurry, to be in a, 126, 19.
Hurts me, it, 162, 8.
Hush, 131, 9.
Hut, 50, 15.
Hymn, 88, 16.
Hypocrisy, 71, 4.
Hypocrite, 71, 3.

I, 95, 27—also, 94, 9—am, 95, 7—
too, 94, 9.
Ice, 79, 7—the river drifts, 75, 1;

82, 17—to break in the, 76, 25—
to go over the, 100, 5.
Idle, to go about, 109, 8.
Idler, 80, 20.
Idol, an, 82, 9.
If, 15, 12; 35, 14; 41, 24—but, 15,
12—only, 15, 12.
Ill, 70, 13, 14—flavored, 71, 5—
natured, 80, 10—pleased, to be,
75, 6—to speak, 69, 9—to take,
75, 6—to treat somebody, 59, 17
—to use somebody, 56, 23—to
use some one, 44, 15.
Imagine, to, 153, 9.
Immediately, 127, 12.
Impatience, to wait with, 23, 11.
Impeachment, 42, 5.
Impotent, 167, 18—to be, 167, 16.
Imputation, 73, 21.
In, 50, 12; 149, 2—some place, 81,
12, 18—the bargain, 47, 21—
there, 16, 19; 22, 23.
Inability, 15, 17.
Inadvertently, 117, 24.
Inanimate, 25, 23.
Incapable of doing, to be, 16, 9.
Incapacity, 15, 17.
Incite one to do something, to, 147,
23.
Inclination, to be against one's, 129,
4.
Increase, to, 43, 8.
Indeed, 9, 1; 18, 23; 26, 7, 8; 30, 7.
Indian, 63, 7—bedstead, an, 143,
21—corn, 27, 7—cradle, an, 19,
18—language, to speak the, 48,
9—shoes, 63, 8—thou, 32, 16.
Indians of the same nation, 64, 23
—northern, 66, 12.
Indifference, 15, 7, 8; 58, 7.
Indifferent, to be, 15, 6—heart and
mind, to be of an, 58, 6.
Indignation, exclamation of, 44, 5,
6; 122, 21.

Indisposed, 69, 18—in mind, to be,
144, 20.
Inferior, it is, 17, 19.
Infirm, 58, 14.
Inform each other, to, 150, 22.
Information, 10, 10; 169, 9.
Inhabitant, 34, 17.
Ink, 30, 22.
Innocence, 57, 1; 107, 11.
Innocent, one that is, 111, 20—suf-
ferer, 102, 17—to be, 107, 10, 16.
Inquire, to, 91, 18—176, 6—of each
other, to, 92, 19.
Instruct, to, 10, 8; 17, 17.
Instruction, 48, 17.
Instrument, to tune an, 60, 24.
Insult somebody, to, 72, 16.
Insulted, the being, 72, 16.
Intercession, 110, 5.
Interpret, 21, 7.
Invisible, 99, 17.
Invitation, 155, 4.
Inwardly, 170, 1.
Ipecacuanha, 78, 12.
Iron, 134, 7—pot, 132, 22; 157, 17
—splitting, 104, 12—wedge, 105,
6—wood, 72, 9.
Iroquois, an, 81, 14.
Irresolution, 11, 21.
Is, as it, 32, 4.
Island, 81, 6—the point of an, 157,
6.
It, 93, 9, 10—is as it should be, 71,
25; 72, 2—is so, 63, 27—is so
much, 90, 13—is there, 48, 6.
Itch, one that has the, 57, 22—to
have the, 57, 21.

January, 21, 11.
Jaw bone, the, 29, 11.
Jealous, 53, 2, 5—of somebody, to
be, 74, 16.
Jealousy, 73, 18; 81, 4.

Jesting, 11, 2.
Jocular, to be, 10, 25.
Joined together, 138, 19.
Joins close together, it, 136, 2.
Joint, 134, 2—of the foot, 26, 13.
Journey, to make a provision for a, 97, 10.
Joy, 173, 13—exclamation of, 48, 23, 24; 51, 4; 121, 9.
Joyful, 173, 15—to be, 173, 12.
Judge somebody, to, 42, 4.
Juice, 177, 10.
July, 50, 14.
Jump hither, to, 148, 13—over, to, 60, 7—over the fence, to, 10, 20; 118, 4.
Jumps, it, 65, 15.
June, 54, 11.
Junk of fire, 118, 3.
Just, 172, 6—alike, 143, 10, 13—here, 51, 6—now, 40, 3—so, 125, 8—to be, 125, 5.

Keep a feast in Indian style, to, 95, 9—a servant, to, 17, 14—each other in remembrance, to, 73, 12—holy day, to, 87, 9—in fellowship, to, 90, 21—one's promise, to 171, 18—or preserve unto somebody, to, 135, 16—somebody, to, 173, 21—watch, to, 102, 7.
Keeper, 99, 11.
Keg, bottom of a, 158, 9.
Kettle, 49, 5—to burn the, 11, 17.
Key, 139, 13; 143, 2.
Kidney, 49, 6.
Kill a bear, to, 96, 8—each other, they, 9, 8—somebody, to, 96, 13—to seek to, 36, 13; 38, 5.
Kind, 141, 17; 174, 20—to be, 141, 14—to each other, to be, 41, 1—to speak, 141, 16.

Kindle, to, 89, 11; 151, 21—a flame within one, to, 89, 10.
Kindness, 147, 15; 174, 19.
Kindred, 60, 22.
King, 123, 13—great, a, 54, 16—to make to a, 123, 14.
Kingdom, 123, 15.
Kinsman, 60, 18.
Kiss, to, 87, 6.
Knee, 46, 18; 111, 2.
Kneel down to, 98, 7—to somebody, to, 98, 8.
Knife, 57, 15; 105, 12—drawing, 60, 13—to cut with a, 43, 18.
Knock, to, 119, 17—at the door, to, 109, 6—down to, 112, 21—in, to, 118, 12—off, to, 19, 1—out, to, 118, 12—somebody on the head, to, 118, 2.
Knoll, a, 154, 2.
Knot, a, 38, 18.
Know, I don't, 136, 24; 137, 5, 17; to, 52, 20; 91, 13; 100, 13; 104, 6; 155, 17; 166, 20—how to do it, to, 98, 27—somebody, to, 100, 12—104, 5—well, to, 175, 11, 13—when, I don't, 137, 5.
Knowledge, 155, 18.
Known, 166, 17—to make, 58, 19; 112, 13.

Labor, 84, 25, 27—hard, to, 11, 23—in vain to, 139, 16—to be burthened with, 149, 11.
Laborer, 84, 26.
Ladder, 30, 21.
Laden, ready, 43, 24.
Ladle, scum, 77, 23—stirring, 35, 13.
Lake, 81, 20; 128, 6—a, 76, 20—over the, 25, 13.
Lamb of God, 139, 24.

INDEX.

Lame, 45, 20; 121, 11—he that is, 121, 12—the, 128, 4—to be, 45, 19.
Lamp, 94, 2—to carry a, 94, 3.
Lancet, a, 113, 15.
Land, bottom, fine, good, 170, 12—rain, 16, 13—to, 25, 17—turtle, 136, 11.
Language, 64, 6—to speak the Indian, 48, 9—to use bad, 70, 1—wicked, 72, 15.
Large, 19, 13; 68, 5; 77, 7, 12, 17—fish, 19, 10—it appears, 77, 18.
Lasciviousness, 12, 23.
Last, at, 73, 14; 169, 23—day, the, 79, 22—evening, 153, 24—summer, 35, 7—time, the, 73, 13; 83, 16—will, 36, 16; 101, 4—winter, 35, 6.
Lasting peace, 14, 6.
Lastly, 73, 13; 169, 23.
Lately, 65, 16; 175, 15.
Lath, 118, 25; 119, 3.
Latterly, 177, 20.
Laugh, they, 44, 19—to, 41, 22—at somebody, to, 10, 23—at some one, to, 12, 16.
Laughs, he, 44, 19.
Laughter, exclamation of, 47, 1; 48, 8.
Law, 64, 12.
Lay hands to something, to, 64, 14—on, to, 26, 18—up one treasure only, to, 95, 12.
Laziness, 99, 20.
Lazy, 99, 19—he is, 41, 13—miserably, 98, 20—to be, 41, 13.
Lead, 136, 20—to, 123, 4—a heathenish life, to, 93, 19—each other, to, 123, 3.
Leaf, 28, 16; 177, 7—over the, 25, 11.
Leaks, it, 176, 20.

Leanness, 17, 20.
Leap over, to, 60, 7.
Leaps, it, 65, 15.
Learn, 17, 19; 149, 18—to become, 166, 26.
Leather, 27, 15—breeches, 27, 17—string, 71, 2; 83, 1; 129, 12.
Leave, 101, 5—behind, to, 95, 10—off, to, 16, 4; 119, 7—out, to, 64, 3—over, to, 18, 6—some one to, 101, 6.
Leaves, 55, 20—come out, the, 167, 19—grow red, the, 68, 26—it is full of, 28, 16—of a tree, 28, 16—turn red, 68, 21.
Left hand, 81, 3—to the, 81, 3.
Leg, 157, 16—the main sinew of the, 93, 23.
Leisure, to be at, 58, 4.
Lend me, 55, 18—to, 53, 12—a hand, to, 164, 6.
Length, 12, 1, 13; 131, 10.
Lenni Lenape, one of the three tribes of the, 148, 12.
Leprous, to be, 31, 26.
Less, 31, 21; 101, 16; 101, 20—to be, 135, 15.
Let alone, 50, 11—it alone, 52, 4—to, 63, 3—he, to, 119, 9—blood, to, 105, 9—somebody have the preference, to, 49, 18—somebody in, to, 75, 19.
Letter, 26, 1; 62, 24; 72, 19.
Level, 129, 5.
Levity, 39, 5.
Liar, a, 10, 14—to make to a, 37, 1.
Liberate, to, 96, 15.
Liberty, 96, 21.
Lice, head, 49, 14.
Lick, to, 99, 10.
Lid, a, 56, 9, 14.
Lie, a, 55, 17—an abominable, 98, 12—to, 10, 13; 42, 20—abomi-

INDEX.   207

nably, to, 98, 11—down, to, 64, 5; 127, 22—down to sleep, to, 38, 10—to have told a ready, 82, 21—on the back, to, 151, 18—sick in a poor condition, to, 58, 15—still, to, 28, 13—with each other, to, 161, 5.

Lies, it, 127, 21; 169, 5—to tell, 36, 17.

Life, 53, 10; 61, 17; 62, 16; 118, 18—he who giveth, 62, 14—he who is the, 118, 19—heathenish, 90, 18—miserable, 58, 13—sorrowful, 149, 9—to depart this, 34, 19—to lead a heathenish, 93, 19—troublesome, 123, 17; 149, 9—word of, 112, 2.

Lift it up, 35, 1—up, to, 23, 15; 118, 9—up the hand, to, 23, 18.

Lifted up, to be, 23, 16.

Light, 42, 11; 60, 17; 149, 16; 151, 20; 152, 2, 3; 164, 20, 23—giving, 114, 8—he who is the, 164, 22—it is, 42, 12—mindedness, 55, 8—to, 89, 11—to be, 164, 21—to make, 22, 26—to somebody, to give, 114, 9.

Lighten, to, 151, 21.

Lightens, it, 124, 14.

Lightning, 124, 15—afar off, 123, 1—bug, 124, 20; 152, 15—it flashes, 124, 18.

Like, 135, 7—as, 32, 18—it, I, 102, 18—manner, 32, 18—manner, in, 169, 15—that, 32, 18—to be in some place, to, 159, 19—to go, to, 160, 13—to hear, to, 160, 14—somebody, 160, 15—unto, 64, 17, 18; 72, 7—what is it, 134, 19.

Likely, it is, 156, 3.

Likes it, he, 174, 21.

Likewise, 33, 11; 169, 15.

Liking, 160, 2.

Lime, 165, 24.

Linden tree, 63, 15; 136, 19.

Line, a, 53, 1—boat, 44, 22—fishing, 19, 3, 4.

Linen, coarse, 19, 12—fine, 172, 20.

Linni Lenape, one of the three tribes of the, 85, 14.

Lip, 168, 15.

Listen, 17, 1; 44, 13—privately, to, 139, 5—to each other, to, 93, 24.

Little, 135, 10, 11, 13; 138, 10; 139, 1; 140, 12, 13—a, 52, 9; 135, 3—and little, by, 20, 26; 21, 1; 141, 18—canoe, 20, 10—dog, 18, 11—further, a, 50, 8—longer, a, 47, 18—man, 63, 18—one, 141, 5—owl, 45, 5—pig, 45, 13—tree, 48, 16—very, 70, 16; 139, 2, 3—while, a, 63, 16—while ago, a, 40, 3; 41, 24; 155, 10.

Live, he who makes, 111, 27—he who makes me, 61, 15—to, 61, 14; 62, 15; 118, 17—blameless, to, 152, 17—by what, to, 154, 18—from, to, 148, 20—on, to, 148, 20—or dwell with each other, to, 163, 16—orderly, to, 152, 17—so long, to, 131, 8—to cause to, 112, 1—to make, 61, 16; 112, 1—until now, to, 114, 10—until now, to cause to, 114, 11—willingly, to, 160, 7—with, to, 163, 4.

Lively, I am, 95, 6—to be, 10, 25—to cause to be, 61, 16.

Living, 118, 20—thing, one, 75, 23.

Lizard, 38, 20; 86, 17.

Lo! 127, 15.

Load, 164, 11—to carry a, 90, 7; 164, 12—to fetch a, 92, 1—somebody with a burden, to, 164, 10.

Loaded, 116, 19.

Loaf, small, 12, 18.

Loathe, to, 98, 19; 133, 7.

Loathsome, to be, 133, 9.

Lock, cock of a gun, 71, 16—to, 83, 11.
Locked up, 56, 7.
Locust, a, 147, 3—tree, honey, 117, 20.
Locusts, 109, 10.
Lodge at one's house, to, 163, 22.
Log, building, 81, 24—for a house, 12, 3—or tree, over the, 25, 10.
Logs, pine, 59, 7.
Long, 20, 4; 45, 24; 46, 2, 8; 122, 11—ago, 62, 2; 65, 17; 171, 14—as, 131, 20—for, to, 37, 22; 38, 2—how, 52, 10—so, 131, 11, 20—timber, 13, 10—to be, 46, 1—to stay out, 45, 21—to think a thing, 46, 7—while, a, 46, 10; 122, 11.
Longer, a little, 47, 18.
Look, 33, 12—painful, 149, 12—sorrowful, 149, 12—to, 10, 12; 64, 24; 112, 24—at each other, to, 113, 5—at somebody, to, 113, 1—back, to, 44, 16; 46, 16—beyond, to, 175, 19—fine, to, 174, 23—for, to, 92, 1—for something, to, 92, 3—friendly, to, 60, 19—hither, to, 114, 17—over, to, 175, 19—steadfastly at something, to, 100, 4—upon as an honor, to, 176, 16.
Looking-glass, 113, 18.
Looking poorly, 10, 22.
Looks black, it, 134, 11—cleanly, it, 116, 2—disagreeable, it, 145, 21—great, it, 77, 18—otherwise, it, 115, 18—quite otherwise, 147, 10—strange, he, 147, 11—strange, it, 145, 21; 147, 5—well, it, 174, 22—white, it, 166, 4.
Loose, to, 169, 8—to cut, 66, 6.
Loosen, to, 40, 13; 59, 15.
Loosening, 59, 14.
Lord, 96, 11—the, 93, 5.

Lose, to, 21, 13.
Loss, 21, 12; 169, 12.
Loss what to do, to be at a, 122, 4.
Loud, to speak, 19, 14; 68, 8.
Love, 14, 19—he that is, 14, 20—if you, 14, 16—better, to, 51, 3—to feel, 14, 21—one another, to, 14, 18—somebody, to, 14, 16.
Lover, my, 31, 7—of hunting, 159, 20.
Loving, 14, 22.
Low, 135, 10, 11, 13, 14—-minded person, 83, 2—-priced, 137, 21—spirited, to be, 101, 13—water, 36, 22.
Lower, to be, 135, 15.
Lowliness of mind, 138, 3.
Lowly-minded, to be, 138, 1.
Luck, to miss one's, 108, 21.
Lucky, 99, 13—the, 153, 23.
Lukewarm, 43, 23.
Luminous, 87, 3.
Lunch, 97, 10.
Lust, to, 36, 15.
Lying, 98, 26.

Madman, a, 37, 3.
Majestic, the most, 34, 6.
Majesty, 17, 10.
Make, I, 73, 23—bread, I, 12, 17—to, 42, 21; 73, 23—85, 1—a great noise, to, 37, 15—a house ready, to, 43, 10—an offering, to, 157, 13—even, to, 60, 14—easy, to, 22, 26—free, to, 96, 15—light, to, 22, 26—ready, to, 43, 14—somebody, to, 157, 10—something, to, 43, 7—something, to be able to, 98, 27—to a chief or king, to, 123, 14—to a liar, to, 37, 1—use of, to, 22, 6; 24, 13; 35, 11—well to, 175, 10—wet, to, 56, 18.

INDEX. 209

Maker, 74, 1.
Makes a terrib'e noise, it, 37, 16.
Male, genitals, 158, 19—of beasts, 63, 20—of birds and fowls, 63, 21.
Maltreat somebody, to, 44, 15.
Mamma, 45, 15.
Man, 51, 6; 63, 17; 112, 5; 155, 15, 19—a rich, 14, 14—a single, 53, 6—chief, 53, 14—cunning, 63, 26—little, 63, 18—old, 84, 22.
Man's cousin, a, 175, 16.
Manfully, 63, 22.
Manifest, 86, 4—to make, 58, 19; 86, 4.
Manifested, to be, 93, 6.
Manifold, 27, 18—in the belly of animals, 113, 14.
Mankind, 112, 5, 6.
Manner, 29, 14—in a heavy, 58, 10—in another, 58, 12—then, in what, 138, 11—to be in a like, 141, 9—to preach in such a, 65, 8.
Many, 28, 7; 68, 4—as, as, 34, 12—as are here, as, 34, 9—nights, 28, 8—there were, 28, 7.
Maple sugar, 13, 17—tree, 128, 10.
March, the month, 77, 25; 127, 7.
Mark, a, 52, 19; 53, 1—to shoot at a, 12, 24; 15, 22.
Marks, one who understands the, 52, 19.
Marriage, 158, 3—his relation by, 155, 7—my, 155, 8.
Married, he is, 158, 5—people, 158, 4—person, 158, 6.
Marry, to, 158, 5.
Marshy, 23, 22—deeply, 46, 6.
Marten, a, 166, 2.
Martyr, 102, 17.
Master, 96, 11—of the house, 155, 23—of, to be, 96, 22—to be one's own, 96, 18.

Mat made of rushes, 20, 20.
Material, corporeal, 79, 4.
Matter, 78, 5; 79, 23; 80, 2—stands, thus the, 91, 2.
Mattery, 80, 3.
Mature, to, 43, 5.
Maul, 104, 16.
May, 139, 12—apple, 74, 19—be, 30, 6.
Me, lend, 55, 18.
Meadow, bog, 129, 2.
Meager, to grow, 166, 26.
Meal, parched, 120, 6; 135, 18.
Mean, 135, 10.
Meaning of the word, 61, 5.
Means, by no, 24, 4, 6; 139, 20.
Meat, 103, 17—a little piece of, 103, 18—a piece of, 103, 17—salt, 130, 19—to cut, 105, 11.
Mediator, 35, 10.
Medicine, 26, 3.
Meditate something good or bad, to hatch or, 42, 20.
Meek, the, 139, 24—to be, 141, 14.
Meet, to, 76, 5; 89, 21—each other, to, 89, 23—somebody, to, 89, 22—somebody to go to, 117, 13.
Meeting house, 76, 7.
Melancholy, to be, 123, 21; 130, 8.
Melt, to, 65, 2.
Melted, 65, 1.
Melts, it, 64, 20.
Member, 134, 2.
Men, wise, 63, 25.
Mend, to, 29, 1; 65, 9—in health, to, 53, 9.
Mended, 27, 21.
Mental anguish, 58, 9.
Mention, to, 159, 16.
Mentioned, 159, 17.
Merchandise, 61, 10; 78, 19.
Merchant, 80, 18.

Merciful, 10, 21; 39, 3; 41, 5—he who is, 41, 4—to be, 40, 2—toward one another, to be, 41, 1.
Mercy, 39, 4; 41, 3.
Merit, 110, 8; 169, 17.
Merry, 173, 15—to be, 44, 7; 173, 12.
Message, 178, 1.
Messenger, 33, 19; 42, 2.
Messengers, 33, 18—his, 155, 12.
Middle finger, 62, 7—in the, 63, 2—of a piece of ground, 61, 18—of the forehead, 62, 6—of the thigh, 61, 13—of winter, 62, 4—the, 62, 3.
Midnight, 62, 5.
Midst, 62, 3—in our, 152, 18; 169, 11.
Might, 152, 24.
Mighty, 17, 22; 18, 1; 46, 12—the, 30, 16.
Mild, 106, 1; 141, 15, 18—God, 139, 24.
Mildness, 169, 4.
Milk, 99, 21—skim, 81, 19—to, 147, 7.
Mill, 135, 19.
Milt, 152, 7.
Mind, calmness of, 15, 8; 55, 12—contrary, 22, 13—lowliness of, 138, 3—made up, to have one's, 125, 10—of one, 71, 22—put me in, 84, 17—the being of one, 95, 19—to be in anguish of, 58, 8—to be indisposed in, 144, 20—to be of a calm, 55, 11—to be of an indifferent, 58, 6—to be of one, 71, 18, 23; 95, 14—to be of one heart and, 95, 18—to be settled in, 72, 3—to be troubled in, 11, 20; 59, 10; 75, 18; 123, 22—to create with the, 42, 18—to have made up one's, 43, 12—to make of one, 71, 19.

Minded, as he is, 33, 21—to be high, 68, 2—to be lowly, 138, 1.
Minister, 115, 4.
Mink, 160, 20.
Miracle, to perform a, 37, 17.
Mire, deep, 46, 5.
Miry, 98, 17.
Misbehavior, 144, 2.
Miscarry, to, 130, 14.
Mischief, to make, 75, 7.
Miserable, 41, 6; 58, 14; 149, 10—life, 58, 13—to be, 41, 8; 58, 17—slave, to be a, 41, 7.
Miserably, to perish, 31, 26.
Misfortune, 177, 1.
Misled, those who have been, 141, 7.
Miss one's luck or chance, to, 108, 21—the time, to, 107, 22.
Mist, 25, 5.
Mistake, to make a, 117, 21.
Misunderstand, to, 144, 8.
Misunderstanding, 144, 9.
Mix clay, to, 23, 25.
Mixed, 156, 18.
Moan, to, 130, 8.
Mock or laugh at somebody, to, 10, 23—somebody, to, 12, 16; 90, 22; 153, 19.
Mocking, 11, 2.
Modest, 135, 13; 138, 4, 9.
Moisteneth, he that, 155, 11.
Money, 45, 1.
Month, 43, 21—in which the deer begin to turn gray, 123, 10—in which the frogs begin to croak, the, 147, 14—of August, the, 159, 15—of falling leaves, the, 119, 13—of March, the, 127, 7—when cold makes the trees crack, the, 77, 1.
Moon, the, 143, 17.
More, 18, 8—by degrees, 21, 15—powerful, 17, 16—still, 50, 7—

INDEX. 211

the, more and more, 20, 26; 21, 1.
Moreover, 24, 5.
Morning, 165, 22—cold, 137, 13; 142, 9—early in the, 15, 10; 16, 6; 131, 2, 3—fine, 172, 5—good, 165, 21—this, 31, 22; 127, 23—unpleasant, 69, 23.
Mortal, 21, 6; 76, 24.
Mortar, 135, 19.
Mosquito, 123, 16.
Moss on trees, 84, 10.
Most, 33, 25—gracious one, the, 34, 2—holy, the, 34, 1—majestic, the, 34, 6—part, for the, 45, 3—powerful, 33, 23; 34, 6.
Mostly, 45, 3.
Moth, a, 103, 19.
Mother, 45, 15; 36, 23—the (of breast), 53, 7.
Mother-in-law, 85, 6.
Motherless, 129, 24.
Mould, bullet, 18, 20.
Mound, a, 154, 2.
Mountain, 150, 6—top of, 123, 7.
Mountainous, 150, 9.
Mouse, 12, 20; 21, 8; 118, 8.
Mouth, the, 153, 13—tied in the, 44, 14—to open the, 142, 23; 147, 20—to shut the, 124, 10.
Moved, 116, 11.
Moves, it, 58, 25—swiftly, it, 59, 20.
Mow, to, 29, 9; 74, 8.
Much, 27, 13; 28, 7; 68, 4; 77, 10, 11—almost too, 36, 10—as, as, 34, 12—as one owes, as, 34, 10—how, 52, 6, 8—more, 18, 8 —so as, 32, 18—too, 168, 8, 9— so very, 49, 17—very, 49, 16, 17.
Mud, 23, 21—deep, 46, 5.
Muddy, 23, 22; 98, 17—creek in a swamp, 74, 21.

R

Mulberry, 165, 4.
Multitude, 77, 9.
Murder, 53, 21—to, 96, 25—secretly, to, 53, 20.
Murderer, 16, 26—a secret, 53, 22.
Murderous, 97, 1.
Muscle, 31, 2; 118, 13—a, 145, 25 —little, 146, 1.
Musical instrument, 12, 11.
Muskrat, 29, 10.
Must, 23, 12.
My, 85, 16.
Myself, 95, 25.
Mystery, 38, 1.

Nail, 87, 15—my, 157, 15—on hand or foot, 157, 15—to drive in a, 39, 19.
Naked, 82, 18; 87, 3; 133, 22—to be, 133, 23—to make somebody, 133, 24.
Name, 153, 10; 169, 19—a, 66, 16 —the, 67, 9—to, 157, 8.
Named, 67, 8; 159, 17—so he is, 32, 17.
Names, one, he, 157, 8.
Narrowly, 154, 21.
Nasty, 98, 21—smelled, 71, 5— talk, 98, 26—to talk, 98, 25—to taste, 98, 16—work, 98, 15.
Nature, to be by, 89, 7.
Naughty, 72, 14.
Navel, the, 99, 2; 163, 17.
Near, 38, 4; 110, 18; 22, 26; 113, 25—by, 41, 14; 110, 19; 167, 24—somebody, to be, 110, 24—the time is, 110, 25—very, 36, 18.
Nearly, 45, 3; almost, 36, 10.
Nearness, 41, 15.
Necessary, 9, 10.
Necessitated, 23, 12.
Neck, 45, 6; 103, 6; 156, 11.

INDEX.

Need, to be in, 101, 17.
Needle, a, 30, 5.
Negro, 94, 11; 134, 6.
Neighbor, 110, 20.
Neither, 165, 1.
Nephew, 66, 7, 23.
Nest, a, 13, 11—bird's, 150, 1.
Net, of yarn, 50, 16—to catch something with a, 13, 7.
Nettle, 157, 1.
Never, 24, 4; 134, 18.
Nevermore, 24, 4.
Nevertheless, 16, 14; 50, 4, 11; 121, 3.
New, 177, 22—it is, 177, 23—shoe, 177, 21.
News, good, 172, 11; 174, 17.
Next year, 36, 12.
Nice, 128, 12.
Nigh, 110, 22—it draweth, 111, 15.
Night, 117, 11—at or by, 97, 16—by, 117, 9; cold, 142, 18—-hawk, 117, 3—it was, 117, 9—last, 143, 16; 153, 24—moderately warm, 136, 23—one, 101, 8—only one, 101, 9—sets in, 117, 12—to go by, 97, 17—walker, 102, 12.
Nights, three, 88, 23.
Nimble, to be, 162, 18.
Nine, 113, 22—hundred, 113, 23.
Ninety, 113, 24.
No, 24, 4, 6; 75, 8, 9; 134, 18.
Nobody, 24, 4.
Noise, it makes a terrible, 37, 16—to make a great, 37, 15—to make an ugly, 98, 13.
Noisy, 98, 26—to be, 10, 25; 98, 25.
Noon, 105, 4.
Nor, 165, 1.
North, 66, 12—side of a hill, on the, 17, 4—wind, 66, 11.
Northerly, 66, 12.

Northward, 66, 12, 13.
Nose, 158, 8—to bleed at the, 79, 12—to blow the, 124, 11—to run at the, 132, 1.
Not, 24, 4; 75, 8; 134, 18—at all, 24, 4; 134, 18; 139, 20—even, 50, 11—only, 130, 15—too dear, 140, 16—yet, 35, 3, 4; 93, 15, 16, 17; 94, 14.
Notch, to, 37, 21—a tree, to, 162, 20.
Nothing, 24, 4.
Notice of, to take no, 175, 20.
Nourishment, 126, 7.
November, 160, 18.
Now, 51, 10, 13, 20; 64, 8; 178, 8—and then, 136, 15; 137, 15—just, 40, 3—till, 51, 13—until, 88, 1.
Nowhere, 75, 8.
Nurse, 92, 24—a, 102, 14—child's, 102, 3—to, 100, 11.
Nut, white hickory, 142, 2.

O, 164, 19—my! 31, 15—that! 178, 9.
Oak, black, 162, 7—Spanish, 19, 11—swamp, 109, 13—white, 161, 13.
Oar, 145, 7—paddle, 136, 16.
Obedience, 25, 21.
Obedient, 25, 22.
Obey, to, 25, 20.
Object, to have one, 95, 14.
Obliged, 23, 12.
Oblique, 116, 5—it is, 116, 8.
Ocean, 54, 15.
October, 119, 13.
Odd, it seems, 147, 5.
Oddness, 145, 17.
Odoriferous, 160, 9.
Of, 149, 3; 177, 11.
Off, to break, 35, 17; 105, 13—to

INDEX. 213

fire, 106, 7—to leave, 16, 4; 119, 7—to take or pull, 46, 25; 64, 4; 68, 20.
Offering, 157, 11—to make an, 157, 13—to somebody, to make an, 157, 10.
Office, an, 64, 11—one holding an, 64, 11.
Often, 20, 3; 136, 15; 138, 22—as, 32, 18—as, as, 34, 11—so, 32, 18; 135, 3.
Oh! 24, 16; 164, 19; 167, 8—that! 51, 14, 15.
Oil, 118, 14—to beat, 118, 15.
Old, 53, 11; 78, 1, 2, 3; 83, 10—field, 77, 26—from use, 78, 4—man, 84, 22—of, 164, 18—to be, 53, 13; 84, 21—tree, 77, 24; 122, 1—woman, 27, 8.
Older people, 53, 11.
On, 50, 12; 149, 2.
Once, 137, 15—more, 61, 2; 101, 7; 146, 24.
One, 71, 24; 75, 23; 76, 4; 79, 17; 95, 16, 17—a certain, 79, 17—another, to love, 14, 18—eyed, 93, 14—holding an office, 64, 11—hundred, 46, 21; 95, 13—living thing, 75, 23—night, 95, 20; 101, 8—of these days, 32, 13—only, 101, 7—person, 71, 21; 79, 19—that is humble, 40, 20—thousand, 140, 5—to become, 79, 20.
One's own person, 96, 24.
Onion, 148, 11—an, 160, 24.
Only, 130, 15, 17—if, 15, 12—one, 71, 24; 76, 4; 101, 7—one, the, 93, 12.
Oozes out, it, 176, 20.
Open, 139, 10; 140, 14; 143, 3—arms, 139, 11—burst, 140, 14—to, 139, 15; 143, 1—to fall and burst, 29, 5—the door, to, 142, 25—the mouth, to, 142, 23; 147, 20.
Openly, 87, 3.
Opinion, 65, 6—to be of, 39, 7; 44, 9; 91, 19.
Opossum, 87, 11; 166, 10.
Opposite, 143, 13; 156, 10—he lives, 156, 10.
Or, 128, 7; 130, 2.
Order, to put a house in, 43, 10.
Orderly person, an, 153, 25.
Orderly, to do, 72, 1—to live, 152, 17.
Original, 63, 12.
Ornament, 173, 20.
Orphan, an, 128, 15.
Other, 136, 21; 137, 4—side, on the, 25, 14, 15.
Otherwise, 58, 12; 85, 15; 107, 25; 108, 6; 115, 17; 144, 14—by far, 85, 15—it looks, 115, 18.
Otter, 45, 23.
Out of, 50, 12; 149, 2—of doors, 56, 6—of this place, 56, 6—to drive, 40, 12—to go all, 154, 11.
Outrun some one, to, 96, 7.
Outstretched, 129, 17—arms, 129, 23.
Oven, an, 38, 17.
Over, 25, 14, 15; 143, 13—frozen, 56, 13—or beyond the hill, 25, 6—the fence, 25, 12—the lake, 25, 13—the leaf, 25, 11—the log or tree, 25, 10—the rain is, 66, 14—the water, 37, 5—there, 25, 14, 15; 37, 5; 50, 5—to leave, 18, 6—to look, 175, 19.
Overcome, to, 18, 5; 109, 19.
Overflowed with water, 120, 8.
Overgrown with weeds, 65, 10.
Overhead, 131, 7.
Overlook, to, 175, 20.
Overseer, 39, 13.
Overset, to, 44, 21.

Owes, as much as one, 34, 10.
Owl, 45, 4—little, 45, 5.
Own, to, 96, 22.
Oysters, 132, 20.

Packed, ready, 43, 24.
Paddle, 145, 7—to, 145, 10.
Pail, water, 153, 17.
Pain, 159, 13—bitter, 162, 4—exclamation of, 31, 15; 52, 23—in the breast, 153, 15—sorrowful, 130, 6—to endure, 73, 1—to feel, 130, 5; 159, 11, 12—to feel great, 14, 5—to feel less, 31, 18—to feel sore, 162, 3—to suffer, 24, 20.
Painful, 11, 24; 25, 3; 149, 5, 6, 10; 168, 16—death, 24, 2—look, 149, 12—to feel, 149, 7.
Pale, 166, 14.
Palm of the hand, 148, 2.
Panther, 12, 15, 16.
Papaw tree, 70, 21.
Parable, 34, 14—to speak, a, 31, 1; 34, 13.
Pardon, to ask, 78, 23.
Parent, 154, 24.
Partaker, the being made, 22, 8—to be made, 22, 7.
Partridge, 119, 18.
Pass by, to, 17, 7; 66, 15.
Pastime, 11, 1.
Pasture, good, 172, 19—to, 100, 18.
Patch, a, 29, 2—to, 29, 1.
Patched, 27, 21.
Path, 21, 3; 56, 25.
Patience, 115, 3.
Patient, 109, 4—the, 139, 24.
Paw, pretty little, 174, 8.
Pay, 109, 20—to, 30, 3, 4—one another, to, 30, 1.
Payment, 30, 1.
Peace, 60, 20—lasting, 14, 6—treaty, of, 173, 3—with one another, to be at, 172, 2.
Peaceable, 60, 21—very, 14, 7.
Peaceful, 60, 21.
Peach, 115, 19.
Peal off the rind of a tree, to, 26, 16.
Pea-vines, 124, 2.
Penetrates my heart, it, 34, 25.
Pent house, 117, 18.
People, 96, 9—among white, 130, 23—married, 158, 4—older, 53, 11.
Perceive, to, 91, 13—somebody, to, 101, 10.
Perdition, 73, 15.
Perform a miracle, to, 37, 17—to be unable to, 16, 9; 107, 18.
Perhaps, 30, 6; 88, 1; 117, 15, 19; 136, 24; 137, 15, 17; 156, 2—then, 111, 19.
Perish miserably, to, 31, 26.
Permit, to, 63, 3, 4.
Perplexed, to be, 58, 8.
Perplexity, 58, 9; 122, 5.
Persecute, to, 36, 13; 38, 5.
Persevere, to, 146, 20.
Person, a blind, 38, 25—a deaf, 38, 24—an orderly, well-behaved, 153, 25—an upright, 125, 6—low-minded, 83, 2—one, 71, 21; 79, 19—pious, 154, 4—white, 151, 15—young, 177, 19.
Personal, 150, 12.
Persons, double plural termination denoting deceased, 91, 1.
Persuade somebody, to, 13, 21.
Petition, 160, 26.
Petticoat, 149, 19.
Pewter spoon, 13, 15.
Pheasant, a, 104, 9.
Physic, 26, 3—good, 153, 22; 170, 9.
Physician, 53, 8.

INDEX. 215

Pick up, to, 76, 10.
Pickled, 132, 5.
Piece, a, 108, 15—of bread, 12, 18—to cut a, 108, 14.
Pieces, rent in, 115, 9—to tear in, 66, 4.
Pierced, 140, 10—through, 126, 11; 140, 11.
Pig, little, 45, 13.
Pigeon, 19, 24.
Pike fish, 54, 5; 121, 17; 145, 11.
Pilgrim, 86, 2.
Pillow, 80, 1.
Pincers, 47, 20—pair of, 136, 3. 12.
Pine, 59, 6—logs, 59, 7—nuts, 164, 9—swamp, 81, 2—tree, 28, 19—white, 116, 15—wood, 28, 19; 59, 17.
Pious person, 154, 4.
Pipe for smoking, a, 49, 9—pumpkin-stem, 119, 25.
Pismire, 33, 8.
Piss, to, 130, 12.
Pitch dark, 14, 9.
Pity, 'tis a, 15, 23.
Place, 30, 10; 139, 18—an uninhabitated, 139, 8—his, 30, 10, 11—in some, 81, 12—in the second, 98, 6—out of this, 56, 6—to, 48, 7—to be in a good, 174, 2—to belong to a, and to be from a, 155, 2—to like to be in some, 159, 19—to sleep on, 12, 9—to watch, a, 102, 9.
Places, in some, 81, 18.
Plain, 80, 17—a wide, 62, 1; 78, 14—on the end of the, 161, 24—without trees, a, 73, 4.
Plainly, to speak, 174, 5.
Plant, to, 47, 10—a large piece of ground, to, 77, 16—unwillingly, to, 129, 7.
Plantation, 47, 9—that side of the, 25, 9.

Planter, 47, 11.
Planting, to be done, 42, 26—to come from, 21, 21.
Play, to, 10, 25; 108, 18.
Please, 15, 12.
Pleased with, to be, 160, 11.
Pleases him, it, 174, 21.
Pleasure, to do a, 160, 4—to do somebody, a, 160, 8—to travel with, 160, 13.
Plenty, 156, 15, 16, 19—of bears, 69, 3—of deer, 14, 4—to have, 156, 17.
Pliable, 169, 2.
Plough, 60, 23.
Plum, the wild red, 105, 5; 132, 16.
Plume of fowls, 84, 9.
Plural termination denoting deceased persons, 91, 1.
Pocket-book, 26, 2.
Point, 161, 22—a sharp, 176, 2—of an island, the, 157, 6.
Pointed, 106, 1.
Poison vine, 121, 2.
Pole, setting, 37, 7.
Pole-cat, a, 130, 11.
Polish, to, 59, 4; 60, 12.
Pond, a, 109, 1.
Poor, 17, 19; 23, 8; 41, 6; 58, 13, 14—to be, 41, 8; 58, 17.
Poorly, looking, 10, 22—to be, 58, 17.
Poplar, 20, 11.
Porch in front of a house, 117, 18.
Possess, to, 61, 11; 89, 4; 103, 22—some one, to, 103, 20; 170, 11.
Pot, 23, 23; 49, 5—with feet, an iron, 157, 17.
Potato, 48, 20, 21—wild white, 166, 11.
Pothook, 49, 3.
Pound, to, 118, 9; 135, 21.

Pour out, to, 133, 15.
Powder, 119, 10.
Power, 146, 9, 17; 153, 24—greater, 17, 10—of endurance, 15, 2—over another, to have, 17, 17—spiritual, 74, 11.
Powerful, 17, 16; 30, 16—more, 17, 16—most, 33, 23; 34, 6.
Prairie, a, 73, 4.
Praise, 20, 6; 25, 19; 67, 15; 73, 8—the being elated by, 19, 8—the receiving of, 67, 14—to, 20, 2; 25, 17; 73, 6, 9—somebody, 25, 18; 67, 12, 13.
Praised, the being, 73, 7; 170, 14—to be, 170, 13.
Pray, to, 109, 21—for, to, 176, 10—for one another, 110, 4—for somebody, to, 110, 2—to somebody, to, 109, 22.
Prayer, 110, 6—house of, 110, 7.
Preach, to, 112, 3, 9—in such a manner, to, 65, 8.
Preacher, 115, 4.
Precious, 67, 16; 152, 25; 158, 22.
Prefer, to, 49, 19; 51, 3.
Preference, to let somebody have the, 49, 18.
Pregnant, to be, 118, 6.
Prepare, to, 43, 14—food, to, 156, 21.
Prepared, to be, 42, 23.
Presence of, in, 33, 13.
Present, at, 112, 8—to be, 111, 23.
Presently, 41, 24; 51, 13; 83, 12.
Preserve, to, 169, 6—one's life until this time, to, 114, 11.
Preserver, 39, 13.
Press, to, 132, 7. 8.
Prettiness, 175, 4.
Pretty, 25, 23; 120, 5; 128, 12; 174, 12; 175, 3, 7.
Prevaricate, to, 107, 14.
Prevent, to, 12, 14.

Price, 61, 21—fair, 140, 16—falls in, 17, 6—to set, a, 61, 20.
Pride, 28, 5; 68, 3; 173, 17—self, 77, 19.
Prison, 56, 11.
Prisoner, to take some one, 91, 6; 136, 17; 142, 3.
Prisoners, 139, 21.
Privately, to hear, 139, 6—to listen, 139, 5—to steal away, 54, 3.
Privilege, 96, 23.
Prize above everything, to, 18, 3.
Probable, 156, 3.
Procreation, 43, 9.
Produce fruit, to, 43, 8.
Profit, 168, 20.
Profits little, it, 73, 22.
Progress, not to, 55, 13.
Promise, to keep one's, 171, 18.
Pronounce well, to, 174, 5.
Proper, 71, 25.
Properly, to do, 72, 1.
Prosperity, 172, 10.
Prostrate, to, 106, 11.
Protect, to, 170, 5.
Proud, to be, 68, 2; 173, 16.
Proved true, it has, 43, 11.
Provision, 86, 12—for a journey, to make, 97, 10—scarcity of, 76, 11.
Prudent, 156, 6.
Puckery, 142, 1.
Pull, to, 105, 23—apart, to, 66, 4—off, to, 46, 25; 68, 20—somebody out of the water, to, 35, 20.
Pulsation, the, 44, 24.
Pulse, the, 44, 24.
Pumpkin, 40, 9; 68, 6—seeds, 158, 21—stem-pipe, 119, 25.
Punk, 105, 15.
Pup, 18, 11.
Pupil of the eye, the, 26, 6.
Purchase, 78, 20—to, 15, 14.
Pure, 40, 5, 6; 63, 12; 115, 16, 21—to be made, 115, 15.

INDEX. 217

Purely, 78, 15.
Purity, 115, 22.
Purpose, it answers the, 140, 21—to be fixed in, 72, 3—to no, 102, 16.
Pursue each other, to, 92, 9—somebody, to, 92, 8.
Push, to, 41, 25—back, to, 45, 10.
Put, to, 48, 7—elsewhere, to, 107, 24—in, to, 116, 18—in a bag, to, 116, 20—me in mind, 84, 17—on, to, 116, 24—on clothes, to, 13, 2—to death, to, 96, 25—under, to, 139, 18—up, to, 103, 22; 172, 24.
Putrid, 80, 3.

Quarrel, 37, 2; 55, 16—to, 55, 15.
Quench fire, to, 23, 26.
Question each other, to, 101, 3.
Quick, be, 131, 9—of hearing, to be, 11, 4.
Quickly, to die, 22, 22.
Quickness, 17, 2.
Quiet, to be, 55, 10.
Quill, 84, 19.
Quit, to, 16, 4; 119, 6—each other, to, 95, 8.
Quite, 78, 15; 82, 14; 85, 15; 139, 20—different, 85, 15—too, 50, 11.

Rabbit, 87, 18; 145, 9.
Raccoon, 88, 12—a, 34, 26.
Raft, 23, 5.
Rafter, 54, 14—on the roof of a house, 64, 13.
Ragged, 117, 25.
Rail, fence, 80, 22.
Rain is over, the, 66, 14—land, 16, 13—showers of, 113, 19—warm, 49, 15.

Rains, it, 133, 17—by showers, it, 119, 16—hard, it, 57, 16—now and then, it, 113, 19; 119, 16.
Rainy, 16, 13—weather, 98, 18.
Raise, to, 97, 15—somebody up, to, 20, 17—the eye, to, 23, 20.
Rakish, to be, 55, 9.
Ramrod, 116, 21.
Ransom, 96, 14.
Rapidly, the water flows, 57, 20—to come from somewhere, 149, 4.
Rare, 92, 14.
Rarely, 92, 14.
Raspberry, 31, 17; 79, 13.
Rat, 19, 9.
Rather, 18, 8; 50, 1.
Rattlesnake, 162, 15.
Raven, a, 160, 5.
Raw, 23, 9, 14.
Rays of the sun, 43, 22.
Reach forth the hand, to, 64, 15.
Read, to, 11, 5, 19; 137, 1.
Ready, 43, 1; 83, 7—all is, 104, 15—laden, 43, 24—packed, 43, 24—to be, 42, 23; 43, 1, 12; 83, 4—to make, 43, 14.
Real, 63, 12.
Reap, to, 74, 8.
Reason, for that, 51, 6—for this, 91, 2; 155, 1—for what, 55, 19.
Reasonable, 140, 16.
Rebounding, the, 44, 24.
Receive, to, 85, 18; 91, 13.
Received, 91, 15.
Receiving of honor and praise, the, 67, 14.
Reception, 91, 14; 154, 19.
Reconciled to one another, to be, 172, 13.
Reconciliation, 76, 8.
Red, 68, 21—bank of a river, 68, 10—bird, 79, 10—cedar, 79, 6—hair, 78, 10—headed woodpecker, 80, 9—looking, 68, 19

—one, the, 78, 13—root, 14, 3
—squirrel, 59, 8; 162, 11—the leaves grow, 68, 26—thread, 68, 23—to dye, 71, 12—yarn, 68, 23.
Redeem, to, 96, 15.
Redeemer, my, 96, 16.
Redemption, 96, 14.
Refuse, to, 45, 10.
Reign, to, 38, 26.
Reject, to, 45, 10.
Rejected, to be, 23, 2.
Rejoice, to, 173, 12.
Rejoicing, word of, 173, 14.
Relate to somebody, to, 24, 1.
Relation, 31, 27—by marriage, his, 155, 7—my, 155, 8.
Relatives, 60, 22.
Release, 59, 14.
Relieve somebody, to, 159, 7—some one, to, 40, 17; 163, 5.
Rely upon, to, 89, 16.
Remain, to, 119, 9.
Remember, to, 82, 3—somebody, to, 73, 10.
Remembered, the being, 73, 11.
Remembrance, 73, 11—to keep each other in, 73, 12.
Remind each other, to, 84, 20.
Rend in two, 29, 4.
Rent, 117, 26—in pieces, 115, 9.
Repair, to, 61, 1; 106, 15.
Repeat, to, 61, 3.
Repeatedly, 165, 1.
Repel, to, 45, 10.
Repentance, 130, 9.
Repentant, to be, 16, 15.
Replace, to, 61, 1.
Replant, to, 60, 25.
Report, bad, 10, 15—of somebody, good, 170, 15.
Reproach some one, to, 72, 16.
Reproduction, 43, 9.
Reproof, 122, 3.

Repulse, to, 45, 10.
Request, 160, 26.
Residence, 12, 8.
Residents, old, 12, 13.
Resolved, to have, 42, 17.
Rest, 15, 17—the, 137, 4—to, 15, 19; 64, 5; 65, 13—happy, to, 15, 18—well, to, 175, 12.
Restore, to, 61, 1.
Restraint, 31, 20.
Rests on something, 28, 9.
Resurrection, 20, 19.
Return, to, 22, 3—something, to, 46, 26.
Revealed, to be, 86, 5.
Revile somebody, to, 72, 16.
Revolves, it, 147, 22.
Reward, 30, 1.
Rhubarb, wild, 77, 2.
Rib, 49, 7—a, 47, 17.
Ribbon, 30, 20.
Rich, 158, 22—man, a, 14, 14—person, 110, 11—to be, 110, 10—to make, 110, 12—woman, 158, 24.
Riches, 110, 13—to enjoy, 61, 11.
Ride on horseback, to, 93, 26.
Rifle, 106, 8; 141, 11.
Right, 71, 25; 96, 23; 125, 12; 171, 17; 175, 7—hand, at the, 63, 10—it is, 71, 26; 72, 2—on the, 169, 18—towards the, 169, 18—tasted, 94, 5—to make it, 143, 11—to the, 63, 10.
Righteous, 125, 4.
Righteousness, 125, 7.
Ring, finger, 126, 12—the bell, to, 124, 6.
Ripe, 40, 8; 140, 22; 160, 23, 27—when it is, 160, 19.
Ripen, to, 43, 5.
Rise up, to, 105, 22.
Rises, it, 109, 17—the sun, 58, 22.
River, 132, 14.—a straight course in a, 125, 1—bank, on the, 178,

7—drifts ice, the, 75, 1—drifts with ice, the, 82, 17—fork of a, 62, 9—great, 54, 17—high bank of a, 14, 11—in the bend of the, 32, 14—large, 77, 14—mouth of a, 124, 3—on the other side of the, 37, 5—or creek, crooked, 120, 10—red bank of a, 68, 10—side, on the, 50, 18—somebody calls from the other side of the, 102, 1—subsides, the, 132, 2—up the, 90, 16—which swells the water of a creek, a rising, 112, 15.

Road, 21, 3—along the, 32, 11—beaten, 56, 25—crooked, 165, 9—fork of a, 62, 12—goes down the hill, where, 155, 6—goes up the hill, where, 154, 13—higher, 119, 19—is crooked, the, 150, 19—one who leaves the, 105, 3—straight, 125, 2—to follow the straight, 125, 18—to go a crooked, 100, 14; 165, 12—to go from the right, 105, 1—to leave the, 105, 3—to run off the, 105, 3—to turn out of the, 105, 2—turns off, where the, 104, 18.

Roads, cross, 75, 11.
Roar, to, 37, 15.
Roast, to, 12, 21.
Roasted corn, 12, 19; 35, 15.
Roasting spit, 144, 21.
Robber, 78, 21.
Robin, 146, 3.
Rock, 111, 26—big, 37, 10—flat, 128, 20—in the cleft of a, 29, 12—somebody, to, 16, 25.
Rocks, full of, 37, 11.
Rocky, 37, 11.
Roll, to, 169, 22—along, to, 17, 9.
Rolls, it, 147, 22.
Room, corner of a, 121, 1—little, 158, 17.
s

Root, 113, 13; 147, 4; 157, 8—red, 14, 3.
Rope, 19, 3; 129, 12—canoe, 44, 22.
Rotten, 16, 12; 174, 7.
Rotten wood, 161, 6.
Rough speaking, 72, 15.
Roughly, to speak, 13, 23—to talk, 75, 13.
Round about, 164, 16, 24; 165, 3—about, to go, 164, 17—all the world, 33, 1—hill, a, 154, 2; 175, 23.
Row, straight, 125, 3—to, 145, 10.
Rub, to, 60, 12.
Rubbed out, 146, 2.
Rule, 38, 28; 64, 12—to, 38, 26.
Ruler, 38, 27.
Rum, 16, 25.
Run at the nose, to, 132, 1—before somebody, to, 96, 7—fast, to, 56, 22—off, to, 168, 17.
Runs out, it, 147, 21—up, it, 60, 16.
Rushes, 132, 6—mat made of, 20, 20.
Rusty, 68, 13.

Sack, 81, 21.
Sacrifice, 157, 11—to, 157, 13.
Sad, to be, 123, 21; 130, 8.
Saddle, 47, 19—bag, 27, 12.
Said, 66, 19—to have said, he is, 66, 18.
Sail down the stream, to, 90, 3—up the water, to, 90, 14.
Saith, as he, 33, 22.
Salt, 132, 4—meat, 130, 19.
Salted, 132, 5.
Saltish, 130, 21.
Salutation, 178, 13.
Salute one another, to, 151, 4—somebody, to, 152, 10—somebody with a present, to, 89, 3.

Saluted, the being, 152, 11.
Sanctified, to be, 115, 15.
Sand, 62, 18—flies, full of, 119, 11—fly, 119, 8.
Sap of trees, 167, 22; 168, 25.
Sarsaparilla, 17, 8—great, 77, 21.
Sassafras, 159, 8.
Satisfaction, to give, 174, 14—to have received, 140, 23.
Satisfied, to be, 44, 4; 140, 17; 23.
Satisfy, to, 141, 1—each other, to, 30, 1—somebody, to, 140, 24.
Sausage, 116, 21.
Save, to, 169, 6; 172, 24.
Saviour, 110, 21; 111, 27; 156, 9.
Savory, 159, 22.
Saw, 43, 15—to, 43, 16—broad and board, 105, 17.
Say, to, 66, 20—among themselves, to, 65, 7—on, to, 18, 10, 18—over, to, 61, 3—to each other, to, 65, 7.
Saying, 66, 21—his, 33, 32—upright, 125, 14.
Scalp, a, 27, 19—to, 74, 6.
Scalped, 74, 7.
Scar, 162, 19.
Scarce, 92, 14.
Scarcely, 13, 19.
Scarcity, 101, 12—of provision, 76, 11.
Scatter, to, 13, 13; 124, 22.
Scattered, those who live, 86, 1.
School, to keep, 133, 12.
Scissors, pair of, 135, 22.
Scold, to, 70, 15; 75, 13—each other, to, 75, 12.
Scour grass, 60, 11; 132, 6.
Scourge some one, to, 131, 17.
Scourging, 131, 18.
Scrape something, to, 60, 12.
Scraped, 146, 2.
Scruple, 144, 4—to, 144, 3.

Scum ladle, 77, 23.
Scythe, 43, 17; 74, 9—a, 29, 8.
Sea, 81, 20—great, 54, 15—on the other side of the great, 37, 4.
Seafarers, 111, 10.
Search, to, 61, 12—after, to, 176, 6.
Searcheth, he that, 31, 23.
Seashore, 126, 4.
Seat, 47, 19.
Sea-tortoise, large, 117, 4.
Second, 98, 4; 137, 4—crop, 73, 17.
Secret, 38, 1—murderer, a, 53, 22.
Secretly, 53, 19—to go from some place, 54, 2—to murder, 53, 20.
See, 65, 14; 66, 9—to, 93, 21; 112, 22, 24—at a glance or for a moment, to, 61, 8—each other, to, 93, 8; 94, 20—there, 127, 15, 19, 24—very well, to 174, 25.
Seed, 166, 24.
Seeds, pumpkin, 158, 21.
Seek, to, 92, 2, 18—for somebody, to, 92, 5—to come, to, 114, 2—to kill, to, 36, 13; 38, 5.
Seeker, 31, 23.
Seem to be far, to, 150, 16.
Seen, to be, 93, 6—well to be, 172, 4.
Seize somebody, to, 91, 6.
Seldom, 92, 14.
Self, 47, 5; 96, 24—pride, 77, 19—shame, 84, 3—suspended, 24, 11.
Sell, to, 71, 14; 78, 18.
Send somebody, to, 17, 11; 42, 3.
Senses, out of one's, 167, 18—to be out of one's, 167, 16.
Sensitive, 19, 7.
Sent, to be, 17, 12.
Sentiment, 65, 6.
Separate, to, 16, 8; 144, 15, 17.
Separated from one another, 141, 10.
Separately, 147, 9, 12.

INDEX. 221

Separation, 62, 10.
September, 54, 12.
Sermon, 33, 15.
Serpents, ye, 29, 20.
Servant, 17, 13—to keep a, 17, 14
—wicked, 69, 14.
Set, a price, to, 61, 20—about wrongly, to, 107, 17—at, to, 147, 23—off by water, to, 18, 12—on, to, 147, 23—something up, to, 21, 20—up, to, 97, 15.
Setting pole, 37, 7.
Settled, 42, 6.
Seven, 97, 23—hundred, 97, 24.
Seventy, 97, 25.
Sew to, 39, 9.
Shad, 127, 7—month, 77, 25.
Shake, of the head, 138, 23, 24—to, 91, 5—hands, to, 123, 5—off, to, 137, 16.
Shallow, 36, 22—water, 139, 4.
Shame, 84, 7—for, 31, 13.
Shameful, 84, 6.
Share with each other, to, 10, 3.
Sharp, 53, 2, 5—tasted, 59, 18.
Sharpen, to, 53, 3; 59, 4.
Sharpener, a, 53, 4.
Shave, to, 87, 17.
Shavings, 128, 14; 168, 14.
Shawano woman, 127, 10.
She, 93, 9, 10—bear, 101, 24.
Sheaves, to bind up into, 21, 17.
Sheep, 79, 24; 80, 14—skin, 80, 15.
Shell corn, to, 110, 14.
Shepherd, 102, 5, 6.
Shepherds, 99, 12.
Shilling, 45, 17.
Shin, 48, 11.
Shin-bone, his, 48, 11.
Shine unto some one, to, 114, 9.
Shines brightly, it, 122, 23.
Shineth from thence, it, 154, 17.
Shining, 42, 9—hither, 114, 8.
Ships, great, 55, 2,

Shiver hickory, 141, 3—to, 101, 21, 22.
Shoe, 71, 6—a new, 177, 21—somebody, to, 72, 4—string, 21, 14.
Shoes, bad, 69, 13—European, 130, 22—Indian, 63, 8.
Shoot, to, 106, 7—amiss, to, 107, 19—at, to, 15, 22—at a mark, to, 12, 24—forth, to, 22, 11; 123, 11.
Shore, along, 50, 18.
Short, 138, 6; 141, 21.
Shorts, 66, 5.
Shot bag, 18, 21.
Shout, to, 106, 12.
Show, to, 17, 18—somebody, to, 66, 1—somebody favor, to, 140, 1—to somebody, to, 176, 8—unto, to, 113, 8.
Showers, it rains by, 119, 16—of rain, 113, 19—of snow and rain in the spring, 132, 19.
Shrunken, 117, 5.
Shut close, to, 45, 8—frozen, 56, 13—the door, 56, 8—the eyes, to, 133, 25—the mouth, to, 124, 10, —up, 56, 7.
Sick, 69, 17, 18—to be, 69, 17; 108, 10; 159, 11—in a poor condition, to lie, 58, 15.
Sickle, 43, 17.
Sickly, to be, 108, 9—to be very, 108, 23.
Sickness, 108, 12; 159, 10—to be a common, 159, 9—to suffer in, 14, 5.
Side, 34, 21; 49, 10—of the great sea, on the other, 37, 4—of the river, on the other, 37, 5—on one, 51, 2—on this, 178, 11—this, 51, 6.
Sides, on both, 156, 10.
Sieve, 110, 16—to, 110, 15.

INDEX.

Sight, 93, 22; 177, 15—good, 173, 5—to have good, 173, 4.
Sign, a, 52, 19, 21.
Silent, 146, 22—he is, 146, 23—to be, 146, 21.
Silk worm, 99, 18.
Simple, 71, 25.
Sin, 70, 8; 87, 19—to, 70, 7; 107, 12; 144, 1.
Sinew, 48, 4; 169, 26—of the leg, the main, 93, 23.
Sinful, 70, 9—behavior, 75, 4—deed, 69, 15.
Sing, to, 88, 15—in company with, to, 163, 7.
Single, 93, 12; 95, 16; 140, 8—man, a, 53, 6—one, a, 95, 15—thing, 140, 8—thread, 46, 19—woman, a, 53, 16.
Singly, 95, 16.
Sinless, to think one's self, 57, 3.
Sinner, 71, 1; 80, 7.
Sister, elder, 85, 16—her, 163, 19—-in-law, 98, 1—-in-law, my, 97, 7—younger brother or, 27, 16.
Sit, to, 175, 22—down, to, 63, 6; 81, 26—still, to, 28, 11; 55, 10.
Sits here, he who, 63, 5.
Situated, to be so, 65, 4.
Six, 46, 22—hundred, 46, 23.
Sixty, 46, 24.
Skilful, 168, 4.
Skim milk, 81, 19.
Skimmed, 74, 15; 81, 16.
Skin, 27, 15—an animal, to, 26, 14—thick, 28, 18.
Skunk, a, 130, 11.
Sky, 111, 25.
Slackens, it, 62, 8.
Slanting, 60, 15; 116, 5, 6—to make, 116, 7.
Slave, to be a miserable, 41, 7.
Sled, 138, 25; 145, 2.

Sleep, to, 38, 9—on, place to, 12, 9—to lie down to, 38, 10—with, to, 163, 22—with one another, to, 161, 5.
Sleeper, 41, 11.
Sleepy, 38, 8—to be, 36, 14.
Sleet, to, 10, 24.
Slides, it, 125, 20.
Slip, to, 82, 5; 168, 12—in, to make, 116, 24.
Slipped off, 143, 19.
Slippery, 168, 11.
Slips, it, 125, 20.
Slowly, 141, 18, 19.
Small, 138, 6, 10—loaf, 12, 18—things, in, 154, 23.
Smallpox, 29, 17—to have the, 29, 16.
Smell, it has a good, pleasant, 160, 10—to, 80, 4.
Smith, 134, 8.
Smokes, it, 121, 4.
Smoking, a pipe for, 49, 9.
Smooth, 168, 10, 11—to cut, 60, 14.
Snake, 11, 11; 122, 14—black, 134, 5—copper, 68, 7; 79, 15—green, 23, 10—horned, 127, 6—red-bellied, 68, 17—striped, 72, 18—water, 76, 16.
Snakeroot, black, 26 11.
Snipe, 117, 14; 131, 1.
Snow, 45, 14—deep, 77, 5—month, 160, 18.
Snows, it, 159, 18—very thick, it, 58, 1.
Snuffers, candle, 139, 22.
So, 32, 18; 33, 5, 11; 64, 17; 89, 24; 91, 2; 169, 20—as, 32, 18; 33, 10; 64, 8, 9, 17—as I, 92, 15—far, 114, 21; 88, 1—far as, 131, 20—far as here, 51, 6—it is, 89, 24—long 131, 11, 20—long as, 94, 13—much, 88, 1—much so, 169, 15—often, 32, 18; 135,

INDEX. 223

3—to be, 65, 4; 169, 21—to do, 65, 4; 169, 21—very 32, 18.
Soaked, 137, 3.
Soft, 106, 1; 137, 3; 141, 18; 169, 2, 5, 7.
Softness, 169, 4.
Sole of the foot, 148, 1.
Some, 16, 11; 135, 3—one else, 115, 17.
Somebody, 24, 14—calls from the other side of the river, 102, 1—good report of, 170, 15—I tell, 92, 16—to, 104, 2—to accuse, 69, 9—to admonish, 41, 21—to, answer, 88, 17—to appoint to an office, 122, 15—to arrest, 136, 17; 142, 3—to be or abide in, 12, 12—to be brought to, 114, 14—to be concerned for, 59, 9—to be glad to see, 106, 9—to be in fellowship with, 163, 12—to be jealous of, 74, 16—to be near, 110, 24—to beat, 105, 8; 118, 21—to betray, 40, 14; 58, 18—to blame, 73, 19—to bless, 172, 9—to bring away, 18, 16—to bring home, 75, 3—to call hither, 177, 13—to carry, 90, 6—to clothe, 11, 16; 116, 17—to come before, 96, 7—to come to, 100, 10—to come up with, 75, 10—to consider about, 113, 2—to conquer, 118, 21—to consider, to be, 153, 8—to cover, 82, 23—to deceive, 11, 7—to design evil against, 83, 14—to despise, 75, 14—to destroy, 154, 9—to direct the wrong away, 69, 16—to distribute to, 10, 4—to do, a pleasure, 160, 8—to do so to, 64, 7—to draw near to, 82, 6—to dress, 111, 4—to drive away, 107, 26—to enlighten, 89, 10—to entreat, 78, 22—to esteem, 67, 12—to fetch, 176, 5—to fetch, over in a canoe, 91, 17—to find out, 94, 6—to follow, 169, 13—to force, 13, 21—to forgive, 86, 9; 106, 24—to forsake, 101, 6—to give light to, 114, 9—to give to, 85, 3—to go in a canoe with, 156, 20—to go to meet, 117, 13—to hate, 128, 21—to have, 103, 20; 170, 11—to hear, 112, 17—to hearken to—177, 4—to help, 40, 17—to help through, 34, 23—to hit, 43, 2—to hold fast, 146, 8—to humble one's self before, 40, 21—to insult, 72, 16—to judge, 42, 4—to keep, 173, 21—to keep or preserve unto, 135, 16—to kill, 96, 13—to kneel to, 98, 8—to knock on the head, 118, 2—to know, 100, 12; 104, 5—to let in, 75, 19—to let, have the preference, 49, 18—to look, 113, 1—to love, 14, 16—to make an offering to, 157, 10—to make, naked, 133, 24—to maltreat, 44, 15—to mock, 12, 16; 90, 22—to mock at, 153, 19—to mock or laugh at, 10, 23—to perceive, 101, 10—to persuade, 13, 21—to praise, 67, 12, 13—to pray for, 110, 2—to pray to, 109, 22—to pull out of the water, 35, 20—to pursue, 92, 8—to put clothes on, 116, 23—to raise up, 20, 17—to relate to, 24, 1—to relieve, 159, 7—to remember, 73, 10—to revile, 72, 16—to rock, 16, 25—to run before, 96, 7—to salute, 152, 10—to salute, with a present, 89, 3—to satisfy, 140, 24—to seek for, 92, 5—to seize, 91, 6—to send, 17, 11; 42, 3—to shoe, 72, 4—to show, 66, 1—to show, favor, 140, 1—to show to, 176,

INDEX.

8—to speak with, 41, 18—to speak evil of, 80, 5—to speak evil to, 80, 6—to spit upon, 124, 23—to sprinkle, 82, 7—to stone, 138, 21—to strengthen, 146, 19—to strike, 96, 12—to take, 91, 12—to take care of, 39, 12; 113, 2—to take, in care, 170, 16—to take, out of the water, 121, 6—to treat, badly, 74, 12—to treat generously, 158, 23—to treat, ill, 59, 17—to touch, 85, 17—to use ill, 56, 23; 70, 6—to use well, 173, 1—to visit, 55, 4—to wait for, 111, 11—to waken, 142, 19—to watch, 102, 4—to whip, 131, 17—to write to, 114, 13.

Something, 55, 19; 140, 8—else, 115, 17—to be able to make, 98, 27—to be concerned for, 59, 10—to catch, with a net, 13, 7—to come or go for, 148, 23—to do just so, 143, 11—to lay hands to, 64, 14—to look for, 92, 3—to look steadfastly at, 100, 4—to make, 43, 7—to return, 46, 26—to scrape, 60, 12—to set up, 21, 20—to spoil, 75, 7; 108, 3—to steal, out of a field, 56, 3—without doubt, 155, 20.

Sometimes, 137, 15; 138, 22.

Somewhere, else, 108, 4, 5—from, 137, 7—perhaps, 137, 5—unwillingly, to be, 128, 19.

Son, 122, 13.

Son-in-law, 92, 4—his, 176, 7.

Sons, my, 100, 16.

Soon, 35, 19; 83, 12; 110, 17, 18—as, as, 58, 20.

Soot, 161, 4.

Sore, 159, 13.

Sorrow, 123, 23; 153, 16—or trouble, 149, 11—to feel, 130, 4; 149, 8.

Sorrowful life, 149, 9—look, 149, 12—pair, 130, 6—to feel, 149, 7.

Sorry, to be, 130, 8.

Sort of stinging fly, 72, 21.

Soul, 83, 15.

Sound, to, 42, 1.

Sounds, it, 64, 1.

Soup, 123, 6.

Sour, 130, 21.

South side of a hill, 145, 14.

Southeast, 36, 1—towards the, 36, 2.

Southerly, 127, 8.

Southward, 127, 8, 9.

Sow, to, 124, 22.

Span, a, 151, 3.

Spanish oak, 19, 11.

Spar, 54, 14.

Spare, enough and to, 156, 15, 16.

Sparkling, 122, 22.

Speak, to, 22, 20—a parable, to, 31, 1; 34, 13—bad to one another, to 75, 12—brokenly, to, 19, 15—civil to, 141, 16—evil of somebody, to, 80, 5—evil, to somebody, to, 80, 6—fast, to, 16, 7; 59, 19—favorably, to, 172, 15—good to each other to, 172, 13—ill of some one to, 69, 9—kind, to, 141, 16—loud, to, 19, 14; 68, 8—of, to, 176, 12—otherwise than the truth, to, 107, 14—plainly, to, 174, 5—roughly, to, 13, 23—the exact truth, to, 125, 15, 16—the Indian language, to, 48, 9—thereof, to, 148, 19—the truth, to, 58, 19—uncivil, to, 75, 13—uncivilly, to, 70, 1—with each other, to, 22, 19—with somebody, to, 41, 18.

Speaking, to blunder in, 117, 16—to break off in, 15, 16; 82, 25—to have finished, 111, 16.

Speaks a good word for us, 172, 12—truly, he, 171, 12.

Spear, 137, 19, 20—a fishing, 100, 9.
Speckled, 124, 17, 19.
Spend in drinking, to, 81, 10.
Spent, day is, 15, 21—it is all, 154, 10.
Spider, 83, 18.
Spike buck, 20, 15.
Spill, to, 133, 14.
Spin, to, 26, 5.
Spins up, it, 60, 16.
Spiral, 141, 11.
Spirit, 83, 15; 145, 18; 170, 2.
Spiritual, 170, 3—power, 74, 11.
Spirituous, 10, 1, 2; 14, 10.
Spit, roasting, 144, 21—upon somebody, to, 124, 23.
Spittle, 131, 19; 134, 14.
Spleen, 152, 7.
Split, 104, 10; 137, 8; 144, 18—off, 141, 10—to, 105, 7—wood, to, 104, 11.
Splitting iron, 104, 12.
Spoil, to, 108, 22—something, to, 75, 7; 108, 3.
Spoiled, 70, 18.
Spoken of, to be ill, 69, 10—well of, to be, 170, 13.
Spoon, 29, 21—little, 137, 23—pewter, 13, 15.
Sport, 11, 1—to make, 44, 7—of some one, to make, 153, 19.
Spotted, 124, 17, 19.
Spread out, 128, 9; 129, 18, 20—to, 128, 8; 129, 19.
Spring, 30, 24; 142, 4—hunt, 132, 18—of the year, 132, 17—this, 32, 10—up, to, 123, 11.
Sprinkle somebody, to, 82, 7.
Sprouts, it, 177, 6—out, 132, 13.
Spruce, 128, 17—forest, 128, 18.
Sprung from, 14, 12.
Square, 47, 23.
Squat down, to, 175, 21.
Squeeze, to, 132, 7, 8.

Squint-eyed, 116, 3.
Squirrel, a, 120, 3—a ground, 21, 8; 47, 16—flying, 26, 10—red, 59, 8; 116, 9; 162, 11.
Stabbed, 140, 10.
Stable cow, 87, 5.
Stallion, 154, 1.
Stammerer, 94, 4.
Stand, to, 97, 18—all around, to, 164, 15—between, to, 35, 9—firm in mind, to, 146, 20—foremost, to, 96, 5—in a circle, to, 165, 2 —up, 97, 18.
Star, 16, 24.
Stay out from home so long, to, 123, 12—out long, to, 45, 21.
Staying, to be weary of, 130, 3.
Steadiness, 28, 12.
Steal, to, 56, 1—away privately, to, 54, 3—something out of a field, to, 56, 3.
Steel, 74, 3—trap, 13, 16; 28, 10.
Steelyards, 120, 20.
Steep, 14, 11—bank, 108, 16.
Step, between, to, 35, 9.
Stick, to, 137, 18.
Sticky, it is, 28, 19.
Stiff, 136, 14; 145, 12.
Still, 16, 14; 50, 2, 4, 11; 121, 3; 146, 24—further, 50, 7—more, 50, 7; 146, 24—or standing water, 28, 14—to be, 55, 13—to sit, 28, 11; 55, 10—water, 55, 14.
Stirred, 116, 11.
Stirring ladle, 35, 13; 116, 13.
Stirs, it, 58, 25.
Stitch, to, 39, 9.
Stocking, 36, 21.
Stolen, 28, 17; 56, 2.
Stomach, 150, 4.
Stone, 13, 14—a, 38, 17—a large, 28, 1—to, 138, 20—to, somebody, 138, 21.
Stony, 13, 18; 35, 5.

INDEX.

Stool, 62, 17.
Stop, to, 12, 14; 65, 24—fighting, to, 16, 2—working, to, 16, 3; 22, 5.
Stopped, 56, 12.
Stopper, 56, 9.
Stops, it, 88, 14.
Stormy, 16, 13—weather, 69, 23.
Story, to tell a straight, 125, 15.
Stove, a, 55, 12—pipe, 30, 25.
Straight, 71, 25; 125, 12—course in a river, a, 125, 1—road, 125, 13—to go, 125, 18—to make, 125, 11.
Straightened out, 143, 19.
Straightway, 119, 20.
Strainer, 131, 23.
Strange, 145, 19, 20; 147, 9—he looks, 147, 11—he seems, 145, 22—it looks, 145, 21; 147, 5.
Strangely, to act, 13, 24—to talk, 13, 23.
Strangeness, 145, 17.
Stranger, 144, 13.
Straw, 82, 15.
Strawberries, 169, 14.
Stream, down, 90, 1—of a reddish color, 68, 15—to go down, 90, 5—to go up, 90, 17—to sail down the, 90, 3—up the, 90, 15—without falls, a, 170, 8.
Strength, 17, 23; 146, 17—he who is, 146, 18.
Strengthen, to, 146, 16—somebody, 146, 19.
Stretched, 129, 18, 21.
Strike, to, 119, 14—each other dead, to, 97, 6—somebody, to, 96, 12—some one, to, 105, 8.
Striking, 113, 11.
String, 19, 3—leather, 71, 2; 83, 1; 129, 12—of Wampum, 127, 18.
Strip one's self, to, 133, 23.

Striped, 125, 9.
Strong, 10, 1, 2; 14, 10; 15, 2; 17, 16, 22; 18, 1; 146, 7, 10, 11—current, 57, 20—to be, 146, 14—to make, 146, 12.
Strongest, the, 34, 4.
Strowd, a, 14, 15.
Struck dead, to be, 97, 5.
Stubbornness, 20, 1.
Stumble, to, 109, 16.
Stump, 143, 18.
Stutterer, 94, 4.
Subdue, to, 18, 5; 109, 19.
Subjects, 96, 9.
Subsides, the river, 132, 2.
Suck, those who give, 99, 15—to give, 100, 2.
Sucking babes, 100, 1.
Suffer, to, 19, 2; 63, 3; 73, 1—hunger, to, 161, 19—in sickness, to, 14, 5—pain, to, 24, 20.
Sufferer, innocent, 102, 17.
Suffering, 25, 1; 73, 2.
Sufficiency, 140, 18; 156, 19.
Sugar, maple, 13, 17.
Suits, it, 71, 26.
Sulphur, 162, 12.
Sultry weather, 99, 16.
Sumach, 27, 3; 44, 12.
Summer, 54, 11; 57, 17; 97, 19—beginning of, 139, 12—duck, 41, 19—hunt, 97, 20—last, 35, 7—this, 32, 10.
Sun, 43, 21—or moon, halo of, 157, 21—rays of the, 43, 22—rises, the, 58, 22.
Sunbeams, 43, 22.
Sunday, 39, 24, 26—after, 15, 20.
Sunfish, 68, 14.
Sunset, 168, 19.
Sunshine, clear, 151, 19—white, 166, 1.
Supper, 148, 9.
Supple, 169, 7.

INDEX.

Supplication, 160, 25—for each other, 110, 3.
Supremely good, the, 34, 3, 5.
Sure, 146, 13—to be, 26, 7, 8; 24, 19—of, to be, 100, 15—of a thing, to be, 125, 10,
Surely, 125, 17.
Surface, on the, 167, 2.
Surly, 80, 10.
Surprise, exclamation of, 31, 9, 12; 48, 22; 121, 8—exclamation of indignant, 31, 16—to, 78, 6.
Surprised, to be, 37, 14.
Surprising, it is, 37, 18.
Surrender, to, 79, 21.
Surrounded, I am, 164, 14.
Suspicion, 81, 4.
Swallow, to, 46, 13.
Swamp, 74, 20; 81, 1—fern, 103, 10—huckleberry, 74, 22—oak, 109, 13—muddy creek in a, 74, 21—pine, 81, 2.
Swan, a, 81, 13.
Sweat by a bath, 28, 15—house, 115, 8; 116, 10—to, 115, 7; 121, 5.
Sweep, to, 145, 4.
Sweet, 159, 22—flag, 113, 12.
Swell, to, 69, 4.
Swelled, 69, 6—to be, 69, 5.
Swiftly, it moves, 59, 20—to go, 57, 14.
Swim, I, 23, 4—to, 23, 4—hither, to, 114, 7—over to, 44, 20.
Swollen, to become, 118, 6.
Sycamore, the, 20, 11.

Table, 121, 14—a, 30, 26.
Take, it, 15, 13—it, here, 67, 10—to, 91, 13—along, to, 39, 10—care, to, 20, 22—care of, to, 39, 14; 59, 11—care of somebody, to, 39, 12—care of some one, to,

T

173, 21—down, to, 64, 4—from, to, 148, 22—hold, to, 39, 8—ill, to, 75, 6—no notice of, to, 175, 20—off, to, 46, 25; 64, 4; 68, 20; 119, 26—or consider somebody to be, to, 173, 7—out of the water, to, 45, 9—somebody in care, to, 170, 16—some one prisoner, to, 136, 17—some one to be, to, 153, 8—together, to, 21, 16.
Taken, the being, 128, 22.
Tale, an amusing, 55, 7.
Talk, nasty, 98, 26—nasty, to, 98, 25—one who likes to, 156, 1—roughly, to, 70, 1; 75, 13—strangely, to, 13, 23—to some one, to, 41, 18—vile, 72, 15.
Tall, 45, 24; 46, 2—as, as, 33, 2—to be, 46, 1.
Tallow, 118, 14.
Tame beast, 152, 21—creature, 29, 6.
Tapering, 106, 1.
Tarry, to, 152, 9.
Taste, 84, 18—it has a fine, 175, 2—of a disagreeable, 71, 7—to, 46, 20; 82, 2.
Tasted, good, 159, 22—ill, 71, 7—sharp, 59, 18.
Tax, 76, 3.
Teach, to, 10, 8, 9; 17, 17.
Teacher, a, 10, 11.
Teaching, 10, 10.
Tear, to, 29, 4; 65, 24—in pieces, to, 66, 4.
Tears, 134, 17.
Teeth, to have good sharp, 41, 23.
Tell, go and, 75, 25—a straight story, to, 125, 15—lies, to, 36, 17—somebody, I, 92, 16.
Temple, 110, 7.
Temptation, 12, 26.
Tempted, to be, 12, 25.

Ten, 83, 3; 140, 4.
Tender, 169, 2, 7.
Tenderness, 40, 18.
Tent, a, 48, 10.
Terrified, to be, 124, 4.
Testament, 36, 16; 101, 4.
Testify to, 113, 8; 155, 20.
Testimony, 113, 9; 155, 21.
Than, 32, 18.
Thank, 39, 16—to, 39, 15.
Thank'e, 21, 10.
Thankful, 39, 17.
Thanks, 21, 10.
That, 88, 1; 90, 13, 20; 91, 2, 3—I, 92, 17—is all, 90, 13—is the way of it, 91, 2—one, 90, 13, 20—or the other, 64, 17—way, 91, 2.
Thaws, it, 64, 20.
The, 88, 1; 92, 20.
Themselves, to say among, 65, 7.
Then, 23, 3; 33, 5; 135, 2; 138, 11.
Thence, 50, 5.
There, 50, 5; 51, 17, 19; 137, 14; 174, 1—from, 50, 5—he who is, 34, 17—it is, 48, 6; 67, 10—over, 50, 5—to be, 12, 7.
Thereabouts, 12, 1; 45, 7.
Thereafter, 169, 23.
Therefore, 51, 6; 91, 2; 94, 24; 149, 3; 155, 1; 177, 11.
Therein, 16, 19, 22, 23.
Thereon, 169, 23.
Thereupon, 89, 9; 169, 23.
These, 51, 12, 16, 18; 93, 18; 97, 2, 3, 4.
They, 93, 11—also, 52, 16.
Thick, 28, 18; 56, 4, 5—136, 14—bellied, 77, 4—board, 28, 18—skin, 28, 18.
Thicket, a, 9, 11; 161, 8.
Thief, a, 52, 18.
Thigh, 118, 5—joint, 66, 2—middle of the, 61, 13.

Thin, 152, 4, 5; 166, 16; 168, 13.
Things, in small, 154, 23.
Think, I, 100, 20—to, 65, 5; 113, 3; 153, 12; 169, 24—a thing long, to, 46, 7—difficult to, 11, 25—disagreeable, to, 145, 16—easy, to, 22, 25—it a long time, to, 46, 7—little of one's self, to, 137, 24; 138, 7—one's self near, to, 110, 23—so, to, 65, 5—so far, to, 115, 1—that one is holy or sinless, to, 57, 3.
Thinks, as he, 33, 14.
Third, 88, 10; 92, 23—time, the, 92, 22.
Thirst, to, 38, 7—to be dry for, 36, 8.
Thirsty, to be, 38, 7.
Thirty, 88, 9.
This, 91, 3; 167, 11; 178, 10—day past, 41, 17—one, 51, 19; 91, 2; 167, 11; 178, 10.
Thither, 50, 6; 64, 2—yonder to, 89, 12.
Thitherward, 91, 2.
Thorn bush, 68, 25—the white, 68, 24.
Those, 97, 2, 3—that had been with him, 157, 9—who live scattered, 86, 1—who weep, 63, 23.
Thou, 52, 17—also, 52, 13—hand! 175, 24—too, 52, 13.
Though, 50, 11.
Thought, 65, 6.
Thousand, 54, 18—one, 140, 5.
Thread, 116, 4—black, 134, 13—red, 68, 23—single, 46, 19—white, 166, 6.
Three, 88, 2, 11—different sorts, 88, 6—fathoms, 88, 4—fold, 88, 5; hundred, 88, 3—nights, 88, 23—times, 88, 8.
Threshold, 35, 2.
Thrice, 88, 8.

INDEX. 229

Thrives well, it, 174, 13.
Throat, 46, 3.
Through, 34, 22—here, 51, 19—there, 91, 2—to drive, 34, 24—to go, 34, 24—to help or carry somebody, 34, 23.
Throw, to, 18, 13—away, to, 107, 2—down, to, 65, 22—water, to, 98, 23.
Thrust, to, 137, 18.
Thumb, 54, 22; 55, 1.
Thunder gust, a, 114, 16.
Thunders, it, 111, 1.
Thus, 169, 20.
Thy, 85, 16.
Thyself, 52, 3.
Tide-ebb, 48, 13.
Tiding, glad, 173, 14—good, 172, 14.
Tie around, to, 157, 4—something, to, 124, 9—well, to, 171, 22.
Tied, 42, 14—about the head, 39, 6—fast, 146, 5—in the mouth, 44, 14—round, 157, 3—together, 135, 23.
Tight, 120, 1.
Till, 131, 11—here, 88, 1—now, 51, 13; 178, 8.
Timber, 54, 14—long, 13, 10.
Time, a long, 20, 4—about that, 64, 8—about the present, 51, 13—about this 112, 8; 135, 5—at any, 48, 1—at no, 24, 4—at the same, 164, 5—at this, 33, 7; 51, 13—at what, 135, 4—at which, 30, 23—bad, 69, 24—in a little, 110, 17—in former, 164, 13—is at hand, the, 143, 12, 14—is near, 110, 25—it is a good, 174, 17—it is a troublesome, 14, 8—the last, 73, 13, 14—the third, 92, 22—to miss the, 107, 22—to think it a long, 46, 7—to this, 50, 2—troublesome, 70, 22; 14, 8.

Times, 139, 19—a few, 52, 7—at all, 9, 3; 50, 17—in olden, 65, 17.
Tinder, 105, 15; 120, 4.
Tipple with one another, to, 80, 23.
Tips of the fingers, 167, 12.
Tired, 126, 20; 128, 2—to be, 126, 14; 161, 23—of, to be, 129, 4.
To, 64, 2.
Tobacco, 56, 24—pouch, 116, 14, 16; 128, 3—strong, 56, 24—twist, 163, 1.
To-day, 33, 6; 51, 13; 178, 8—once, 32, 10—some time, 32, 10; 155, 10.
Toe, 173, 19; the great, 122, 19.
Toes, fork of the, 60, 9—tops of the, 167, 14.
Together, 136, 6—again, to come or to be, 61, 4—it does not join, 144, 14—joined, 138, 19—to be, 163, 16—to bring, 76, 6—to take, 21, 16—with, 38, 7; 89, 6.
Toil, to, 11, 23.
Token, 52, 21.
To-morrow, 16, 5; 151, 11; 165, 23, 25.
Tongue, 158, 20.
Too, big, 168, 7—much, 168, 8, 9—thou, 52, 13—you, 52, 15.
Tooth, 161, 7—holes, 121, 18.
Toothless, 80, 19; 87, 1.
Top, at the 167, 4—of anything, the, 167, 13—of the hill, 166, 28—of the house, on the, 167, 1—or the, 167, 2, 3.
Tops of the toes, 167, 14.
Torch, 94, 2—to go with a, 94, 3.
Torment, 73, 2.
Tormented to death, to be, 9, 9.
Torn, 115, 9; 117, 26; 143, 19—violently, 143, 19.
Touch somebody, to, 85, 17.
Tough tree, 169, 1.
Toward, 41, 14; 65, 12—here, 89, 12—where, 91, 2.

INDEX.

Towards, the right hand, 169, 18—the southeast, 36, 2—where, 135, 1
Town, 149, 13—dilapidated, 78, 1.
Towns round about, the, 112, 11.
Trader, 80, 18.
Trail of an animal, the, 130, 18.
Traitor, 40, 16.
Transgress, to, 144, 1.
Transgression, 107, 15; 108, 2.
Trap, 55, 6—steel, 13, 16; 28, 10.
Travel about, to, 86, 3—alone, to, 92, 25—at night, to, 97, 17—badly, to, 75, 21—with, to, 163, 21—with pleasure, to, 160, 13.
Traveler, frequent, 80, 20; 86, 2.
Traveling, difficult, 14, 24—to have bad, 11, 22.
Tread under foot, to, 29, 7—upon, to, 21, 22.
Treasure only, to lay up one, 95, 12.
Treat, to, 61, 9—friendly, to, 173, 2—somebody badly, to, 74, 12—somebody generously, to, 158, 23—somebody ill, to, 59, 17—some one badly, to, 70, 6.
Treatment, kind, 170, 4.
Treaty of peace, 173, 3.
Tree, 48, 18; 79, 5—a hollow, 150, 26—bark of a, 49, 1—barren, 79, 3—birch, 157, 7—butt end of a, 158, 10—gum, 135, 20—heart of a, 159, 6—leaves of a, 28, 16—linden, 63, 15; 136, 19—little, 48, 16—old, 77, 24; 122, 1—pine, 28, 19—red beech, 126, 18—the elm, 11, 3—to notch a, 162, 20—to peel off the rind of a, 26, 16—tough, 169, 1—with a fork, a, 62, 11—yellow wood, 162, 10.
Trees, moss on, 84, 10—sap of, 167, 22; 168, 25—the inner bark of, 157, 18.

Tremble, to, 91, 5; 101, 22.
Trembling, 101, 23.
Trench, 150, 23.
Trespass, 144, 2.
Tribute, 76, 3.
Trifle, 154, 22.
Trifles, in, 154, 23.
Trouble, 122, 8; 123, 20, 23; 149, 11—to, 131, 14.
Troubled, to be, 85, 10—to be, in mind, 11, 20; 59, 10; 75, 18; 123, 22; 149, 11—to feel, 123, 18, 19.
Troublesome, 11, 24; 56, 21—it is a, time, 14, 8—life, 123, 17; 149, 9—time, 14, 8; 70, 22—to come in a, time, 124, 1.
Trough, 46, 11—big, 28, 1.
Trout, 74, 18.
True, 62, 19; 63, 27; 171, 12, 17—certainly, 125, 17—it has proved, 43, 11—it is, 54, 10—it is certainly, 91, 2—not at all, 24, 4—saying, 171, 21—to be, 125, 5—word, 171, 21
Truly, 54, 9, 13; 171, 16—he speaks, 171, 12.
Trust, 89, 19—to, 89, 16; 95, 21, 23.
Truth, 171, 19—he who is, 171, 20—to convince of the, 171, 15—to speak the, 58, 19; 107, 14—to speak the exact, 125, 15, 16.
Tub-washing, 39, 2.
Tune an instrument, to, 60, 24.
Turbid, 86, 25.
Turkey, 145, 3—cock, a, 26, 12; 45, 18—buzzard, 19, 16.
Turn, to, 59, 2—about, to, 44, 17—back, to, 59, 2—out of the road, to, 105, 2—the wrong side out, to, 22, 27.
Turned, 116, 12—about, 44, 18.
Turnip, 48, 20.

INDEX. 231

Turtle, 147, 16—dove, 80, 11—land, 136, 11.
Twenty, 98, 5.
Twice, 98, 3.
Twig, 79, 2; 131, 5.
Twilight, 68, 16; 69, 1.
Twin, 36, 3.
Twisted, 116, 12.
Two, 97, 21—days ago, 98, 9—days hence, 98, 10—hundred, 97, 22—sorts, 98, 2—to rend in, 29, 4.
Twofold, 98, 2.
Tying, 36, 4.

Ugly, 70, 11, 12.
Unable to bear, to be, 129, 16—to perform, to be, 16, 9; 107, 18.
Unanimity, 95, 19.
Unawares, 156, 22.
Unbeliever, 93, 20; 111, 21; 113, 16.
Unbending, 145, 12.
Unburnt brick, 165, 27.
Uncertain, 122, 9—to be, 122, 6.
Uncivil, to speak, 75, 13.
Uncle, an, 128, 11.
Uncommonness, 145, 24.
Unconcerned, to be, 15, 6.
Under, 34, 18—47, 12—the hill, 16, 17.
Understand, to, 112, 12—each other, to, 100, 8—well, to, 174, 26.
Understanding, 94, 7; 100, 7—to be of good, 156, 5; 175, 13.
Uneasiness, 123, 20.
Uneasy, to be, 75, 18.
Unexpectedly, 156, 22.
Unforeseen, 117, 24.
Unfortunate, 107, 23—to be, 70, 2.
Unhappiness, 70, 3.
Unhappy, 70, 5—to be, 70, 2—to make, 70, 4.

Uninhabited place, an, 139, 8; 140, 2.
Union, 71, 20.
United, 71, 22.
Unity, 71, 20.
Unless, 41, 24.
Unlike, 144, 16; 147, 9.
Unlucky, 99, 13; 107, 23—he is, 148, 24.
Unpleasant, morning, 69, 23—to be, 145, 16.
Unpleasing, uncommonly, 145, 22.
Unripe, 23, 1.
Unruly, 56, 16; 156, 14—to be, 156, 13.
Unseen, 99, 17.
Untie to, 40, 13; 59, 15.
Until, 114, 21; 131, 20—here, 114, 21—now, 88, 1; 112, 8.
Unto, 114, 21.
Untractable, 24, 8.
Untwisted, 46, 19.
Unusual, 147, 9.
Unwilling, 129, 6—to be, 129, 3—to give, to be, 152, 20—to go, to be, 129, 13.
Unwillingly, 129, 6—do it, 100, 17—to be somewhere, 128, 19—to plant, 129, 7—to work, 129, 8.
Unworthy, 94, 1.
Up, hill, 154, 14—lift it, 35, 1—there, 167, 3—to give, 16, 4; 119, 6—to rise, 105, 23.
Upland, 63, 9; 64, 21—hickory, 54, 6.
Upon earth, 13, 1.
Upright, 172, 6—person, an, 125, 6—saying, 125, 14—to be, 125, 5.
Uprightness, 172, 7.
Upward, 49, 4.
Usage, kind, 170, 4.
Use, bad language, to, 70, 1—for firewood, to, 139, 7—of, to make, 22, 6—24, 13; 35, 11—old from,

INDEX.

78, 4—somebody ill, to, 56, 23; 70, 6—somebody well, to, 173, 1—some one ill, to, 44, 15.
Useful, 22, 10.
Usual with one, as is, 33, 9.

Vagabond, 80, 20.
Vain, in, 22, 1; 102, 16—labor in, 139, 16.
Vale, a, 105, 16.
Valley, a, 105, 16—in the, 105, 18.
Valuable, 18, 2; 158, 22.
Value, 61, 19, 21—high, 68, 1—to, 14, 23; 67, 19—some one, to, 67, 12.
Vanish, to, 83, 9.
Vein, a, 86, 18.
Venture to go, to, 13, 20.
Verily, 54, 9, 13.
Very, 49, 16; 54, 9—good, 49, 16—little, 70, 16; 139, 2, 3—long ago, 164, 13—much, 49, 16, 17—much so, 49, 17—near, 110, 19—peaceable, 14, 7.
Victuals, 86, 12.
View, to, 137, 10.
Vile talk, 72, 15.
Vine, poison, 121, 2.
Violent, 14, 10.
Viper, 122, 14.
Virginian, 27, 23.
Visible, it is plainly, 174, 24.
Visit, to, 55, 5—somebody, to, 55, 4.
Vociferation, exclamation of, 49, 11, 19; 103, 15.
Vomit, to, 73, 3; 79, 25—to take a, 79, 26.
Vomiting, 79, 27.
Vouchsafe, to, 138, 5.

Wade, to, 143, 9; 147, 2.
Wages, 109, 20.
Wagon, 141, 12.
Wait, to, 111, 12—for somebody, to, 111, 11—for with much concern, to, 29, 3—with impatience, to, 23, 11.
Waited, he, 114, 1.
Waken somebody, to, 142, 19.
Wakening, 142, 20.
Walk, to, 12, 2; 61, 14; 119, 2, 5—about, to, 86, 3—alone, to, 92, 25—fast, to, 58, 2—humbly, to, 138, 2—to begin to, 119, 1—to make, 61, 16—with, to, 163, 9.
Walker, 112, 10—night, 102, 12.
Walketh, he that, 112, 10.
Walking, good, 175, 1—road, 21, 3.
Walnut, 120, 12—black, 120, 13—white, 104, 17.
Wampum, 45, 1—belt of, 103, 3—string of, 127, 18.
Want, 101, 12, 18—to, 37, 22; 101, 17.
Wanting, 101, 16, 19, 20.
Wantonness, 156, 14.
War, 69, 8; 94, 19; 143, 4—chief, a, 50, 10—time, 69, 24; 143, 6—to begin, 102, 13—to go to, 76, 9—whoop, the, 16, 21.
Warm, 43, 23, 25; 57, 24—house, 43, 26; 44, 1—one's self, to, 25, 16—the hands, to, 21, 18—thyself, 159, 3.
Warped, 150, 18.
Warrior, 94, 18; 143, 5.
Wash, to, 40, 7; 57, 5, 13—one's self, to, 57, 8.
Washed, 40, 5.
Washing tub, 39, 2.
Wasp, 20, 12.
Wasp's nest, a, 150, 1.
Watch a place, to, 102, 9—somebody, to, 102, 4—to keep, 102, 7.

INDEX. 233

Watchful, to be, 92, 21.
Watchman, 99, 11; 102, 8; 156, 4.
Water, 76, 15—beech, 165, 19—clear, 57, 11; 87, 4—deep, 27, 22—deep dead, 120, 17—down the, 90, 4—falls, the, 48, 12—flows rapidly, the, 57, 20—from the, 44, 23—high, 27, 22; 28, 4; 77, 3—is rising, the, 114, 6—low, 36, 22—overflowed with, 120, 8—over the, 37, 5—pail, 140, 6; 153, 17—shallow, 139, 4—snake, 76, 16—still, 55, 14—still or standing, 28, 14—this side the, 148, 15—to boil, in till dry, 48, 14—to go by, 118, 16—to go down the, 90, 2—to make, 133, 10—to pull somebody out of the, 35, 20—to sail up the, 90, 14—to set off by, 18, 12—to take out of the, 45, 9—to take somebody out of the, 121, 6—to throw, 98, 23—tumbles down from a precipice, 133, 21—turtle, 147, 16.
Watereth, he that, 155, 11.
Watermelon, 30, 19.
Water-snake, 46, 4.
Way, a little this, 148, 17—by the, 22, 12; 32, 12; 167, 23—that, 148, 18—this, 51, 6; 148, 14, 18 —to hunt by the, 168, 2.
We, 53, 17; 97, 8—also, 52, 14—94, 10—too, 94, 10.
Weak, 126, 20; 127, 3, 11; 128, 1, 2; 167, 18—hand, 126, 22—it is, 126, 21—to be, 126, 14; 167, 16.
Weakly, 72, 13; 126, 20—look, 126, 23—to be, 119, 12.
Weakness, 126, 15, 23.
Wealth, 110, 13.
Weary of staying, to be, 130, 3.
Weasel, 124, 13.

Weather, bad morning, 69, 12—clear, 87, 2; 172, 1—mild, 168, 27—rainy, 98, 18—stormy, 69, 23—sultry, 99, 16—ugly, 98, 18 —very hot, 57, 18—warm, 172, 1.
Wedge, iron, 105, 6.
Weed, the bitter, 157, 1.
Weeds, 65, 11—overgrown with, 65, 10.
Week, 39, 25—this, 32, 10.
Weep, those who, 63, 23.
Weepers, 63, 23.
Weeping, 63, 24; 124, 5—to come, 114, 15—to go about, 109, 7—to go away, 18, 14.
Weigh, to, 120, 19.
Weighty, most, 18, 7.
Well, 9, 1; 18, 23; 30, 24; 38, 3; 51, 5, 7, 9; 142, 4; 171, 5; 175, 7—behaved person, a, 153, 25—cut, 175, 7—hewn, 175, 7—it goes, 171, 8—squared, 175, 7—to be, 171, 1, 6—to be always, 152, 16—to be seen, 172, 4—to make, 171, 4; 175, 10—to use somebody, 173, 1.
West, 176, 14—wind, 64, 19.
Westerly, 176, 14.
Westward, 176, 15.
Wet, 98, 24; 133, 5; 137, 3—ground, 124, 24; 133, 3, 4—to make, 56, 18; 98, 23; 131, 4.
Whale, 76, 17.
What, 33, 5; 55, 19—may it be, 55, 19—then, 55, 19—to do, 31, 24—we are destined for, 32, 7.
When, 145, 13.
Whence, 135, 1—he came, 154, 20 he is, from, 177, 12—to come from, 103, 25.
Where, 31, 8; 34, 8; 135, 1, 6; 138, 11—else, 108, 4—I am, 34, 15—it is, 35, 8—it is to be got from, 176, 18—the road goes up

INDEX.

the hill, 154, 13; 155, 6—towards, 135, 1—we are, 12, 8.
Whereabouts, 135, 1.
Wherefrom, 135, 1.
Wherever or whither I go, 31, 8.
Whether, 35, 14.
Which, 24, 14—then, 135, 6.
While, a little, 63, 16; 90, 8—a long, 46, 10—a very little, 141, 20—ago, a little, 40, 3; 171, 11—in a little, 89, 15, 20—yet a little, 47, 18.
Whip somebody, to, 131, 17.
Whippoorwill, 121, 10.
Whisper, 122, 16.
White, 151, 8, 16; 166, 5, 13—frost, 103, 1—it looks, 166, 4—oak, 161, 13—person, 151, 15; 166, 12—thorn, the, 68, 24—thread, 166, 6—walnut, 104, 17—yarn, 166, 6.
Whither, 34, 8—I go, 31, 8.
Whitherwards, 135, 1.
Who, 24, 14—I am, 35, 12—is it, 24, 15—is there, 24, 14—then, 24, 14—was with him, 163, 15.
Whole, 27, 11; 82, 4, 11, 14—to make, 106, 15.
Wholly, 78, 15, 16; 82, 13; 144, 23.
Whoop, the war, 16, 21.
Whooping cough, 9, 5—to have the, 9, 6.
Whoredom, 12, 23.
Why, 55, 19; 121, 7—not, 121, 7—perhaps, 121, 7.
Wicked, 78, 7, 8—act, 69, 15—language, 72, 15—man, 82, 24—servant, 69, 14.
Wickedness, 71, 8.
Wide, 10, 6; 150, 15—as, as, 32, 19—as the world is, as big and, 33, 1—plain, a, 62, 1; 78, 14.
Widow, 128, 13, 15.

Wife, his brother's, 163, 11—my, 158, 1.
Wild, 24, 8—apple, 142, 22—bay, 35, 18—cat, a, 145, 15—cherry, 87, 13—goose, 52, 1—hemp, 47, 13—red plum, the, 105, 5.
Wilderness, 26, 9—in the, 139, 9.
Will, last, 36, 16; 101, 4.
Willful, 15, 1.
Willing, be, 38, 3—I am, 102, 18—to be, 64, 10.
Willingly, 160, 6—I do, 102, 18—to go, 160, 13—to hear, 160, 12—to live, 160, 7.
Win, to, 168, 22.
Wind blows hard, the, 56, 19—ceases, the, 15, 24—comes from a particular quarter, 177, 2—comes from thence, the, 176, 13—in the belly, 109, 9—moderately warm, 168, 26—north, 66, 11—southerly, 127, 5—the east, 12, 4—west, 64, 19.
Window, 31, 3.
Wing, 175, 16, 17.
Wink of an eye, 134, 1.
Winter, 66, 10—last, 35, 6—middle of, 62, 4—this, 32, 10.
Wipe off, to, 146, 4.
Wiped out, 146, 2.
Write to somebody, 114, 13.
Wisdom, 168, 5; 178, 2.
Wise, 65, 3; 156, 6—man, 156, 7; 168, 6—men, 63, 25; 156, 8—to be, 156, 5.
Wisely, 67, 1.
Wish, 36, 13.
Wished for, 15, 5—it is to be, 36, 7; 15, 3.
Witch, 102, 12.
Witchcraft, 72, 10, 11.
With, 89, 6; 149, 3; 164, 5—it, 47, 21.
Withered, 127, 1, 4.

INDEX.

Withers, it, 126, 21.
Within, 16, 19, 22, 23; 148, 3; 170, 1.
Without, 56, 6.
Witness, to bear, 113, 8.
Wittiness, 67, 2.
Wolf, 83, 6; 142, 8.
Woman, 103, 9—a single, 53, 16—elderly, 53, 15—old, 27, 8—rich, 158, 24—the breasts of a, 101, 11—young, 177, 24.
Woman's cousin, a, 103, 2.
Womb, 16, 16.
Wonder, exclamation of, 52, 2—to, 37, 14; 173, 8.
Wonderful, 33, 17; 52, 2; 74, 10; 145, 19; 173, 9—it is, 173, 10—it seems, 173, 11—work, 37, 13.
Wonderfully, to behave, 13, 24.
Wonders, to do great, 37, 12.
Wood, basket, 26, 15—boat, 20, 11—cutter, 74, 5—full of, 35, 9—he fetches, 91, 7—piece of, 135, 8—pine, 59, 7—rotten, 161, 6—to chop, 74, 4—to come from cutting, 22, 2—to fetch, 91, 9—to split, 104, 11—white, 136, 19.
Woodcock, 80, 16.
Woodpecker, 108, 19; red-headed, 80, 9.
Woods, 140, 2.
Woody, 135, 9.
Word, 22, 18—fine, 172, 11—for us, he speaks a good, 172, 12—meaning of the, 61, 5—of life, 112, 2—of or from the, 154, 16.
Work, 17, 15; 84, 27—good, 170, 19—nasty, 98, 15—to, 84, 25—to come from, 21, 24—to do dirty, 98, 14—to finish a, 42, 13—unwillingly, to, 129, 8—with, to, 163, 8—wonderful, 37, 13.
Working, to stop, 16, 3; 22, 5.
Works well, it, 174, 11.

World, as big and wide as the, 33, 1—at the end of the, 31, 14—end of the, 157, 19—round, all the, 33, 1—the, 112, 5.
Worm, 86, 22—little, 86, 23—rain, 49, 15—silk, 99, 18.
Worn out, 83, 10.
Worship, 110, 6—to, 109, 22.
Worth, 61, 19—nothing, 23, 8.
Worthiness, 169, 17.
Worthy, to be, 33, 3; 169, 16.
Would that! 51, 14.
Wound, 12, 5; 82, 1—to bind up or dress a, 11, 18.
Wounded, 12, 6.
Wrangle, to, 144, 19.
Wrenched, 143, 19.
Wrinkled, 117, 5.
Write, to, 62, 20, 25.
Writer, 63, 1.
Writing, 72, 19.
Written, 62, 22, 23—as is, 32, 6.
Wrong, hearing, 144, 11—side out, to turn, 22, 27—to do, 144, 5—to do it, 108, 3—to hear, 144, 10 to make, 107, 17; 144, 5.
Wrongly, to set about, 107, 17.

Yarn, black, 134, 13—net of, 50, 16—red, 68, 23—white, 166, 6.
Yawn, to, 124, 21.
Ye, 53, 18—also, 52, 15.
Year, 36, 11—next, 36, 12—spring of the, 132, 17.
Yearling, 20, 15.
Yeasts, 109, 11.
Yellow, 162, 12, 13.
Yellow-wood tree, 162, 10.
Yes, 26, 7, 8; 29, 19; 30, 7; 45, 2; 52, 11; 54, 10—exclamation of approval, 45, 2.
Yesterday, 148, 10; 172, 16.
Yet, 16, 14; 18, 22; 24, 17; 34,

20; 45, 25; 50, 4, 11; 121, 3; 146, 24; 178, 4—a little while, 47, 18—more, 18, 8; 121, 3; not, 35, 3, 4; 93, 15, 16, 17.
Yonder, 50, 5; 174, 1—to thither, 89, 12.
You, 53, 18—too, 52, 15.
Young buck, 24, 18; deer, 72, 20 —of a bird or fowl, the, 21, 9.
Younger brother or sister, 27, 16.
Zealous, 133, 6.

www.ingramcontent.com/pod-product-compliance
Lightning Source LLC
Chambersburg PA
CBHW020805230426

43666CB00007B/859